The Management of Peace Processes

Ethnic and Intercommunity Conflict Series

General Editors: **Seamus Dunn**, Professor of Conflict Studies and Director, Centre for the Study of Conflict, and **Valerie Morgan**, Professor of History and Research Associate, Centre for the Study of Conflict, University of Ulster, Northern Ireland

With the end of the Cold War, the hitherto concealed existence of a great many other conflicts, relatively small in scale, long-lived, ethnic in character and intra- rather than inter-state has been revealed. The dramatic changes in the distribution of world power, along with the removal of some previously resolute forms of centralised restraint, have resulted in the re-emergence of older, historical ethnic quarrels, many of which either became violent and warlike or teetered, and continue to teeter, on the brink of violence. For these reasons, ethnic conflicts and consequent violence are likely to have the greatest impact on world affairs during the next period of history.

This new series examines a range of issues related to ethnic and inter-community conflict. Each book concentrates on a well-defined aspect of ethnic and inter-community conflict and approaches it from a comparative and international standpoint.

Rather than focus on the macrolevel, that is, on the grand and substantive matters of states and empires, this series argues that the fundamental causes of ethnic conflict are often to be found in the hidden roots and tangled social infrastructures of the opposing separated groups. It is the understanding of these foundations and the working out of their implications for policy and practical activity that may lead to ameliorative processes and the construction of transforming social mechanisms and programmes calculated to produce long-term peace.

Coming out of Violence Project

General Editors: **John Darby**, INCORE (Initiative on Conflict Resolution and Ethnicity) University of Ulster, and Kroc Institute, University of Notre Dame, and **Roger Mac Ginty**, University of Lancaster

Titles include:

John Darby and Roger Mac Ginty (*editors*)
THE MANAGEMENT OF PEACE PROCESSES

The Management of Peace Processes

Edited by

John Darby
INCORE, University of Ulster and
Kroc Institute, University of Notre Dame

and

Roger Mac Ginty
University of Lancaster

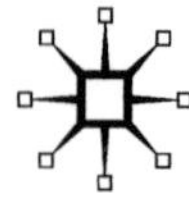

Published by PALGRAVE
Houndmills, Basingstoke, Hampshire RG21 6XS and
175 Fifth Avenue, New York, N. Y. 10010
Companies and representatives throughout the world

PALGRAVE is the new global academic imprint of St. Martin's Press LLC Scholarly and Reference Division and Palgrave Publishers Ltd (formerly Macmillan Press Ltd).

Outside North America
ISBN 0–333–80039–7

In North America
ISBN 0–312–23198–9

This book is printed on paper suitable for recycling and made from fully managed and sustained forest sources.

A catalogue record for this book is available from the British Library.

Library of Congress Catalog Card Number: 99–059427

10 9 8 7 6 5 4 3 2
08 07 06 05 04 03 02 01

Printed and bound in Great Britain by
Antony Rowe Ltd, Chippenham, Wiltshire

Contents

List of Tables

List of Figures

Acknowledgements

The authors acknowledge with gratitude the financial support provided by the European Union, UNESCO's Culture of Peace Programme and the Northern Ireland Central Community Relations Unit. John Darby was awarded a Fellowship at the United States Institute of Peace during a key period of the project. We are also grateful for administrative support from INCORE at the University of Ulster. Thanks are also due to Gillian Robinson, Mike McCool, Desiree Nielsson and Dennis McCoy. Many key players – politicians and policy-makers – in various peace processes were interviewed on the basis of anonymity. Their patience and goodwill is gratefully acknowledged.

List of Abbreviations

AIDMK	Anna Dravida Munetra Kazam
ANC	African National Congress
AWB	Afrikaner Weerstandsbeweging
APLA	Azanian People's Liberation Army
AZAPO	Azanian People's Organisation
BAC	Basque Autonomous Community
BJP	Bharatiya Janata Party
BNLM	Basque National Liberation Movement
CAIN	Conflict Archive on the INternet
CCOO	Comisiones Obreras
CGDK	Coalition Government of Democratic Kampuchea
CODESA	Congress for a Democratic South Africa
CPSR	Center for Palestine Studies and Research
DAAD	Direct Action Against Drugs
DOP	Declaration of Principles
DUP	Democratic Unionist Party
EA	Eusko Alkartasuna
EE	Euskadiko Ezkerra
EHNE	Euskal Herriko Nekazarien Elkartea
ELA	Eusko Langileen Alkartasuna
EPDP	Eelam People's Democratic Party
ETA	Euskadi 'ta Askatasuna
FF	Freedom Front
GAL	Grupos Antiterroristas de Liberación
GDP	Gross Domestic Product
GEAR	Growth, Employment and Redistribution
HB	Herri Batasuna
IDASA	Institute for a Democratic Alternative for South Africa
IDF	Israeli Defense Forces
IEC	Independent Electoral Commission
IFP	Inkatha Freedom Party
IK	Iparretarrak
IPKF	Indian Peacekeeping Force
IRA	Irish Republican Army
IU	Izquierda Unida
JMCC	Jerusalem Media and Communication Center

JVP	Janata Vimukthi Peramuna/Peoples Liberation Front
KAS	Koordinadora Abertzale Sozialista
LAB	Langile Abertzaleen Batzordeak
LTTE	Liberation Tigers of Tamil Eelam
LVF	Loyalist Volunteer Force
MK	Umkhonto we Sizwe
MNLF	Moro National Liberation Front
MPLA	Popular Movement for the Liberation of Angola
NGO	Non-Governmental Organisation
NIC	Newly Industrialised Country
NIS	National Intelligence Service
NP	National Party
NPC	National Peace Council
PA	Palestinian Authority
PA	People's Alliance
PAC	Pan Africanist Congress
PAGAD	People Against Gangsterism and Drugs
PIOOM	Interdisciplinary Research Program on Causes of Human Rights Violations
PLO	Palestine Liberation Organisation
PNV	Partido Nacionalista Vasco
PP	Partido Popular
PSE	Partido Socialista de Euskadi
PSOE	Partido Socialista Obrero Español
PUP	Progressive Unionist Party
SACP	South African Communist Party
SADF	South African Defence Force
SAP	South African Police
SDLP	Social Democratic and Labour Party
SDU	Self-Defence Units
SF	Sinn Féin
SLFP	Sri Lanka Freedom Party
SLMC	Sri Lanka Muslim Congress
TEC	Transitional Executive Council
TRC	Commission on Truth and Reconciliation
TULF	Tamil United Liberation Front
UDA	Ulster Defence Association
UDP	Ulster Democratic Party
UFF	Ulster Freedom Fighters
UGT	Unión General de Trabajadores

UNITA	National Union for the Total Liberation of Angola
UNP	United National Party
URNG	Guatemalan National Revolutionary Unity
UUP	Ulster Unionist Party
UVF	Ulster Volunteer Force

Notes on the Contributors

John Darby is Professor of Ethnic Studies at the University of Ulster and Senior Research Fellow at INCORE (Initiative on Conflict Resolution and Ethnicity). He is also President of the Ethnic Studies Network, an international network of more than 500 academics. He was previously Director of the Centre for the Study of Conflict at the University of Ulster and the founding Director of INCORE. He has published 8 books and more than 80 articles on ethnic conflict and the Northern Ireland conflict, including *Scorpions in a Bottle: Conflicting Cultures in Northern Ireland*, (1997). In 1998 Darby was a Senior Fellow at the United States Institute of Peace, and was appointed as a Visiting Professor at the Kroc Institute in the University of Notre Dame in 1999.

Tamar Hermann is Senior Lecturer in Political Science at the Open University of Israel and Director of the Tami Steinmetz Center for Peace Research, Tel Aviv University, Israel. She was leader of the Israeli research team of the International Study of Peace Organisations, sponsored by the Aspen Institute, Washington, DC. She has published extensively on Israel, politics, public opinion and foreign policy making, and the Israeli peace movement.

Roger Mac Ginty is lecturer at the Richardson Institute for Peace Studies at the Department of Politics and International Relations, Lancaster University. Previously he was co-ordinator of the Coming Out of Violence research project based at INCORE (Initiative on Conflict Resolution and Ethnicity) at the University of Ulster.

Ludger Mees is a lecturer in the Department of Contemporary History at the University of the Basque Country. His main publications include *Nacionalismo vasco: Movemento obrero y cuestión social* (1992) and a number of book chapters and journal articles on modern social movements and Basque nationalism.

David Newman is Professor of Political Geography and Chairperson of the Department of Politics and Government at Ben Gurion University of the Negev, Israel. He is editor of *Geopolitics* and contributes a weekly political commentary column to the *Jerusalem Post*. He has published extensively on territorial issues relating to the Israel–Palestine conflict and peace process. His latest book is *The Dynamics of Territorial Change: a Political Geography of the Arab–Israel Conflict.*

Paikiasothy Saravanamuttu is Executive Director of the Centre for Policy Alternatives, Columbo, Sri Lanka. He is also a visiting lecturer in international relations at the University of Colombo.

Pierre du Toit is Associate Professor at the Department of Political Science, University of Stellenbosch, South Africa. He has published extensively on conflict resolution in divided societies, constitutional rules for conflict management, theories of bargaining and negotiation, the dynamics of ethnic conflict, and state building and democratic stability. Following a fellowship at the United States Institute of Peace he published *Democracy and State Building Southern Africa – Botswana, South Africa and Zimbabwe* (1995).

Introduction: Comparing Peace Processes

John Darby and Roger Mac Ginty

Example is the school of mankind, and they will learn at no other.

(Edmund Burke, *Letters on a Regicide Peace*, 1796)

Westphalia was a peace, not only the end of a war. In itself, it was an extraordinary, drawn-out business, much more of a 'peace process' than a rapid treaty. These days, we are suddenly very interested in how peace is made. The delegates in Westphalia had been negotiating for four long years before the documents were ready to sign, during which many more thousands died. The process was handled by something like our own 'proximity talks', the technique used at Dayton for Bosnia, in Northern Ireland before Good Friday, in some of the Israel–Palestine talks. The combatants sorted themselves out into two sides. The 'Imperialists', broadly Catholic and pro-Habsburg, settled into the cathedral city of Muenster, while the northerners and Protestant rulers housed their delegations at Osnabrueck, a few miles away.

Courtiers galloped back and forth between the cities with fresh drafts or new clauses, and sometimes an august diplomat made the journey. The main delegations never actually met at all. Finally, on 24 October, 1648, the grand signings took place – separately. The terms of the Peace were proclaimed and read to the crowds. Cannons fired from the walls of Muenster, and the cathedral bells boomed over the flat, sodden countryside. The war was over.

(Neal Ascherson, *Independent*, 8 September 1998)

Introduction

Mention the term 'ethnic' and you are likely to hear one of two responses: references to either folk songs, beads or rustic costumes, or to violence. The second response has probably gained dominance in recent years. International developments since the end of the Cold War – in the former Soviet Union, Sri Lanka, Bosnia, Rwanda and Burundi – may mark out the 1990s as the decade when ethnic violence crept out from under the carpet and came to haunt us again.

Shadowing this spectre was another phenomenon, less frequently observed. In the last few years a number of durable and traditional ethnic conflicts seemed to lurch along the continuum from violence towards settlement, or at least compromise. The 1990s witnessed a unique moment in history, when a number of persistent ethnic conflicts was transformed into a less violent stage.

- Perhaps the most dramatic has been the rapid move in South Africa towards free elections and majority rule in April 1994. The constitutional settlement has significantly shifted the emphasis to the need for fundamental social restructuring and more equitable distribution of resources, and the process towards a more lasting peace continues.
- In the Middle East, talks between Israel and the Palestine Liberation Organisation (PLO) have provided sufficient momentum for the transfer of territory and a level of autonomy. The Oslo Accords have subsequently been undermined by political suspicion and by violence, but it is premature to write off the peace process there.
- The long-standing conflict in the Basque Country is showing cautious signs of moving towards resolution. After years of violence, concessions by the Spanish government have given the Basques greater, if not complete, control over their own affairs. Euskadi 'ta Askatasuna (ETA) ended its violent campaign in September 1998, by which time it had lost the support of most Basques.
- The declaration of the Irish Republican Army (IRA) ceasefire in August 1994 ushered in the start of a cautious peace process in Northern Ireland. Despite the ending of the IRA ceasefire, the process continued and culminated in the Good Friday agreement in 1998. The post-agreement problems continue, but so does the momentum of the process.

These are the front-page cases. Behind the headlines the process of making peace has been transformed during the 1990s. Over the course of the 11 years between 1988 and 1998, at least 38 formal peace accords were signed which aimed at resolving internal conflict in 33 states. Some of these agreements were fresh attempts to resolve conflicts which had existed before and during the Cold War. Other more enduring conflicts, such as Northern Ireland, New Caledonia and Western Sahara, had scarcely been touched by the struggle between the superpowers.

These agreements were not evenly spread geographically. Nineteen took place on the African continent and 12 of these involved Sub-Saharan African states. It is also worth noting that the African agreements included several of the more successful attempts at conflict settlement, including those in South Africa, Namibia and Mozambique. Elsewhere, there were two each in South Asia and Central Asia/former Soviet Union, four apiece in Europe and East Asia/Pacific, three in the Middle East, and five in Latin America/Caribbean. To look at it from another aspect, most post-war conflicts were in the Global South, and all but three agreements – Northern Ireland, South Africa and Israel–Palestine – came from Third World or formerly Second World states.

All of the accords dealt with conflicts which were mainly concentrated within national boundaries, as distinct from wars between neighbouring states. This does not mean that external powers were not involved in their settlement; indeed, none of the conflicts was free of external influence. Nor does it mean that all the conflicts concerned the entire geographical territory of a state; some were confined within a region of a state. By this perspective 29 of the accords were national pacts, while 9 addressed sub-national disputes, usually between the state and an ethnic minority.[1]

What's in an accord?

In all of these places the ending of violence has brought new problems as well as new opportunities, not least of which is the threat that it may return. When violence ends in durable violent conflicts, the policy agenda shifts radically from military containment towards a new set of problems which have not previously been faced: how to include ex-paramilitaries in political negotiations; how to handle such sensitive issues as amnesties, political prisoners, the decommissioning of weapons and the policing of divided societies; and the problem of economic reconstruction.

Every conflict has its own distinct culture, history, attitude and social development, but the issues confronted in peace accords are often quite similar. The accords share universal themes – ceasefires, the inclusion of armed participants in negotiations, disarmament, amnesty for political prisoners and reform of the security branches of government. The issues of autonomy and human rights are constants, and elections are usually necessary for the ratification of the agreement. Socio-economic development, if it features at all, is usually cast in a secondary role. Internationally, the removal of foreign forces and the return of refugees may draw formerly hostile third-party states into the negotiations.

The ending of violence is often regarded as the principal objective in a peace process, or at least as an important first step towards settlement. In many processes, including South Africa, Israel–Palestine and Northern Ireland, ceasefires were preceded by secret negotiations between the representatives of guerrillas and either government or other intermediaries. Even when secret negotiations led to ceasefires, the resulting talks were almost inevitably carried out to a background of disruptive and destabilising violence by more extreme spoiler groups and dissidents. Ceasefires never eliminate violence completely, and the continuation of violence may feed the distrust which is a feature of most internal peace negotiations. In particular, it takes time to remove the suspicion that those representing ex-paramilitaries are prepared to call their soldiers into action to influence the negotiations or to remind other negotiators of their power. This highlights differences about whether security-related issues such as amnesties or the release of prisoners should be introduced at an early stage as confidence-building gestures for paramilitaries, or if arms decommissioning should be a precondition in order to reassure constitutional politicians.

Serious negotiations often do not begin until each side has attempted to maximise its bargaining position through military offensives. Paramilitary groups may attempt to demonstrate their strength and staying power in order to persuade the government that military victory is impossible. In Angola, both the opposition National Union for the Total Liberation of Angola (UNITA) and the government Popular Movement for the Liberation of Angola (MPLA) launched military offensives to win back territory and deter the other from securing a military victory in preparation for negotiation. In the case of more established regimes like those in Mexico, the Philippines, Russia, Israel, Guatemala and Cambodia, government policies shifted between limited and total warfare. The campaigns of militant rebels such as the Moro National Liberation Front (MNLF) in the Philippines, the PLO in Israel, the IRA in Northern Ireland, the Coalition Government of Democratic Kampuchea (CGDK) in Cambodia and the Guatemalan

National Revolutionary Unity (URNG) ultimately led to more forthright negotiations. However, new offensives can also interrupt the peace process, and did in Angola, Liberia and Rwanda.

A key component of many settlements is the early release of prisoners. Some go further and include the integration of former combatants into the national armed forces and/or police, a transition often linked to the demobilisation of troops and decommissioning of weapons. A new unified armed force was established in Angola under the Bicesse Accord. A proportional balance between the military was agreed in Mozambique, while the People's Liberation Army of Namibia and the Southwest Africa territorial force were merged into a National Defense Force in Namibia. There are many other examples: Tuaregs in Niger, the new South African security arrangements, the United Tajik Opposition in Tajikistan, the CGDK including some Khmer Rouge in Cambodia, and the amalgamation of the MNLF into the Armed Forces of the Philippines. These attempts at integration did not always succeed. Notable failures include those attempted by the Mondou Accord in Chad and the Conakry Accord in Sierra Leone. In Sudan defecting troops fired on the government troops with whom they had recently amalgamated. Amalgamation was unable to prevent genocide in Rwanda.

In many cases the accords outlawed discrimination or recognised the rights of a group to exist, while some countries have taken the further step of forming truth and reconciliation commissions. The 1996 Philippines agreement and the agreements in Latin America placed a special emphasis on the protection of human rights – indeed Guatemala has probably the most extensive consideration of human and indigenous rights of any agreement. Reconciliation commissions were incorporated into the agreements in Mozambique and South Africa, and discussed in Chad. Discriminatory legislation was repealed in South Africa and Namibia, and a Victims Commissioner was appointed in Northern Ireland. There – as in a number of other cases including El Salvador, Guatemala, Nicaragua and Haiti – the peace agreement went far beyond political and constitutional agreement. The agreements included undertakings to review security arrangements, emergency legislation and the criminal justice system, as well as professionalising the police and armed forces.

International organisations and peace processes

Over the last decade the number of UN-brokered agreements has declined in relation to other approaches to peace accords. The United

Nations was directly involved in 16 of the 38 accords agreed between 1988 and 1998; the other 22 had no substantive UN involvement. Within this broad pattern, however, there has been a significant shift away from UN involvement. Six of the ten peace agreements (60 per cent) signed during the first five years resulted from UN initiatives. Only 10 of the 28 agreements (36 per cent) signed during the following six years involved the UN. The change in pattern has been accelerating; of the 15 agreements reached since the start of 1996, all but 2 were agreed without UN assistance.

Economics and strategy both had a say in this abrupt shift. The United Nation's peacekeeping budget dropped from $3 billion in 1995 to $1 billion in 1998, and the international political will for extensive peacekeeping operations has greatly diminished. At the same time the UN's peacekeeping strategy, notably in Cambodia and El Salvador, was gradually shifting towards a multi-dimensional approach. This was based on a stronger attempt to secure consensus rather than to impose force. It required co-operation between the state and the international community, and between UN peacekeepers and a host of other actors, including civilian police and non-governmental organisations. The UN was involved in peacemaking, peacekeeping and peacebuilding, sometimes simultaneously. The UN mission was 'not merely to create conditions for negotiations between the parties, but to develop strategies and support structures that would bring about a lasting peace'.[2]

It seems likely that the UN's peacekeeping role will continue to diminish. In the immediate future the most common form of peacemaking will fall more heavily on the Non-Governmental Organisation (NGO) community, individual states and protagonists. More significantly, the shift from UN peacekeeping towards internally negotiated peace processes is the most significant development in international conflict reduction since the mid-1990s.

Peace processes – what are they?

'There is no such thing as a peace process', thundered Ian Paisley at the Democratic Unionist Party (DUP) conference in 1998, not for the first time. Nor was he the only politician in Northern Ireland to suggest this. Every peace process is punctuated by claims that it has ended or never started, for reasons of either frustration or tactics. It is not an easy charge to sustain or refute, because there is no universally agreed definition of a peace process. When does a process start? What constitutes an irretrievable breakdown? When can one claim it has been successfully completed?

It is important to distinguish between the common characteristics of peace processes and their essential characteristics. Ceasefires and secret negotiations may stimulate negotiations, but often fail to do so. The core dispute is often, but not always, about demands for and opposition to greater devolution. Some peace processes are heavily influenced by local external actors, other hardly at all. There are no rules about how many internal parties are sufficient to deliver a durable agreement, although most recent negotiations have tended to include as many parties as are willing to abjure violence.

Looking at these common features, it is possible to identify five essential criteria which define a peace process.

1. *The protagonists are willing to negotiate in good faith*
   At some stage the protagonists have made a conscious choice (often at leadership level) to engage seriously in negotiations, as distinct from approaching them as the continuation of war by other means. This is not always an easy decision, due to residual mutual suspicions, and the ultimate test is the Protagonists' willingness to sustain a process despite inevitable setbacks.

   Willingness to negotiate does not imply an inevitable outcome. What is inevitable is the tension between the negotiators' needs both to co-operate and to compete with each other. The success or failure of a peace process is determined primarily by the management of this tension.
2. *The key actors are included in the process*
   The definition of 'key actor' is determined by the local peculiarities, but three empirical observations are constant. First, meaningful negotiations include the existing government of the area in question. Second, they include those paramilitary groupings which command significant support or an electoral mandate; third, they include all elements which have the power to bring about the downfall of an agreement. The third consideration – the inclusion of veto-holders – is the most controversial and subjective. It makes a distinction between mainstream paramilitary groups and spoiler groups, and recognises that the distinction may be altered by time. Significant spoiler groups may opt out or be excluded, to be admitted later under certain conditions – a morally ambiguous concession which, it might be argued, encourages spoiler violence. The uneasy principle

of 'sufficient consensus', devised during the South African process, provides a useful test for admission.

3. *The negotiations address the central issues in dispute*
The central issues dividing the participants, usually constitutional, are sometimes deferred until procedural or confidence-building measures have been agreed. But agreement to include the fundamental issues is an essential criterion of a peace process.
4. *The negotiators do not use force to achieve their objectives*
Violence precedes peace processes and continues as an unavoidable background during them, and the willingness to continue negotiations in spite of disruptive violence is a crucial test. A peace process cannot progress if any of the participant parties continues to be systematically involved in political violence. Consequently it must include explicit agreement by participants not to engage in violence in order to gain an advantage in the negotiations.
5. *The negotiators are committed to a sustained process*
A peace process is distinguished from a truce or a treaty by its duration. Above all else, it is a *process*. It must be able to withstand pressures, sometimes violence, from without. Peace processes are often suspended, sometimes for a substantial period. The decision as to whether it continues or has been terminated depends on the extent to which the key actors regard it as a feasible approach to resolving their differences.

Outside these general principles peace processes follow greatly varied directions. Pre-negotiation contacts may be used to test the ground, and may involve external or internal mediators. The official process usually begins with a public announcement and often with a ceasefire. Once started, the rules and sequence of negotiation are determined by negotiators who, by definition, have little experience of negotiation. It is not essential to start with a defined constitutional or political outcome for the process, but a peace process cannot be regarded as completed unless a political and constitutional framework has been agreed. Even if it is, the detailed implementation presents other opportunities for failure. Throughout, the process is likely to run into periods, sometimes extensive, of stalemate. The ultimate test of its durability is its ability to retain all of its key characteristics and to leave open the possibility of restoring momentum.

The study of peace processes

Until the 1970s the study of ethnic conflict rested uncomfortably in an academic space somewhere between sociology and international relations, until Glazer and Moynihan's *Ethnicity*,[3] published in 1976, identified a space for it. Since then it has elbowed itself into an expanded empirical and theoretical space, tracking the growth of ethnic violence since the 1980s.

The initial emphasis was on country-specific studies, and especially on the causes and dynamics of ethnic violence.[4] The five conflicts which are the focus of this book, for example, have attracted a level of empirical research which shows no sign of abating. These empirical building blocks have illustrated a dynamic ethnic cycle from conflict prevention through violence to conflict management and resolution and, ultimately, to post-settlement peacebuilding. The substantial and rapidly growing literature on conflict resolution has been reviewed by Miall, Woodhouse and Ramsbotham (1999).

Paralleling these empirical studies is a growing number of important analyses of the changing patterns of international violence, notably by Gurr (1993) and Geller and Singer (1998). Two recent longitudinal studies in particular have moved on from analysis of recent and current worldwide violence towards the analysis of its ending. The Uppsala project identified 66 armed conflicts which were terminated between 1989 and 1996. The terminations were classified into three groups:

a. Peace agreement	19
b. Victory	23
c. Other outcome	24

The project did not attempt to distinguish ethnic from other conflicts, and, although the vast majority was internal conflicts, the total also includes international wars. 'Peace agreement' was defined as 'an arrangement entered into by warring parties to explicitly regulate or resolve the basic incompatibility'.[5]

The 1997 PIOOM (Interdisciplinary Research Program on Causes of Human Rights Violations) World Conflict map identified 22 'peace accords and ceasefires' since the mid-1990s. Most of these remain volatile, and repeated violations are reported. To quote PIOOM, 'A Peace Accord does not automatically mean an end to violence. A number of High Intensity Conflicts still figure on the current list of Low Intensity Conflicts, while others have fallen back to the level of Violent Political Conflicts.'[6]

These quantitative studies have been supplemented by a welcome rise of interest into how it might be ended. Zartman (1995) focused on negotiation within the process, while Doyle, Johnstone and Orr (1997) explored multidimensional peacekeeping in Cambodia and El Salvador, primarily from a UN perspective. Hampson's 1996 study of five peace settlements, again all involving the UN, singled out the role of third parties as especially important and laid proper emphasis on the importance of implementing as well as signing agreements. There is still a dearth of comparative work on the successful management of peace processes. As Zartman put it, 'negotiation theory must be further developed, tested against situations of internal conflict, and refined accordingly, so that deductive guides to the potentialities for negotiation can be established'.[7]

The coincidence of these developments across the world, and the emergence of a literature on internal peace processes, provides an opportunity for comparative research. It also provided the foundations for the 'Coming Out of Violence' research project on which this book is based.

The Coming Out of Violence Project

Background and aims

'Coming Out of Violence' set out to explore the transformation from violence to agreement in ethnic conflict. It monitored the peace processes as they evolved in five selected areas, in order to identify those factors which accelerated or frustrated them, and to distinguish between the regional and universal. One of the paradoxes of ethnic conflict is that each conflict is essentially parochial, with its own history and social context, but shares with other conflicts similar characteristics and problems. 'Coming Out of Violence' aimed: to provide an empirical base for comparative study; to develop a better theoretical understanding of peace processes; and to assist those – policy-makers, politicians, international organisations, NGOs and community groups – who are currently dealing with these problems, and who will be in the future.

In each area under study a distinguished academic or team monitored the peace process as it evolved or collapsed over a two-year period. All were working to an agreed methodology, which made allowances for local differences. The partners participating in the study were: John Darby and Roger Mac Ginty, INCORE, University of Ulster; Pierre van der Post du Toit, University of Stellenbosch; Tamar Hermann, Tami Steinmetz Center, Tel Aviv University, and David Newman, Ben Gurion University; Ludger Mees, Universidad del País Vasco-Euskal Herriko Unibertsitatea, Bilbao; and Paikiasothy Saravanamuttu, Centre for Policy Alternatives, Colombo.

The principal aim of the research, and the factor which determined the selection of the five case studies, was to reach a fuller understanding of how peace processes are initiated, how they evolve and what factors support or frustrate their success.

All research involves selection bias. The five areas participating in 'Coming out of Violence' were not selected at random. They were chosen to achieve certain objectives. It is, of course, possible to argue that a different selection would produce different conclusions, well illustrated by the apt title of Barbara Geddes's article 'How the Cases You Choose Affect the Answers You Get'.[8] Our approach is to explain as honestly as possible our criteria for selection, and to let the reader judge. 'The deficiency of many comparative studies', as Horowitz put it, 'may not be selection bias as much as it is the failure to be explicit'.[9] Three main criteria determined the selection of the five cases.

First, they were durable ethnic conflicts. Previous studies of peace processes have often focused on those which involved UN interventions. The focus of this research was on internal peace processes, those where the main motor came from within the parties in dispute rather than international organisations.

Second, the five areas were selected because they had embarked on a peace process or were likely to do so. No two peace processes start and finish in the same time span – indeed it could be argued that the year 1994 marked both the elections which ratified the South African process, and only the start of the Northern Ireland process with the first ceasefires. This raises the risk that external factors, which affect all peace processes, had altered the context to the point where comparisons are invalidated. In effect, however, all five processes were creatures of the 1990s, and were played out within the same post-Cold War international context.

Finally, the 'Coming out of Violence' project was distinctive in adopting an evolutionary as opposed to a retrospective approach. This creates a number of problems in the selection of cases. It is difficult to forecast if a process is likely to continue – peace processes are notoriously vulnerable to violence and political extremism. The advantages, however, are considerable. The participating researchers were able to record the unvarnished views and reactions of participants at various points as processes stumbled along the road to agreement or breakdown. Such concepts as 'ripeness', for example, are more sensitively assessed contemporaneously than retrospectively.

These reasons have, we hope, produced what Collier and Mahoney called an appropriate 'frame of comparison' for the research.[10] The reader should be aware of what falls outside the frame, those subjects which we excluded from our concern, as well as what is included. Those interested in the UN's role in peacemaking, for example, should be aware that this is not the subject of this book, and should read the findings in conjunction with studies which address that concern. Nor should research into emerging peace processes be regarded as a laboratory study. Its aims are more modest. It is to provide insights into an increasingly important category of peace processes.

The approach

The monitoring process involved the collection and classification of newspaper cuttings, official documents, relevant legislation and policy papers, and academic commentaries. An e-mail discussion allowed useful and speedy debate on critical methodological and definitional problems. Each participant established a reference group of politicians, activists and others who have special insights into developments. The aim was to record immediate responses to developments rather than retrospective wisdom, and to provide an inside commentary on the problems involved in peacebuilding. The end result was a longitudinal survey of emerging or collapsing peace processes.

The themes

The success or failure of any emerging peace process depends on the interaction between a wide range of variable influences. The balance and the interaction is different in different settings and may alter significantly as each evolves, but elements of all are likely to have influence on the outcome. For the purposes of this research the main influences were divided into six main themes:

- violence and security issues
- economic factors
- the role of external actors
- popular responses
- symbols and ritual
- progress towards political/constitutional agreement

Violence and security issues

The most obvious threat to any peace process is that violence may start up again. Indeed it seems likely that a combination of factors would make its return inevitable: an entrenched culture of violence; the continuing presence of arms; failure to move towards successful negotiations and compromise; and unwillingness to remove the security apparatus erected during the period of violence. The key question then is the resilience of the peace process itself, and its ability to continue, despite a resumption of violence, and perhaps to engender further ceasefires. The ending of a ceasefire does not necessarily mean the ending of a peace process.

Economic factors

One of the ironies of any peace process is that the ending of violence often carries a peace deficit rather than a peace dividend. The promise of new investment may not compensate for jobs and incomes lost as a result of the termination of hostilities – police, soldiers and extra security personnel – thus leaving discontented and volatile armed elements to threaten the stability of the peace process.

The role of external actors

External actors, including the UN and regional organisations, may also have a negative or positive effect on the outcome of a peace process. If a neighbouring country feels that its interests may be threatened by either instability or change induced by ethnic violence, it may be tempted to intervene or influence events. Alternatively, a common desire to encourage a stable accommodation may act as a spur towards agreement. Similarly, diaspora populations may finance warring parties or act as mediators between them.

Popular responses

A common feature in many societies suffering from ethnic violence is a popular desire for peace. This is often frustrated by its inability to influence either those using violence or those engaged in political discussions. The success or failure to mobilise popular opinion, and the strength of civil society, are often important factors in determining the outcome of a peace process.

Symbols and ritual

Ethnic conflicts rapidly take on symbolic expression – flags, songs, cultural affiliations, religious and linguistic revivals. The symbols and rituals add an additional layer of complexity that has to be unravelled. Symbols have an equal importance in binding wounds during and after a peace process.

Progress towards political/constitutional agreement

Political discussions aimed at reaching agreed constitutional and political structures sometimes start while violence is still prevalent, or follow the declaration of a ceasefire. A common sticking point is an insistence on preconditions – insistence on abjuration of violence or decommissioning, or the inclusion of certain parties in the negotiation process. Once the parties reach the table, they are confronted by disagreements about the management of the process and ultimately about their contradictory constitutional and political objectives. Underlying the process is basic mutual mistrust.

This list is neither comprehensive nor weighted. In some settings, for example, interventions by neighbouring states have been a critical determinant of progress, while in others tardy political progress or a continuation of violence have been more influential. It is precisely the variety of influences, and the interaction between them, which is the central justification of this project.

The literature on peace processes is unbalanced in favour of United Nations intervention, and the five cases described in the following chapters may illuminate the growing proportion of peace processes which are primarily the result of voluntary internal negotiations. Among the problems inherent in selecting on-going processes is the impossibility of forecasting how they are likely to develop. In retrospect, the five areas illustrate almost the entire spectrum from success to failure. The 1994 elections in South Africa still stand out as a most remarkable voluntary transfer of power; the revolution was neither entirely radical nor entirely peaceful, but now appears to be irrevocable. There are still major obstacles to overcome before the 1998 Good Friday Agreement in Northern Ireland can be claimed as either irrevocable or completed, but it has moved the conflict on to a different level. It may be too soon to claim a great deal from the Basque process, but the 1998 ceasefire by ETA and the increased willingness of the Spanish government to contemplate negotiations bears certain resemblances to the situation in Northern Ireland two years earlier. At the time of drafting this book, many observers have declared the Camp David Accord dead and the Wye River agreement on its death bed; an air of despondency dominates, and the process has certainly decelerated, but it is sometimes overlooked that the Israel–Palestine dispute has accomplished what many other intractable conflicts have not – the transfer of both territory and authority to the Palestinians. Only in Sri Lanka is it difficult to find any evidence of change or reasons for optimism; the main antagonists have not yet reached the essential turning point which initiates all peace processes – the realisation by both sides that they cannot achieve their objectives by force, or that the price of military victory is not worth the reward.

Notes

1 Internal Peace Agreements: 1988–98 (date of most important accord)

UN		Non-UN (national)		Non-UN (sub-national)	
1998	Namibia	1989	Lebanon	1992	Mali
	Western Sahara I	1991	South Africa	1995	Niger
1991	Angola I	1992	Czech Rep./ Slovakia	1996	Mexico
	Cambodia				Philippines (Moro)
1992	El Salvador	1993	Afghanistan		
	Mozambique		Israel/Palestine I	1997	Bangladesh
1993	Ethiopia/Eritrea	1994	Djibouti		Russia
	Haiti	1995	Nicaragua	1998	New Caledonia
	Rwanda	1997	Chad		Northern Ireland
	Somalia I		Sierra Leone		Philippines (NDF)
1994	Angola II		Somalia II		
1995	Bosnia		Sudan		
	Guatemala	1998	Guinea-Bissau		
	Liberia		Israel/ Palestine II		
1997	Tajikistan				
	Western Sahara II				

2 M. W. Doyle, I. Johnstone and R. C. Orr (eds), *Keeping the Peace: Multidimensional UN Operations in Cambodia and El Salvador* (Cambridge: Cambridge University Press, 1997).

3 N. Glazer and D. P. Moynihan (eds), *Ethnicity* (Cambridge: Cambridge University Press, 1976).

4 Northern Ireland, perhaps an extreme case of academic overload, illustrates the level of research activity and publications. Three registers of research into the conflict indicate no slowing-down of interest since the 1970s: in 1972 there were 175 projects, rising to 517 in 1981 and to 605 in 1993. A similar pattern applies in Israel–Palestine and South Africa.

5 M. Sollenberg, *States in Armed Conflict* (University of Uppsala: Department of Peace and Conflict Research, 1997), p. 32.

6 *PIOOM* (The Interdisciplinary Research Program on Causes of Human Rights Violations) (University of Leiden, 1997).

7 I. W. Zartman (ed.), *Elusive Peace: Negotiating an End to Civil Wars* (Washington DC: The Brookings Institute, 1995), p. 4.

8 B. Geddes, 'How the Cases You Choose Affect the Answers You Get', in J. Stimson (ed.), *Political Analysis* (Ann Arbor: University of Michigan Press, 1990), pp. 131–50.

9 See Chapter 12 in Donald L. Horowitz's book *The Deadly Ethnic Riot* (California: University of California Press, forthcoming).

10 D. Collier and J. Mahoney, 'Insights and Pitfalls: Selection Bias in Qualitative Research', *World Politics*, 49, 1 (October 1996), pp. 56–74 (68).

1

South Africa: In Search of Post-Settlement Peace

Pierre du Toit

Introduction

'(T)here are no shortcuts to political salvation.'[1] S. P. Huntington's admonishment has strong relevance for places such as Northern Ireland, Israel/Palestine, South Africa, Sri Lanka and the Basque Country of Spain. Each of these cases has seen numerous attempts at resolving apparently intractable conflicts which have endured for decades, if not centuries. Some have, in recent times, produced a measure of success. For others, salvation remains elusive. This research forms part of a larger comparative study of these five cases with the substantive focus on the comparative success in each case at effectively emerging from violent conflict. South Africa features in this company as a case which has experienced a relative measure of success in dealing with its fundamental conflicts, culminating in the inauguration of a new democratic constitution in 1994. The relevant question now is whether this watershed agreement has inaugurated enduring political salvation or whether it is only likely to produce ephemeral relief from violence and instability. The focus on coming out of violence, in this case then, will apply mostly to instances and events of *post-settlement violence*. The descriptive narrative will proceed along six tracks: actual events of violence, negotiated agreements (particularly constitutional rules) relevant to violence and its containment, economic factors, external factors and symbolic factors which bear on violence, and popular responses which emerge from, or are related to, events of public violence.

The analysis is guided by the presupposition that, in order to account for the emergence from violence, one has to consider the nature of the process which led to the entry of the society into violence, as well as the process which lead to the agreements aimed at containing such violence.

Theoretical perspective

The theoretical perspective selected for this chapter is a state-centred one. Emphasis will be placed on the state as a site of conflict, as an agent of conflict, and also as an agent of conflict resolution. Two characteristics of states guide this perspective. The first is that states, by definition, set formal rules for the conduct of others and for themselves. This applies to the conduct of public violence (war) as well as its curtailment and containment (peace). The second is that states have, in the modern age, served as the pre-eminent units of democracy. Each will be elaborated briefly.

First, states, by definition, try to monopolise the means of violence in a society, and also try to be the sole party to use violence publicly. They set rules for the use of violence inside states and between states. The latter is referred to as the rules of war, and these rules serve to classify some cases of public violence as acts of war and others as acts of crime, separate combatants (soldiers) from non-combatants (civilians) and differentiate prisoners of war (and by extension, political prisoners) from criminals. Inferred from these rules are requirements that non-combatants are not legitimate targets, that civilian populations are to be disarmed, and that crime is distinguished from war. These rules were intended to guide the conduct of war *between* states, but the rise of low intensity conflict *within* states has made the relevance and application of these rules a highly contested issue.[2] South Africa's descent into public violence, and its attempts at extricating itself from such violence, is traced with particular reference to the decay, collapse and attempts at reassertion of the state-sponsored rules of war and of peace.

Secondly, democratic regimes, in the modern era, are embedded in the more comprehensive institutional framework of national states.[3] These states have come to serve as the pre-eminent units of democracy. Where states have succeeded in upholding their claims to sovereignty and secured the monopoly on the means and use of public violence, they have served to buttress democracies against the impact of undemocratic forces. Likewise, state agencies have been well capable of delivering public goods equitably, a primary requirement of democratic citizenship. The general insight relevant to this project is that the management of democratic transition needs to take particular care in protecting those state institutions within which the new democratic regime is to be inaugurated, and which are required to protect this regime against anti-democratic forces who are intent on using means of violence against democratic institutions.

The context: South Africa's violent transition (1984–96)

The conflict phase

South Africa's transition to democracy entails a transition from war to peace. This war, especially from 1984 till 1994, can be characterised as a Low-Intensity Conflict, with the deliberate violation of the state-sponsored rules of war.

The war was never officially declared or officially terminated. Only one set of combatants (the South African Police [SAP], the South African Defence Force [SADF] and related security agencies) represented a state, while the others (such as the African National Congress [ANC], Afrikaner Weerstandsbeweging [AWB], and the Pan Africanist Congress [PAC]) claimed to represent 'peoples'. In some cases the justification for actions was found in a cause, expressed in terms conveying the notion of a 'just war'.[4] Both the armed forces of the state and of the liberation movements targeted civilians (while both hold that this was not a matter of policy).[5] Both saw the arming of civilian populations as essential to their overall strategies, with both high and low technology weapons being deployed.[6] Some military actions carried intended symbolic meaning.[7] Targets were attacked through both physical violence and through methods of social dislocation.[8] Finally, in some cases military projects were financed through criminal activity.[9]

All of these actions were conducted in terms of two contending doctrines. The South African state proceeded from the 'total onslaught' doctrine with the corresponding strategy and tactics of the 'total strategy'.[10] This strategy entailed the mobilisation of large sectors of the white population through military conscription against the perceived communist threat. The ANC/SACP alliance formalised its position in terms of the 'Peoples' War' doctrine, with the concomitant strategy and tactics of 'ungovernability'.[11] The overall attack on the fabric of society was guided by the notion of the 'four pillars of the struggle', that is, international isolation of the country, mass mobilisation of the domestic population, creation of underground structures to conduct the campaign of ungovernability, and guerrilla warfare.[12] The combined effect of these doctrines in action was to create an almost omnipresent insecurity among the civilian populations on both sides of the apartheid divide. Comprehensive economic sanctions, large-scale labour strikes and trade union militancy impacted negatively on employment, investment and economic growth, deeply affecting economic security and the prosperity of many civilians. Successive states of emergency, clandestine actions by 'death squads', and large-scale detentions without trial, accompanied by deaths in detention, unsolved disappearances of detainees, massacres, assassinations and necklace murders all contributed to the actual threats to the physical security of civilians.

Prenegotiations

Talks about talks (1985–90)

The aim of talks about talks is to try to engage the opponent in a debate/discussion on whether to try to solve their conflict through a process of formal negotiations instead of continued confrontation. The visible cycle of revolt and repression of the 1980s, with its escalating levels of public violence, as depicted above, made the prospects of talks of any kind seem very remote. Yet these talks did occur, and were conducted amidst the rising tide of polarisation and confrontation.

Talks about talks in South Africa had a number of distinctive characteristics. The talks were held informally, in the sense that the participants did not act as official representatives of political organisations. They met as 'private individuals', in their 'personal capacities'. The meetings were secret: the general public never got to know about it, and the meetings were also often unknown to some members of the ANC and/or National Party (NP) government. These events therefore held low exit costs: parties could establish contact with little responsibility for maintaining it. They could break off discussions without great damage to themselves. These contacts were initiated by individuals without setting any preconditions for contacting one another. The objective of the meetings was to find agreement on the pre-conditions for formal negotiations. The process proceeded along two tracks. These can be depicted as 'The Mandela initiative' and 'The intermediaries'. A third, very public track ran parallel to these secret processes, and can be called 'The civil society initiative'.[13]

The earliest formal positions on the preconditions for negotiation were contained in statements by the then State President, P. W. Botha, in 1986, requiring the ANC to renounce violence as a necessary prerequisite for negotiations. The ANC responded with the 1987 Harare Declaration setting the following conditions for negotiation:

- the unconditional release of all prisoners
- lifting of all bans on restricted organisations

- removing all troops from the townships
- ending the state of emergency
- ceasing of all political executions (death penalty for convicted murderers)

It appeared to be a case of a deadlocked confrontation. As early as 1983, however, a debate had started within the ranks of the Afrikaner *Broederbond* (a secret organisation of Afrikaner elites, dedicated to the pursuit of white Afrikaner interests) about a future beyond apartheid. The argument was advanced that apartheid had become counter-productive to the survival of white South Africans, and that a future without apartheid had to be constructed. This document introduced the notion that a non-zero-sum outcome to the conflict in the country could be found, or, at least, was worth looking for.[14] Nelson Mandela provided them with the opportunity to explore this possibility.

a) The Mandela initiative

During the course of 1985 Mandela wrote a letter from prison to the then Minister of Justice, Kobie Coetsee, arguing for the need for discussions between the ANC and the NP government. In late 1985 Mandela took ill and was hospitalised for surgery. Coetsee paid him an unannounced surprise visit. The meeting was significant for a number of reasons. The hospital was 'neutral ground' where both participants assumed 'neutral roles'. Mandela was able to break free from being a prisoner, and was, first and foremost, in that context, a patient. Likewise, Coetsee could step out of his role as minister, and became a visitor. Nobody was exposed to losing face. The bona-fide reason for the meeting was a humanitarian one. Yet this courtesy call also conveyed a more fundamental gesture: a sign of goodwill to Mandela to indicate willingness to explore the issue further.

By 1987 Mandela was given his own house on the Pollsmoor prison grounds, and granted secret daytrips outside the prison. As meetings increased Coetsee established a committee of individuals, heavily weighted with members of the National Intelligence Service (NIS), to proceed further. The main issues of discussion between them were:

- that the process would not be conducted through third-party mediation, such as the failed Eminent Persons Group sent by the Commonwealth in 1986 (to this Mandela agreed)
- the terms of Mandela's release
- the role of violence (in general terms) as a means to an end

- Mandela's views on Communism
- Mandela's views on majority rule
- Mandela's general view on a future South Africa
- Mandela's views on the role of South Africa's neighbouring states in the process of change

From the government's point of view, they were trying to size up Mandela as a potential negotiating opponent, probing for his bottom line, trying to find issues on which he was flexible, and those on which he stood firm, looking for an approach reflecting reasonableness, even-handedness, good faith and willingness to meet the other party half way. No doubt he was doing the same. During this process, however, they were also drawn into redefining their own positions, finding their own fall-back positions, conceptualising ideal and realistic settlements, defining a future, post-apartheid South Africa. Central to this intellectual exercise was the quest to perceive a middle ground, where both parties could find a mutually profitable settlement. In short, both parties had to engage in redefining themselves, the opponent and the nature of the conflict.

As the meetings progressed, the topics of discussion also shifted to more concrete issues on the preconditions for formal negotiations. The salient issues on the agenda of these meetings were: the question of the release of political prisoners, as a precondition for further negotiations, the removal of restrictions on the ANC (then still banned), and the issue of violence, as a precondition for formal talks and as an obstacle to mutual trust.

By March 1989 the matter had progressed so far that Mandela sent a detailed memorandum to P. W. Botha proposing the start of formal negotiations if the government would drop the following three demands: that the ANC reject violence, that the ANC break links with the South African Communist Party, and that the ANC should abandon the concept of majority rule. In turn he argued that the fears of whites should be taken into account and that these fears should, and could, be reconciled with the principle and practice of majority rule.

A few weeks later De Klerk succeeded Botha as State President, and the Committee/Mandela meetings drew to a close. In its final report the Committee concluded that they had found what they were looking for. According to one analyst their assessment was

> that Mandela was a man of integrity, and a man with which the government could deal with, keeping in mind that he was immovable

> on some issues. This [report] served an important role later in convincing the government to engage Mandela in talks, without having to worry that he would continuously shift between positions.[15]

b) The intermediaries

The meeting of minds with Mandela was not sufficient to get formal negotiations going. The ANC in exile was led by Oliver Tambo, and there was only intermittent contact with Mandela in prison inside South Africa. The government therefore needed information about the ANC in exile. Given the need for low exit costs, the need to avoid loss of face by appearing to be weak in making the first move and the need for intermediaries became clear. This became available in 1987.

A series of meetings between British business leaders and the ANC produced a spin-off when they facilitated a meeting between influential Afrikaners and the ANC in London in 1987. A committee of NIS came to know of the planned meeting and contacted the Afrikaner side (led by Professor Willie Esterhuyse) to report back to them. Esterhuyse agreed to do so, but not as an informant. He would act as an intermediary, an informal messenger, making it known to the ANC that he was to convey their views to the South African state. (It is notable that this NIS committee was set up a year before the one which held the series of talks with Mandela.) This made it possible for both the Afrikaner opinion leaders and the ANC and the NIS to retain low exit costs – all parties could disavow the talks, should it become public, and all could gain from an exchange of information without having any formal status to the proceedings.

Eight meetings were held between these parties from October 1987 to July 1990. The issues which formed the substance of the talks changed perceptibly. At the second meeting the list of topics explored included the ANC's stance on the conduct of violence and their preconditions for formal negotiations. A number of their policy positions also entered the agenda. These included the ANC's economic policy, their policy on minority rights, and their views on the complex issue of so-called 'black-on-black' violence. Closely related to this was the concern about the ability of ANC leaders to pacify and moderate their more militant followers. Finally, the relationship between military and civilian powers in South Africa, both present and future, also came up for discussion.

Many of these topics were explored by way of scenario building and the examination of hypothetical events. This amounted to a similar dynamic as in the case of the Mandela initiative: the opposing individuals were able to size one another up, to establish personal trust, to gauge the good faith of the opponent, to find the negotiable and non-negotiable items in the agenda of the opponent, and to communicate their own bottom lines, and their own positions which were open to compromise. This could be done at little cost, as the actual conversation dealt with imaginary situations, with scenarios with a 'what if' and 'if this/then that' quality.

During the next meetings additional, even more detailed issues were added to the talks, thus bringing the scenarios even closer to the actual prevailing circumstances. These included talks on matters of both process and substance: the release of Mandela; white support for change; divisions within the NP government regarding the ANC; the suspension of the armed struggle; the timetable for transition; the influence of the SACP in the ANC; the views of the ANC on power-sharing; the status of Mandela in the ANC (then still led by Oliver Tambo); and the lifting of sanctions.

The general pattern is that as these talks about talks progressed the items for discussion became narrowed down to ever more specific matters relating to the actual start of formal negotiations. The end result was that some parties came to redefine their perceptions of their opponents, of themselves and of the nature of the conflict. Above all, they came away with a conviction that their opponents were not zealous fanatics, but reasonable stakeholders, open to negotiate on the basis of reasonable persuasion, horse trading and mutual concessions.

c) The civil society initiative

Both these tracks of talks about talks were conducted in the utmost secrecy. In the public view the landscape was one of deadlock, escalating violence and a mutual demonising of one another. A number of individuals and organisations felt the need to put pressure on the government to move towards negotiations. They did this through a series of unsanctioned private, yet highly publicised meetings with ANC members outside the country. The best-known one being the 1987 meeting with the ANC in Dakar, Senegal, organised by the Institute for a Democratic Alternative for South Africa (IDASA). In total about seventy-five such meetings took place between 1985 and 1989.[16] After the 1990 breakthrough many of these individuals congratulated themselves on their influence in bringing the government 'to its senses'. They were unaware of the Mandela initiative, however, and of the initiatives taken by the intermediaries. In the actual sequence of events, their initiative followed the previous two. They in fact did little to move the primary antagonists to the negotiating table. This is not to say that their efforts were of no value. Their value lies in sensitising the government's constituency to the prospect of a breakthrough, and they helped to undo some of the demonising which had been part of the era of conflict. In short, they contributed to moulding public opinion to be receptive for the changes which took place after 1990.

On 2 February 1990 De Klerk announced the unbanning of the ANC, SACP, PAC and related organisations. Nine days later Mandela was released. The terms set by the ANC had been met. Now the onus was on them to reciprocate. This Mandela did. A day after his release from prison he declared in a speech that whites were considered to be fellow South Africans, and that the ANC, aware of their anxiety and sense of insecurity, was prepared to address the matter.[17] Talks about substantive talks could begin.

Talks about substantive talks (1990–3)

The engagements now became formal. Whereas the previous talks were about whether to negotiate, now they were about setting (negotiating) the conditions for formal constitutional negotiations. Most of these dealt with immediate security issues, and dealing with them amounted to confidence-building measures. This series of agreements culminated in the National Peace Accord, the most comprehensive non-aggression pact of this phase on negotiations.

The Groote Schuur Minute of May 1990 bound parties to work towards a commitment to suspend violence as a means to achieve political goals. A number of specific items bear on this issue:

- agreement to establish a working group that had to find definitions for 'political offences' and for 'political prisoners', and set up a process for their release
- the arrangement for temporary immunity from prosecution under then operative laws for senior ANC members
- the review of security laws and a repeal of the state of emergency
- the setting up of channels between the government and the ANC in order to curb violence

The Pretoria Minute of August 1990 built upon this and contained the following agreements:

- suspension (note, not renunciation) of armed violence by the ANC
- an undertaking by the government to allow for the return of exiles

- an undertaking by the government to release all political prisoners by 30 April 1991
- the intention by all to form structures to deal with violence at all levels (a precursor to the National Peace Accord)
- an undertaking by the government to lift the State of Emergency in Natal
- the establishment of a working group to deal with the implementation of the suspension of armed action
- an agreement to start with exploratory constitutional talks
- recognition that other parties would have to be brought into the process

The following guidelines were agreed on in searching for a definition of a *political prisoner*:

- A need to examine and consider the specific circumstances of every case.
- The acceptance that 'common' crimes could also be regarded as political offences in view of:

  i) the motive of the offender;
  ii) the context in which the offence was committed;
  iii) the nature of the political objective;
  iv) the legal nature of the offence (that is, which specific laws were broken);
  v) the object of the offence;
  vi) the link between the offence and the political objective being pursued;
  vii) the question whether the offence was committed with/under the approval/endorsement/instructions of the relevant institution, organisation or movement

The D. F. Malan Accord of February 1991 contained a yet more precise definition of what was entailed in the 'suspension of armed action' and of 'related activities' by the ANC. It stipulated that no more:

- attacks with firearms, explosives and incendiary devices would take place
- infiltration of arms and personnel would be undertaken
- underground structures would be set up
- statements inciting violence would be made

- threats of armed action would be made against opponents
- military training would be conducted inside the country

The agreement also accepted that democratic transition obliges all participants to act peacefully, which entails that:

- No political party or movement should have a private army
- All South Africans should be free to hold peaceful political demonstrations and marches
- All violence and intimidation should be eliminated from mass action campaigns
- All actions agreed upon must conform with current South African law

The National Peace Accord of September 1991 was the most detailed non-aggression pact of this phase in the negotiations, and covered the following items:

- a comprehensive code of conduct for political parties
- a specific code of conduct for the security forces, comprising:

  i) detailed principles of conduct for the police;
  ii) prohibitions on covert operations by any organisation;
  iii) constraints on the use/display of dangerous weapons;
  iv) rules pertaining to the setting up of self-protection units

- a Standing Commission of Inquiry into public violence and intimidation
- a National Peace Secretariat and Regional Dispute Resolution Committees (Peace Committees)
- a National Peace Committee

Substantive negotiations

The Congress for a Democratic South Africa (CODESA I) saw the start of formal constitutional negotiations in December 1991. The protracted, tortuous process of convergence in negotiating positions by the opposing parties, from 1991 to 1994, will only be discussed in brief detail here, partly because of a lack of space, and as it has been dealt with thoroughly in the work of Sisk.[18] Only a short outline of events and issues will be presented, followed by some reasons why the negotiations failed at the first attempt, but then succeeded.

The CODESA negotiations centred on two interrelated issues. The first one concerned matters of process. The ANC wanted elections for a constitutional assembly held under the authority of an interim government of short duration, which then would proceed with negotiating the new democratic constitution. The NP wanted the CODESA assembly to negotiate a constitution for an interim government of unspecified duration. This government would set up another multi-party forum to negotiate the final constitution, on terms set by themselves. The second issue was the exact structure of such an interim constitutional authority.

These negotiations broke down when the ANC withdrew in May 1992. The massacre of ANC followers in the township of Boipatong on the East Rand later that month moved the ANC and its alliance partners, the SACP and COSATU, to call off talks indefinitely. Then followed their 'mass action' campaign, aimed at mass protest marches to specific symbolically laden sites of the apartheid state. This was the so-called 'Leipzig option', of inducing incumbents to capitulate through the sheer volume of public rejection of their claims to legitimacy. These events escalated into violent confrontations between the police/army, ANC alliance protesters and the local authorities at every specific site. The culmination of these marches was to be the mass march on Bisho, the capital of the Ciskei black 'homeland' government. On the day, the marchers broke ranks and deviated from their authorised route. Ciskei soldiers opened fire, killing 28 marchers.

This proved to be a decisive turning point in the negotiation process, creating new impetus on the main protagonists to get back to the table, and to find agreement there. The ANC called off its mass action campaign, and the NP and ANC entered into bilateral talks. The Bisho experience was a sobering one for all parties concerned, and allowed both the NP government and the ANC alliance to reassess their approach to negotiations.

According to Friedman, CODESA failed because both entered the negotiations with flawed assumptions. Each thought it was going to *talk the opponent into submission*: 'many in the "establishment" camp assumed that the ANC had come back to join the existing order; many in the "liberation" fold believed that the exiles and prisoners had returned to take the NP's surrender'.[19] Each *overestimated its own strength*, and underestimated those of the opponent. This calamity eventually proved to be an expensive, but invaluable learning experience: 'the nightmare which followed the breakdown of CODESA instilled a sense of humility, sobriety and realism in both government and ANC leaders, and impressed upon them the dangers of delaying a settlement'.[20]

The parties regrouped in January 1993 to restart constitutional negotiations. This time deliberations were steered by a bilateral agreement between the ANC and the NP, reached in September 1992, following the events at Bisho. This agreement about matters of process committed both parties to convene multi-party talks to negotiate a constitution for an interim government to be established after elections. This government would then also act as a constitutional assembly to negotiate a 'final' constitution. This constitution would have to comply with principles drawn up by the multi-party talks.

This time round negotiators reached agreement. The following reasons for this success can be advanced. The first is that conditions of high levels of *mutual dependence* existed between the contenders, and the negotiators were aware of the mutual vulnerability this created. This interdependence was primarily found in the economic structure of the modern economy, with every stakeholder being drawn into the intricate web of relations generated by market activities and private enterprise. The power implications of such mutual vulnerability, expressed as 'mutual hostageship', was not lost on the negotiators.[21] They recognised (especially after the mass action campaign that ended in the Bisho massacre) that their structural position made the safety, security and well being of each contingent upon the extent to which the other was able to enjoy these benefits. Each held a negative veto on the other. To make the country ungovernable for the opponent, so they learned (following the mass action campaigns of 1992), became a roundabout way of making the country ungovernable for yourself.[22]

The second reason is that the negotiators perceived the outcome, as yet unclear, to be one with a *win–win result*. 'Whites are fellow South Africans, and we want them to feel safe.'[23] These remarkable words were spoken by Nelson Mandela, a day after his release from prison, and illustrate the point. De Klerk expressed a similar view in declaring that the process was about reconciling both minority concerns and majority expectations. Both consistently maintained this public stance throughout the negotiation process.

The *mutually hurting stalemate*, keenly experienced by all contenders, was a third factor in accounting for the negotiated settlement. This stalemate had set in by late 1989, and was experienced in both political and military terms. Neither party could eliminate the other from the political terrain, nor could any one attain a decisive advantage through continued confrontation, while the costs of the continued stalemate continued to rise for both parties. A way out of this stalemate appeared in late 1989 with a change in NP leadership, the dramatic change in the international environment with the fall of the Berlin Wall and effective pre-negotiation which allowed parties to revise their perceptions of one another.[24] Some time during the CODESA negotiations this mutually hurting stalemate was unlearnt, as both the NP and ANC alliance lost their sense of judgement about the balance of power at the negotiating table. This was quickly relearned during the mass action campaign.

When talks were restarted in early 1993 some *innovative negotiating rules* prevented another breakdown. These rules were firstly the rule of 'sufficient consensus'. By this was understood that 'consensus was sufficient if the process could move on the backing of only those who supported a proposal. Disagreement would be recorded; dissenters could remain in the process, await its outcome, and then decide whether to support it.'[25] The effective working of this rule presupposed a high level of trust among negotiators and a strong all round commitment to finding a mutually acceptable solution.

The second rule, of *Bosberade* ('bush summits'), proved to be another successful negotiating innovation. These were negotiating events with a uniquely South African touch. Parties in the process who encountered fundamental differences of opinion would retreat to undisclosed, remote, yet luxurious game parks. There, in seclusion, away from the pressure of audiences, in the African wildlife setting, they could break deadlocks, debate matters of principle, plan strategy and work on new proposals. These summits were mostly bilateral, but were also held as intra-party events, where the internal cohesion of negotiating teams could be patched up.

The third important negotiating rule was the establishment of *'the channel'*. The deliberate deadlock-breaking mechanism consisted of a planning committee, with the specific task of preventing deadlocks from breaking the momentum of the process, and its sub-committee, 'the channel'. The planning committee met behind closed doors, and no minutes were taken of their deliberations. The channel became even more crucial. Initially, it comprised three members (one each from the Inkatha Freedom Party [IFP], the ANC and the NP). After the IFP withdrew from the negotiations, the representatives of the other parties continued to meet. The membership never altered. These two individuals, Mac Maharaj from the ANC and Fanie van der Merwe of the NP, worked very closely, meeting every day, so as to review proceedings of that day, to consider problems, to anticipate others, and to formulate new initiatives with which the negotiators could start the next day. The deadlock-breaking skills of these two individuals became so renowned that, as the process evolved, it became virtually standard practice to 'channel' divisive or contentious issues to them.[26]

The final, inadvertent innovation was the *negotiated election*. The 1994 election, in terms of the standards prevailing in established Western democracies, should have been declared null and void. The procedural requirements of a 'free and fair' election were simply not met. To give but one example, the monitoring authority identified up to 165 no-go areas, where one party effectively denied other parties access to a particular group of voters.[27] Yet all parties accepted the process and the outcome, despite all of them being aware of the indiscretion committed by some of the major parties. The deal was done by the parties accepting the vote count as it was announced by the officials, not by contriving a particular count. And it emerged

> not necessarily by politicians huddling with commissioners, but by the simple fact that parties had withdrawn all complaints. This was not the result of spontaneous self-renunciation – one IFP leader has described privately in detail the meeting between it and the ANC where the two agreed to drop complaints against each other.[28]

A fifth set of factors conducive to the success of the negotiations was the role of astute *leadership*.[29] De Klerk succeeded Botha in late 1989, providing a new generation of leadership to the NP. General Constand Viljoen became the effective leader of the white right wing in 1993 with the death of Andries Treurnicht, the leader of the white Conservative Party. Both of these leaders were able to take their followers into the negotiating process, and to get them to the ballot boxes at the election. Viljoen, in particular, can be singled out, for he, as leader of the Freedom Front, was able to draw the white right-wingers into the process at a very late stage in early 1994, after all other attempts to do so had failed. On the liberationist side Mandela towers above all.

The quality required of leadership in these negotiations was to be able to perceive the condition of 'mutual hostageship', to recognise the mutually hurting stalemate, and from there to set in motion the self-negating prediction. The self-negating prediction refers to the capacity of negotiators to be aware of the destructive conflict potential of their societies, and to be motivated by this awareness to co-operate with opposing negotiators in order to avert such conflict. This they did. As Friedman puts it: 'However bitter conflict became, however unbridgeable the divide between negotiating parties seemed to be, somehow the abyss always seemed to hold less appeal than the option of shifting ground.'[30]

The rapidly changing *international context* of the late 1980s changed crucial aspects of the negotiating environment. De Klerk and the ruling NP's strategic calculation of the ANC as a threatening insurgent force with Marxist superpower backing could make way for a different estimate. The fall of the USSR deprived the ANC of its logistical support, both in military and economic terms. The accompanying collapse of communist regimes in Eastern Europe profoundly discredited the ideology of the ANC's alliance partner, the South African Communist party. In De Klerk's assessment, the ANC became a force that could be contained and moderated, and talked into a power sharing settlement within which the NP and its supporters could be secure.[31]

Deliberate ambiguity is another tactic which contributed to the success of the negotiating process. Some potentially divisive issues, which could even deadlock negotiations, were dealt with by transferring them to the agenda of the first elected government. Issues such as the composition of the civil service, the exact form that policies of affirmative action would take and the details on the integration of the armed forces were not addressed in detail. This left the outcome unclear and ambiguous, allowing stakeholders to continue to perceive matters in win–win terms.

Finally, the negotiators dealt with the problem of an imbalance in institutional bargaining power in an imaginative way. This they did not by making use of external third-party mediation, but by creating new institutions geared to managing the transition. At issue was the unequal structural power of the prospective negotiators in 1991. The NP was occupying the state, and planned to act as negotiator within a process which the state would manage. The ANC objected, arguing in the metaphor of the time, for a need to *'level the playing field'*. This meant that to cancel out the strategic advantage of state incumbency, new institutions would have to be created. It was only in late 1992 that the NP agreed to this demand, and in the 1993 negotiations it was agreed to establish a Transitional Executive Council (TEC), a multi-party council, which would manage the process once agreement on the constitution had been reached. This council would oversee the inaugural 1994 election, to be administered by another new body, the Independent Electoral Commission (IEC). This commission took over the tasks of the state Department of Home Affairs, which had run all previous elections, and which the ANC rejected as partisan. The task was to produce a competent, impartial and politically neutral administration of the election. In this the TEC and IEC duly failed, in part because the latter had to be assembled from scratch just three months prior to the election. The task was just too big, and time and resources too few. The alternative, however, would have been to stick with the tainted institutions of the state, or to request international bureaucracies (UN) to conduct the election, both options with other grave shortcomings.

The implementation phase: coming out of violence? (1996–8)

Events: violence and security

Political violence. The patterns of violence which resulted from the Low-Intensity Conflict which started in the 1980s can be seen from the following statistics.[32] The overall number of political violence fatalities from 1 September 1984 up to the end of December 1997 stands at 23 609.[33] The annual casualty rate varied greatly over this time, escalating during the 1980s, and peaked in the decisive transition years of 1990–4. After 1994 the death rate dropped dramatically, as can be seen from the accompanying graph. (See Figure 1.1)

Up to 1990 the conflict was structured primarily by the state-imposed system of apartheid. A more or less clear-cut line demarcating the state from its opponents structured the conflict into a polarised confrontation between two sets of antagonists. After 1990, with the unbanning of the liberation movements and the weakening of the South African state, the landscape of conflict became more fractured, with new lines of confrontation emerging in the ensuing political vacuum. Violence then increasingly found expression in the forms of:

- massacres (one group of attackers kill five or more people in a single assault)
- political assassinations, more often than not aimed at mid-level community-based leadership, or state officials such as police officers
- intimidation and forced mobilisation for mass demonstrations
- attacks by township youths organised in so-called Self-Defence Units (SDUs)
- revenge attacks by the residents of hostels on perceived enemies
- attacks on rail commuters
- minibus taxi wars
- warlordism[34]

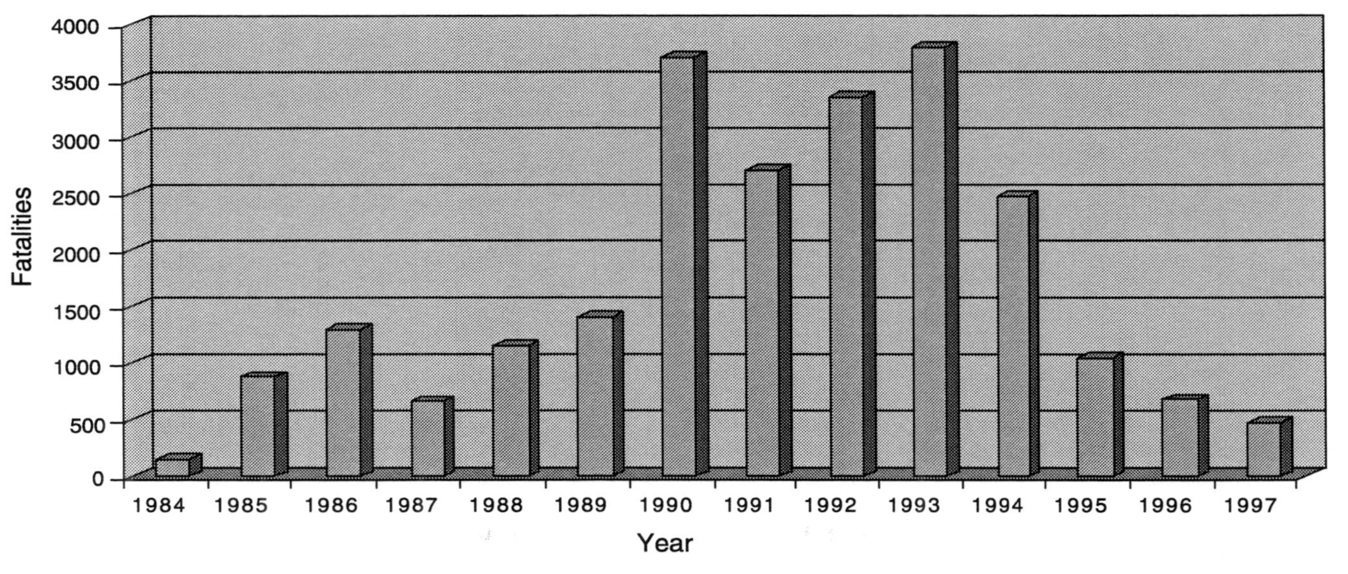

Figure 1.1 Political fatalities in South Africa, 1984–97
Source: Adapted from *Fast Facts*, 2/97 (February 1997), p. 3, and E. Sidiropoulos et al., *South Africa Survey 1997–98* (Johannesburg: South African Institute of Race Relations, 1998), p. 51.

During this era various means of attack were used ranging from explosives through to the use of various firearms, especially AK-47 assault rifles, handguns, stones and the torching of people and property.[35]

Crime

Overt political violence declined rapidly after the 1994 elections, but was soon overtaken by the dramatic rise in violent crime. Crimes to the person (assault, murder, rape and robbery) had been on the rise since the advent of political protest in 1984/5 but had been obscured (and probably under-reported) by the overt anti-apartheid political confrontation. After 1994 the rise in crime (as reported) not only continued, but accelerated. The long-term rise from 1974 to 1995 in assault has been by 24 per cent, murder by 119 per cent, robbery by 171 per cent, rape by 149 per cent, housebreaking by 223 per cent and the theft of motor vehicles by 275 per cent.[36] Expressed slightly differently, every day saw 52 people murdered, a rape committed every 30 minutes, armed robbery every 11 minutes, and a car was stolen every 9 minutes.[37] In total numbers, 1995 saw 18983 reported murders, 36888 rapes, 10839 car hijackings, and more than 45000 armed robberies with aggravating circumstances.[38] Other kinds of violence persisted or escalated. Taxi wars, for instance, continued to flare up. In 1994 taxi-related violence accounted for 199 deaths, in 1995 for 236, and in 1996 for 338.[39]

Community violence

Some of the criminal violence took place within a communal context, in the sense that the agents of violence were organised, with support bases in particular regions/urban areas, and found support among particular sections of the general populace. Most prominent of these communal agents engaged in violence has been PAGAD (People Against Gangsterism and Drugs), a vigilante organisation based in Cape Town (in the area known as the Cape Flats), which draws almost exclusive support from the coloured Muslim community. PAGAD emerged in 1996 and went into action with the public execution of an alleged drug lord in Cape Town. Since then PAGAD has been in conflict with the state as well as a number of the major gangs in Cape Town.

Criminal gangs form an integral part of the social structure of the poorest sections of Cape Town's population. Their origin can be traced to the social dislocation experienced by the coloured community of Cape Town when they were relocated onto the Cape Flats during the 1950s and 1960s.[40] Although their emergence is generally accounted for by the reference to the invidious effects of the apartheid system, a striking aspect of post-apartheid South Africa is that these gangs did not disperse or wane in any way after the end of apartheid. On the contrary, they appear to have increased in number, and in strength. According to one police report, in late 1996, there were about 137 gangs in the Western Cape region, with a combined membership of between 30 000 and 50 000. About 100 of these gangs were operating in the Cape Flats. Some of these gangs are drawn into larger crime syndicates of which about 481 were said to be in operation in the country in mid-1996.[41] Criminal gangs are, by definition, immersed in a culture of violence, and this culture does not appear to have been fundamentally affected by South Africa's transition towards democracy.

One area of conflict which almost defies classification is the communal violence experienced in the Qumbu and Tsolo regions of the Eastern Cape Province. Police records for this rural area show 905 murders from 1994 to June 1996 and 314 cases of attempted murder reported to the authorities.[42] This resulted from a conflict which originated in stock theft, and then rapidly escalated into cycles of reprisals, retaliation and vengeance in which vigilante organisations, members of the provincial government and even the police were implicated. According to an official investigation, by 1997 entire villages had completely abandoned hope of any authority being able to secure their safety, and they resorted to lawless actions on their own account.[43]

Communal conflict with a more recent political origin emerged in the Richmond area of KwaZulu/Natal. A regional leader of the ANC, Sifiso Nkabinde, was accused in a confidential report by the SADF of engaging in establishing a private army in the Richmond area, of setting up hit-squad activities and of engaging in gun-running. Nkabinde was expelled from the ANC during mid-1997, and arrested and charged for the murder of 18 persons in late 1997.[44] On 30 April 1998 he was acquitted on all charges, and released. The presiding judge dismissed the case of the state, describing state witnesses as 'liars', and cited police irregularity and improper conduct in their handling of the case.[45] Nkabinde returned to Richmond and joined the United Democratic Movement. Violence also returned. By the end of August 1998 23 more people were killed in three separate massacres. None of the assailants has been arrested.

White farmers became another very specific target of violent attacks. In 1995 there were 551 reported attacks on farms and smallholdings, resulting in the death of 121 persons. In 1996, 468 attacks lead to the death of 109 farmers. In 1997 these attacks declined to 347, in which 85 farmers lost their lives.[46]

Finally, yet another notable category of public violence that relates to community life is that associated with witchcraft. This occurs almost exclusively in the Northern Province of the country, and from the early 1990s there has been a steady rise in the number of reported incidents. These incidents include so-called *muti* murders, where the aim is to obtain bodily parts for use in potions which are then assumed to acquire magical properties. Other kinds of violence are witch purging, in the form of expulsion, destruction of property and also murder, and labelling of people as witches. From 1990 to April 1995 445 such cases were reported to the authorities. In 1996 it rose dramatically to 1182 reported cases, and then again declined in the first half of 1997 to 321 cases. The number of deaths which emanated from these events are not easily ascertained, but the official estimate for the year April 1994 to April 1995 stands at 228, declining to 24, 17 and 11 in the following years.[47]

There are a number of significant features to this overall picture of criminal violence, which are relevant to accounting for post-settlement violence in South Africa. The first is that of persistent reports of police involvement in crime. It was revealed officially that in the year and a half up to May 1996 800 allegations of police involvement in corruption were investigated, resulting in the arrest of 170 officers. In 1995 there were 833 complaints of assault laid against the police, resulting in 241 convictions. And in the two years leading up to September 1996 the Gauteng Province alone investigated 8300 criminal cases in which members of the police were implicated.[48] These convictions serve as evidence of state weakness, with state officials unable to uphold their own rules.

The second is the extent to which the civilian population has been armed. A UN report calculated that civilian-owned arms in South Africa stands at a ratio of 84 per 1000, which converts to an estimate of 20 per cent of all households owning a firearm. Official sources also conceded that almost 20 000 convicted criminals were owners of licensed firearms.[49] The extent to which the society is saturated with illegal firearms is difficult to assess accurately, but police estimated that there were about 4 million weapons in the country held illegally by the end of 1997.[50] Some indication of the kind of weaponry in civilian hands is provided by statistics of such arms confiscated by the police. In 1995 the police seized 16 291 unlicensed firearms, an increase of 10 per cent on the previous year. This included 1392 AK-47 assault rifles and 256 sub-machine guns. During the same year 508 explosive devices were confiscated, which included hand grenades, mortars, limpet mines and RPG-7 projectiles.[51]

These two factors, an armed civilian population, ready to use these weapons and the primary law enforcement agency of the state that is, to some extent, unable to comply with the laws it has to enforce, are early indicators of state weakness. The state cannot effectively exercise a monopoly on the means of force, and cannot stick to its own rules. State weakness is a crucial factor in accounting for South Africa's problems of post-settlement violence. In the next sections the sources of state weakness will be examined.

Negotiated settlements and constitutional rules relevant to security and policing

South Africa's negotiated settlement clearly did not provide it with a set of law enforcement institutions able to meet the challenge which emerged after the transition to democracy. The Nedcor study on crime found that

> of every 1000 crimes committed in South Africa, only 450 were reported, 230 were solved and 100 were brought to trial. Of those prosecuted, only 77 were convicted, of whom 33 were imprisoned but only eight served sentences of two years or longer. Of the eight imprisoned, only one would be rehabilitated.[52]

What were the weak links in the negotiated settlement?

The first weak link is arguably to be found in the process of negotiation itself. A striking feature of the process was the number of non-aggression pacts made between the South African government of the time and the ANC. This culminated in the signing of the National Peace Accord in September 1991. The Accord set out a code of conduct for political parties and movements and a set of rules applicable to dangerous weapons and paramilitary groups. Briefly, the Accord did not demand that arms caches be revealed and handed over to the state, only that firearms should not be carried and/or displayed in public gatherings (sect. 3.6). Nor did the Accord disband paramilitary units, but only required such units to be renamed as 'self-protection units'. The relevant clause read that

> all individuals [have] the right to protect themselves and their property, and to establish voluntary associations or self-protection units in any neighbourhood to prevent crime and to prevent any invasion of the lawful rights of such communities. This shall include the

> right to bear licensed arms and to use them in legitimate and lawful self-defence.
>
> (sect. 3.7.1)

Nor was the state obliged to disband its agencies engaged in covert operations. The only relevant stipulation was that 'The government shall not allow any operation by the security forces with the intention to undermine, promote or influence any political party or political organisation at the expense of another by means of any acts, or by means of disinformation' (sect. 3.5.2). The Accord also stopped short from committing the ANC to move from a suspension of violence to a renunciation thereof, and did not oblige them to reveal their arms caches. To what extent this Accord effectively contained public violence during the transition, and inhibited the continuing violence after the transition, is very difficult to assess. It can be argued that had more stringent measures been settled on, the availability of firearms, and the organisational units intent on deploying them, would have been notably curtailed. The counter-argument is that the Accord, weak as it was, represented the art of the possible, at that time, and no stronger set of constraints could have been agreed on.

The 1993 constitution, seen to be the most tangible product of the settlement, is, in general terms, an admirable example of liberal constitutionalism. It contained, amongst others, a chapter on fundamental rights, the first in the country's history. Section 25, the longest in the entire chapter, contains extensive rights awarded to detained, arrested and accused persons. (This is perfectly understandable, given the nature of the conflict which preceded negotiations. Many of the negotiators, with Mandela as the supreme example, had spent many years in prison, without any constitutional protection from abuse and with little recourse to the courts for remedial action.) One crucial item in the list of rights granted to arrested persons deals with the conditions of bail and release. Section 25(2)(d) reads that every person arrested on the suspicion of having committed a crime and having been brought to court and charged accordingly is 'to be released from detention with or without bail unless the interests of justice require otherwise'. This put the onus on the state to give reasons for not releasing suspects, and compelling the state to do so if reasons could not be presented. The record shows that some criminals used this constitutional opening to continue their careers in crime. In 1995, the year after the constitution came into force, 6217 people arrested for criminal activity were found to be out on bail for previously charged offences.[53] In 1996 the laws on bail were amended, and the 1996 constitution reversed the onus of argumentation and burden of proof to the defendant.

The 1996 constitution defines the security services of the state as consisting of the police service, defence force and the intelligence services. The task of the police is described in the constitution as to 'combat and investigate crime, to maintain public order, to protect and secure the inhabitants of the Republic and their property, and to uphold and enforce the law' (sect. 205[3]). The objectives of the defence force do not specify crime and public order. Instead, 'the primary object of the defence force is to defend and protect the Republic, its territorial integrity and its people in accordance with the Constitution and the principles of international law regulating the use of force' (sect. 200[20]). In pursuing these objectives the composition and operations of these two forces are guided by two important guidelines. Firstly, both services must, in their membership, like the public service in general, 'be broadly representative of the South African people' (sect. 195[1]). In practical terms, this means that the *racial composition* of the country be reflected in the personnel profile of the respective forces. Secondly partisan bias in the security services is discouraged by section 199(7) which stipulates that

> neither the security services, nor any of their members may, in the performance of their functions – (a) prejudice a political party interest that is legitimate in terms of the Constitution; or (b) further, in a partisan manner, any interest of a political party

These two guidelines attempt to enhance legitimacy and effectiveness. The latter stipulation can be considered to be a mild application of the principle of *gelding,* and is intended to promote impartiality in the ranks of the security services. Given the history of political conflict, and the post-settlement emergence of community-based conflict, the need for non-partisan security forces is obvious. However, these very limited restrictions are significantly weaker than even those contained in the 1993 constitution. There the prescription is that no member of the defence force shall 'hold office in any political party or political organisation' (sect. 226(6)). And while police activities beyond the law have apparently not (yet) infringed on party-political activity, these constitutional constraints have not succeeded in preventing their activities from entering the domain of community conflicts which are gang related.

The police service did act with some energy in response to the rise in criminal violence after apartheid. In May 1996 the National Crime

Prevention Strategy was launched. Its most visible objective was a campaign to arrest 10 000 of the country's most wanted criminals. A month after the launch of the project the police announced that more than 7000 of these persons had in fact been taken into custody. Closer scrutiny revealed, however, that 2099 (29.5 per cent) of them had again been released on bail![54] Other aspects of the strategy included additional legislation prohibiting the carrying of firearms in public, extending government control over public gatherings and demonstrations, upgrading of equipment, a witness protection programme and steps to contain the spread of the gang activity within the prison system.

This effort by the police has been hampered by a lack of resources. The most immediate was a lack of training. In mid-1996 the national commissioner of police stated that only 25 per cent of the force's detectives were adequately trained. Another press report had it that 40 per cent of the police officers in Johannesburg did not possess a driver's licence, and that about one-third of them did not have a matric pass. Furthermore the force was understaffed by about 15 per cent during the crucial first years of the transition. This state of affairs was exacerbated by the moratorium on the recruitment of new personnel which had been introduced in 1994. This moratorium was lifted only in May 1997.[55]

Unlike the police, who during the transition did not have to come to terms with a rival, parallel and contending police formation within the ranks of the liberation forces, the defence force had to deal with an extensive programme of integrating the forces of the apartheid state with those of the liberation forces. This programme is crucial to the containment of post-settlement violence. The progress in this regard, for the period under review, is as follows. The process of integration of these forces had, by early 1996, swelled the ranks of the defence force to just over 100 000 members, with, amongst others, the absorption of 16 450 former liberation army members (mostly MK [Umkhonto we Sizwe]) into the force. August 1996 was to be the final cut off date for the recruitment of MK members. This overall force size was considered to be too large, and the target was to reduce it again to about 90 000 full-time members by the year 2000. This would involve voluntary release of former MK members, who would receive severance packages. The integration of other forces had not proceeded at the same pace. A start at drawing members of the self-protection units of the IFP into the defence force was only made by June 1996, and funds were made available for the recruitment of only 2200 individuals from their ranks.

The integration of members of Azanian People's Liberation Army (APLA), the military wing of the PAC, had met with the least success. The defence force reported in March 1996 that only 3963 of the estimated 6000 members of APLA had formally joined. About 11 500 members from the former homeland armies had also joined by late 1996.[56]

Despite the constitutional delimitation of tasks assigned to the police and the defence force, the latter had regularly provided personnel to help the police. During 1996 about 4000 troops were deployed daily throughout the country to help combat crime. The province of KwaZulu-Natal alone made use of 1600 troops daily. Border controls were also staffed by the defence force, who deployed 2700 troops on a regular basis for this task.

The integration of former military and paramilitary personnel is crucial to the containment of post-settlement public violence. The ANC has claimed that members of the security services of the former government have become active in violent crime after 1994, while the NP has responded with the assertion that former MK members are engaged in armed robbery. Circumstantial evidence, in the form of arrested suspects with MK and/or SADF backgrounds, tends to support both claims.[57] A more serious claim that has been made is that some former MK members have been operating in violent crime under the direction of ANC politicians.[58] Should this be confirmed, then the level of state weakness in responding to crime is not merely of *active encouragement* but also, to some extent, *collusion*. To date this has not been conclusively substantiated, but the Minister of Safety and Security has gone so far as to admit that 'we are clearly dealing with highly organised syndicates, of which some of the members have military backgrounds, either as former members of the liberation armies or as former and even serving members of the statutory armed formations'.[59]

The general point to be made is that some former members of MK and the SADF and their respective paramilitary off-shoots, the Self-Defence Units and Bureau for Civil Co-operation, have not been drawn into the discipline of the state and society in the post-settlement era. Given their expertise in weaponry, given the availability of weapons, and given the social context of poverty and unemployment, these individuals have strong incentives to re-engage in public violence, albeit this time for personal gain. Following from this, the general lesson to be learnt from the South African case is that the terms of the constitutional settlement, as well as the process of transition, must aim to disarm paramilitary units (by enforcing the disclosure of arms caches, closing conduits for arms smuggling, etc.) and aim to enlist as many as possible of their personnel into the security forces of the state. To the extent that this was not achieved in the South African settlement, the state was weakened, and the post-apartheid democratic regime had to confront armed civilians with anti-democratic agendas whom the state could not contain effectively.

Economic factors

Some of the incentives for violent crime lie in conditions of poverty, inequality and unemployment. South Africans experienced overall rising standards of living up to the early 1980s. Since then economic life has become less secure. The curve in GDP per capita growth (see Tables 1.1, 1.2 and 1.3) is revealed in the fact that in 1996 South Africans were about 23 per cent richer (in real terms) than they were in 1960, but still 16 per cent worse off than they were in 1981. This trend is also revealed in the changing pattern of per capita personal disposable incomes, which declined between 1980 and 1990 by 7.1 per cent and between 1990 and 1996 by a further 2.6 per cent.

The pervasiveness of poverty is reflected in the findings of a study which shows that by late 1995 53 per cent of the population were found among the poorest 40 per cent of households. The richest 20 per cent of households in the country were earning 19 times more than the poorest 20 per cent of households.[60] Data on unemployment varies according to the definition used. According to an expanded definition used by official sources, South Africa had an overall unemployment rate of 29.3 per cent in 1995. The rate varies strongly according to race. Among Africans the rate stood at 36.9 per cent while 22.3 per cent of

Table 1.1 Real GDP: 1960–96

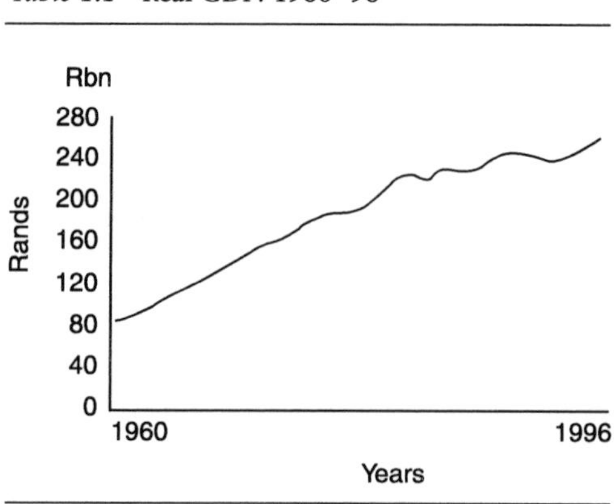

Table 1.2 Real GDP per head: 1960–96

R
10000
8000
6000
4000
2000
0
Rands
1981
1960
1996
Years

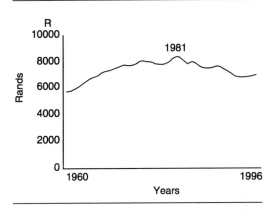

Table 1.3 Real annual economic growth: 1960–96

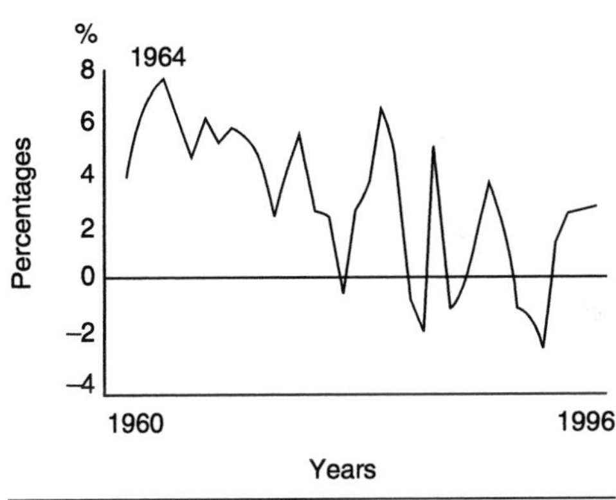

Source: E. Sidiropoulos et al., *South Africa Survey 1996–97* (Johannesburg: South African Institute of Race Relations, 1997), pp. 655–6.

coloureds, 13.4 per cent of Asians and 5.5 per cent of whites were unemployed. Given the disparities in size of these racial groups, this meant that about 87 per cent of all unemployed people were Africans, 8 per cent were coloureds, 3 per cent whites and 1 per cent Asians.[61]

The causes of this economic decline are multiple, and the impact of more or less 'pure' economic factors, such as the decline in the gold price from its all-time high in 1980, are difficult to isolate from factors associated with the turmoil of the violent revolt and transition from 1980s onwards. Nonetheless, conspicuous factors worth considering are the deliberate attempts to divert foreign investment capital away from South Africa, as part of the more comprehensive programme of economic isolation of the country, the worsening investment profile of the country resulting from domestic violence and turmoil, and increasing militancy in the domestic labour market. The overall impact of the sanctions campaign on the democratic transition therefore needs to be judged with care. To the extent that sanctions could have contributed to the pressure on the apartheid regime to get to the negotiating table it counts as a positive force. (The political impact of sanctions is considered in the next section.) However, such short-term benefits have to be weighed up against the longer-term impact, especially relevant to the issue of post-settlement violence, and to the overall process of democratic consolidation. The proposition to consider is that to the extent that sanctions contributed to conditions of economic decline, unemployment, inequality and both relative and absolute poverty it generated incentives to those people with access to weapons, and skills in using them, to engage in violent crime. Contingent upon the strength of this proposition is the recommendation that outsiders should be careful in employing economic sanctions as an inducement towards democratic transition. It may serve the immediate objective of getting recalcitrant incumbents to the negotiating table, but it can also produce the paradoxical effect of undermining the economic system to be inherited by the new democratic regime. To escape this paradox, international sanctioneers would have to invest massively into the economy in the immediate post-settlement era.

Whatever the sources of rising unemployment, the result is that the expected peace dividend has not materialised for many South Africans. Statistics cannot really provide adequate measurement of the resulting disillusionment. The intuitive sense of African journalist Maja Mokoena, a long-time exile, upon revisiting Soweto on 16 June 1998, to commemorate the 1976 uprising, captures this mood as well as any:

> What I experienced in 1998 was a far cry from the fervour and energetic defiance of 1976. These emotions have been replaced by a complacency I would expect only from a defeated nation – a complacency reminiscent of the late 1960s ... Most Sowetans, unemployed for more than 10 years, feel left out by the new government ... How did this unemployment situation happen? For starters, we can blame the wholesale retrenchments of the pre-election era ... Blame

> also lies squarely on the government's incompetence at managing the economy for growth ...[62]

External factors

South Africa's prospects for economic growth and the concomitant redress of poverty, inequality and unemployment are very closely tied to its position and performance in the global economy. Likewise, the ability of the state to disarm violent civilian formations such as vigilantes, gangs and crime syndicates is also contingent upon its relations with states within the southern African region and the wider global environment.

South Africa's industrial economy has, from its takeoff with the diamond and gold mining industries, been tied to international markets. International economic sanctions moved to isolate the domestic economy, and in part succeeded, especially after 1986. The political impact of sanctions needs to be considered separately. The careful analysis by Trevor Bell finds support for the proposition that

> the possibility clearly remains that sanctions had a significant political impact in various ways, not dependent on their constricting the economy. One obvious possibility is that, though sanctions might not actually have been causing significant economic change, the mere threat of intensified sanctions contributed to political change.[63]

According to Bell the threat of such sanctions only achieved effective leverage after the end of the Cold War. While the bipolar rivalry existed, South Africa could always credibly counter Western threats of sanctions with the argument that the Soviets were ready to move into Southern Africa should the South African government fall. After the fall of the Berlin Wall the USA remained unchallenged as the only superpower, and the threat of Soviet influence disappeared. The USA could effectively present the De Klerk government with an ultimatum: negotiate or face comprehensive sanctions.

The economic impact of sanctions notwithstanding, except for 1986 and 1991, exports grew every year, accelerating rapidly after 1994, with an overall increase of 42 per cent between 1985 and 1996. Imports rose by 94.8 per cent over the same period. To hold its own in this competitive arena the economy would, amongst others, require consistent large foreign capital investments. This in turn requires an investor-friendly domestic environment. The Government has gone a substantial way in delivering this, with its macro-economic plan titled Growth, Employment and Redistribution (GEAR). This entails a policy of economic orthodoxy, combining fiscal austerity, wage restraint, export promotion and lower bank rates as inducements to direct foreign investment, employment creation and overall economic growth. The projected targets for the year 2000 include a growth rate of 6 per cent, and job creation of 400 000 per annum. These targets present an enormous challenge, given the extent of the global competition for investment capital, and South Africa's own stagnant level of productivity, which dropped by an average of 0.1 per cent per year for the period from 1970 through to 1994.[64] Many of the reasons for economic under performance remain: hostility between labour and management, racism on the shop floor, inadequate training, a workforce loathe to identify with the issue of raising productivity, and volatile industrial relations.

The issue of arms smuggling and gang warfare also has an international dimension. Above (p. 35), it was mentioned that the state estimated that by mid-1996 there were 481 crime syndicates operative in the country. The same source had it that at least 187 of these syndicates were operating internationally, and 125 of them were active in sub-Saharan Africa. South Africa has thus been classified as being both a *home state* to domestic criminal organisations and also a *host state* to Zairean, Chechen, Nigerian, Chinese and Italian criminal organisations.[65] Many of these are entangled in the regional and global network of the illegal trade in arms. This trade is at the core of the post-settlement violence in South Africa.

The forces of globalisation and of democratic transition have opened up new opportunities for transnational criminal organisations, at the expense of state sovereignty. One of the most lucrative fields of operation has been the illegal arms trade. Historically, this trade was subject to some stringent controls. On the supply side the major powers controlled production and movement of armaments. On the demand side, the ability of non-state forces to obtain weapons, even if they could circumvent supply side controls, was limited by their incapacity to obtain the financial means of payment. After the end of the Cold War, so it is argued, both forms of control have collapsed. On the supply side, a glut of weapons has flooded the market, some from the demise of totalitarian and authoritarian regimes, some from the expanding commercial arms industry, and some from flawed processes of disarmament and peacemaking. This has lead to a downward spiral in prices, making small arms easily affordable, thus opening the demand side of the market. An AK-47, for example, can be bought in Uganda for the price of a chicken, in Angola and Mozambique for the equivalent of a bag of maize, and in Namibia for about SAR50.00 (the equivalent of US$10.00).[66]

South Africa finds itself in one of the more active regions in the global small arms black market. The Low Intensity Conflicts in the Southern African region, ranging from those which lead to the independence of Namibia, Zimbabwe, Angola and Mozambique, and the subsequent civil wars in the last two generated a huge influx of weaponry into the region. The winding down of these civil wars did not, however, succeed in effectively withdrawing these arms from the arena. The UNOMOZ operation of the UN in Mozambique (1993–5), in particular, failed dismally in its disarmament objectives, partly due to a lack of will and assertiveness on the side of the peacemakers. The UN succeeded in disposing of less than 190 000 of the estimated 1.5 million AK-47s distributed to the civilian population during the course of the civil war.[67] The remaining ones became available for entry into the black market for small arms in South Africa. Despite concerted efforts by the state to remove this weaponry from society, the public remains armed, and organisations geared to use these arms continue to do so. One of the key rules of peace, a disarmed civilian population, therefore remains an unachieved objective.

Illegal immigrants who enter South Africa from the rest of Africa, and from other continents, add another set of external factors which impinge on the country's efforts at extricating itself from post-settlement violence. Estimates about the number of illegals in the country vary widely and wildly, ranging from a low 2 million to a high estimate of 8 million. Whether their presence is a positive contribution to peace, development and stability, or a factor exacerbating the already existing problems of unemployment, crime and competition for housing, education and welfare is a hotly disputed issue, with strong claims being made on both sides. Official statistics for 1994 showed that 14 per cent of general crimes were committed by illegal immigrants, 12 400 of whom were arrested in that year.[68] Public opinion towards these illegals will be discussed below.

Popular responses

Public opinion

At the core of South Africa's negotiated transition to democracy was the attempt to move away from a racially ordered state and society towards a democratic order in which citizenship would not be tied to racial identities dictated and imposed by the state. This objective was achieved, to the extent that both the 1993 and 1996 constitutions subscribed to the ideal of non-racialism. The social diversity in society, a combination of race and culture, remains. Legal racial classification has fallen away. In metaphorical terms, the society, in the immediate post-1994 euphoria, was depicted as 'the rainbow nation', expressing the conviction (yearning) that race has ceased to be the salient social identity. Has this become fact?

In a nationally representative opinion survey conducted shortly after the 1994 elections the following question was put to the respondents: 'How important is your culture, history and values to you?' Seventy-nine per cent of the respondents indicated that it was important to them. In 1996 this survey was repeated, and the affirmative response to the identical question was 90 per cent. This sentiment appears to seep into people's self-identification as well. Only 17.3 per cent of the respondents in the 1996 survey identified themselves in the first instance as 'South Africans', an identification one can take to be compatible with the notion of the 'rainbow nation'. The other respondents selected race or culture as first-order indicators of identity.[69] The salience of race and culture has therefore not only persisted in the political culture of the society, but may even be on the resurgence. If one accepts that negotiated transitions can produce fundamental changes in a very short time, but that political culture changes more gradually, then the task of implementation and consolidation can become the true pivotal stage in democratisation. Deliberate, concerted policy actions are required to maintain the momentum created by the negotiators, and to let it permeate through to the citizenry on all sides of the political divide.

The overall priorities of the public in the immediate post-settlement era rapidly moved away from issues directly related to their newly acquired status of democratic citizenship. Physical and economic security rapidly became first-order concerns. The 1995/96 World Values Survey probed respondents' views on the most desirable priorities for the country. From a list of 18 items, democratic concerns only entered the list at number 12 (Giving people more say in their work and their community).[70] The full list is presented in Table 1.4.

Concern with security issues found expression in a number of other avenues as well. Support for the reinstatement of the death penalty is one. In 1995 the Constitutional Court ruled that the death penalty violated the right to life, dignity and equality, and abolished it accordingly. A 1995 national opinion survey found that 62 per cent of the

Table 1.4 1995/96 World Values Survey: Overall priorities – most desirable*

1.	Making sure all people are fully employed	27.8
2.	Maintaining a high rate of economic growth	13.9
3.	Providing shelter for all people	12.0
4.	Fighting crime	8.7
5.	Making sure that everyone can go to school	7.8
6.	Maintaining law and order	7.2
7.	Providing land for all people	4.3
8.	Providing clean water for all people	3.2
9.	Providing everyone with enough food to eat	3.1
10.	Fighting rising prices	2.9
11.	Making sure that everyone is adequately clothed	2.2
12.	Giving people more say in their work and their community	1.7
13.	Maintaining a strong defence force	1.3
14.	Making society friendlier and less impersonal	1.2
15.	Keeping cities and countryside beautiful	1.0
16.	Giving people more say in government	0.8
17.	Protecting freedom of speech	0.7
18.	Creating a society where ideas count more than money	0.3
		Total N: 2935**

*Percentages: numbers do not add up to 100 owing to rounding.
**Total number of respondents who filled in the questionnaire item.
Source: Hennie Kotzé and Pierre du Toit, 'Public Opinion on Security and Democracy in South Africa after Transition: the 1995/96 World Values Survey', *Strategic Review for Southern Africa*, 19, 2 (November 1997), pp. 52–75 (67).

total population were in favour of its reinstatement. By July 1996 this had increased to 71.4 per cent.[71] Changes in opinions on the police also reflect security concerns. In 1995 the police were held in high esteem, and respondents in the World Values Survey ranked them second only to the churches as public organisations in whom they had confidence.[72] Declining police performance, however, appears to be whittling away at the public support. A July 1997 survey of victims of crime in Johannesburg found that more than 60 per cent of victims of assault were dissatisfied with the way police responded.[73] Only slightly removed from direct security issues is the matter of public resentment against illegal immigrants. This has been measured at both the elite level and that of the general public, and also across the range of party support. A 1995 survey of elite respondents found 88 per cent of them supportive of stricter action against illegals.[74] Another survey in 1997, probing a different aspect of attitudes towards illegal immigrants, found that social distance towards illegal immigrants from Africa was consistently high, amongst all racial categories of respondents.[75]

Public action

Changing attitudes and opinions represent one measure of the public's response to their post-settlement environment. Direct action is another measure. One form of direct response to an environment in which economic and physical security is threatened is that of self-defence. Some of these responses have already been dealt with and will only be briefly mentioned again. Vigilante action is a direct, informal and often illegal defence mechanism which has been resorted to by a number of communities. When they effectively 'take the law into their own hands', they, paradoxically, become part of the problem which they set out to remedy: to protect citizens against violent forces which break the laws of the state.

A more measured response has been the rise of the private security industry. This industry has grown dramatically, but accurate estimates of its size appear to be unavailable. One source reports the number of personnel in this sector at 110 000, while another one puts it as high as 280 000 members, which is more than the police and defence force combined.[76] This response is only a partial solution to the problem, as privatised security offers protection only to those who can pay for it, thus perpetuating the problem of inequitable delivery of what is essentially a public good.

By far the most appropriate response to date has been the initiative called Business Against Crime. This is a corporate business project, financed by the business sector, and aims to bolster police effectiveness through the provision of logistic and organisational support. Thus far, this support has taken the form of donations of motor vehicles, closed circuit television cameras, cellular phones, accommodation, cash donations and the setting up of regional communications networks.[77] This initiative serves to strengthen the state and its capacity to provide security to all citizens, not by breaking the law, but by increasing state capacity to enforce the law.

Symbolic factors

Essential to peace are public policies which deal with symbolic matters in an evenhanded and equitable manner. These symbols should, ideally, celebrate, commemorate and dignify what is seen as a decisive, even watershed achievement. The achievement in this case is the dissolution of the contest for hegemony, and the finding of agreement on who constitutes 'the people' who are to be governed democratically, the nature of the state in which this people are to be located, and the constitutional rules which will shape the democratic regime. This has wide application, whether in the realm of language policy, historical and/or religious days of significance to particular communities (and therefore candidates for public holidays), places of symbolic importance, the names of public places (airports, dams, city parks, towns, cities, etc.), or the official symbols of the state (heraldic emblems, flags, anthems, bank notes, even the name of the state).

Opposing formations have to deal with the past. This has a symbolic as well as practical dimension. Practical considerations relate to dealing with 'war crimes', often stated as 'gross violations of human rights'. Procedures involving disclosure, amnesty, indemnity, reparation and reconciliation are relevant here. The symbolic dimension bears on the overall moral assessment of the actions and objectives of the various adversaries, to means and to ends. Can one or more party lay claim to having pursued a 'just war', which may then be used to legitimise the use of immoral means? Is one or more party, and by implication community, obliged to accept collective guilt for actions taken by individuals during the conflict? Is accountability to be established on an individual basis, or is it to be understood in systemic terms, with culpability therefore to be assigned accordingly?

South Africa's transition was accompanied by some striking symbolic moments. The new flag, first unveiled at the inauguration of Nelson Mandela as the new President, and the opening of the first democratic parliament were all choreographed to convey the uniqueness of the events, and the fact that they emerged from a particular kind of process, that is, a negotiated settlement which was produced through the politics of compromise. However, except for the flag, the other symbolic gestures were all part of ephemeral events, with little enduring presence.

Somewhat more permanent were a number of other changes. A new set of banknotes, depicting the Big Five of the African bushveld (Lion, Leopard, Elephant, Rhino and Buffalo), were issued in 1993. These met some of the requirements of appropriate symbols: neutral, attractive and truly indigenous. Neutral ground was also found in the renaming of public spaces such as airports with bland, and rather uninspiring substitutes: D. F. Malan Airport became Cape Town Airport, Jan Smuts Airport became Johannesburg International Airport. Even more original, and more romantic, was the renaming of places with names from the language of a virtually extinct culture, that of the San (Bushmen), the original autochthonous inhabitants and owners of the country. The outstanding example is the renaming of the H. F. Verwoerd Dam to the Gariep Dam.

By far the most daunting challenge facing South Africa is to come to terms with its violent past. This holds important symbolic implications. In 1995 the official Commission on Truth and Reconciliation (TRC) was established to examine the country's past and to ascertain the nature and extent of the gross violation of human rights during this era. The commission's work has been dogged with controversy throughout, and remained so till the release of its final report. The major issues in dispute, each bearing on the extent to which the rules of war and peace were upheld or not, can be mentioned briefly.

- Claims to having engaged in violent acts in pursuit of a 'just war'. This claim is advanced by the ANC and PAC, but is challenged by the NP and IFP.
- Acceptance of collective guilt. The ANC, and, at times, the chairperson of the Commission, has insisted that white South Africans, and particularly Afrikaans speakers, accept collective guilt for the injustices of the past. This has been refused by the NP, FF (Freedom Front) and various liberal NGOs who point out that the TRC Act does not make allowance for this.
- Claims and denials about responsibility for civilian deaths. Both the liberation forces and the then South African government conducted actions which have led to civilian deaths. Both stand accused of having done so as a matter of deliberate policy. Both deny it. (See pp. 18–19.)

The findings of the TRC, released on 29 October 1998, bear on a number of the above issues. The major findings, quoted from the report, are:

i) The predominant portion of gross violations of human rights was committed by the former State through its security and law-enforcement agencies';
ii) 'The Commission endorses the position in international law that apartheid as a form of systematic racial discrimination and separation constituted a crime against humanity';
iii) '[P. W.] Botha contributed to and facilitated a climate in which the above gross violations of human rights could and did occur, and as such is accountable for such violations';
iv) 'The former government deliberately and systematically destroyed state documentation over a number of years';
v) 'During the period 1982–94 the Inkatha Freedom Party ... was responsible for gross violations of human rights committed in the

former Transvaal, Natal and KwaZulu... Chief Mangosuthu Buthelezi is held by this Commission to be accountable in his representative capacity as the leader...'

vi) 'The Commission... finds that in the period 1990–94 the ANC was responsible for: killings, assaults and attacks on political opponents including members of the IFP, PAC, AZAPO (Azanian People's Organisation) and the SAP... and therefore finds that the leadership of the ANC and MK must take responsibility, and be accountable for gross violations of human rights.'

vii) 'The Commission finds that Mrs. [Winnie] Madikizela-Mandela herself was responsible for committing [such] gross violations of human rights';

viii) 'The commission finds PAC action directed towards both civilians and whites to have been a gross violation of human rights for which the PAC and APLA leadership are held morally and politically responsible';

ix) 'The killings of [76] IFP office-bearers amount to a systematic pattern of abuse... for which the respective structures of the UDF, ANC and MK are held accountable'.[78]

Every major participant was therefore denied the emotional gratification of being accorded a morally exalted status. None can claim the symbolic high ground as their own. These findings caught some political actors unaware, and did not meet with their approval. F. W. De Klerk succeeded through a High Court action to have findings about his alleged transgressions deleted. The ANC leadership unsuccessfully sought a High Court ruling to have the release of the entire report blocked. Nelson Mandela famously took issue with his own party's objections (that the struggle against apartheid was being criminalised) and backed the findings of the Commission. The controversy is bound to persist. Future research will show how valid these findings are (that is, how close to the truth the TRC got) and future events will reveal whether reconciliation has been served or not. The option of a blanket amnesty (which will invalidate the entire TRC process) is already being mooted by a number of political actors.

The essence of a symbol which is both inspiring and neutral is hard to find. According to Horowitz, Malaysia succeeded in finding this, and the Malaysian coalition carries with it '... a mystique' which embodies an 'enduring memory of a watershed achievement'.[79] This symbolic image still eludes South Africa. Whether the TRC will be able to generate such a mystique remains to be seen.

Conclusion: Towards new rules of peace?

The problem of post-settlement violence in countries negotiating their transition to democracy should not be underestimated. In the case of South Africa this problem emerged from a number of factors. The first and probably most important one is that very few negotiators appeared to be aware of the prospect of post-settlement criminal violence of the order which emerged after 1994. On both sides of the table they appeared to be unaware of the long-term impact destabilising doctrines of 'ungovernability' and of 'total strategy' were going to have on both state and society. Therefore, when they negotiated for new constitutional rules, there was an element of naivety in their deliberations. They negotiated for democratic constitutional rules with little awareness of the profound breakdown in the state-driven rules for the conduct and containment of public violence, which they themselves had violated so consistently in the conflict leading up to the negotiations. The result is that some constitutional rules were quite unable to function in containing post-settlement violence. This momentum towards violence was further pushed forward by adverse economic conditions, a regional context saturated with small arms, and a public who responded in part, by taking vigilante actions, intent on protecting themselves where the state was seen to be inadequate.

Post-settlement violence can be dealt with more effectively if negotiators are adequately aware of its prospect, and if they deal with it in anticipation. The negotiation process must secure the strength of those state agencies which will be essential to implementing the negotiated settlement, once made. And the settlement itself must take care in producing constitutional rules which limit the access to the means of violence by non-state actors. Democracies can flourish only in states that are able to deal effectively with non-state forces hostile to democracy, and who are intent on using violence to pursue their ends. The South African case shows that both the domestic process and outcome had shortcomings. In addition, a regional and international dimension to the settlement was required.

This may require innovative solutions to deal with the following issues. Firstly, spoiler violence. This usually occurs as a form of violence with which to undermine peace agreements. In South Africa, as the data on political violence suggests, the most intensely violent years were those during the transition, that is, 1990–3 (p. 33). Spoilers were therefore probably engaged in undermining the *process* of searching for peace, rather than the *outcome* in the form of an agreement. Protecting the process, especially when the opposing parties themselves have yet to establish mutual trust, is a tall order. When the state is viewed as a partisan body by one or more of the negotiating parties (which was the view of the ANC), external agencies appear to offer the only remaining units of power able to try and contain spoilers.

This leads to the second issue, that of external support. Given the above problems of mutual trust and spoiler violence, the need for early external support for the process of peacemaking is urgent. The CODESA negotiations broke down (pp. 26–8) because each party still pursued victory on its own terms, by talking the opponent into submission. Had this mutual misperception been broken down earlier, subsequent violence could have been prevented. Early trust-building mechanisms, endorsed by outside agencies, are vital.

Dealing with the massacre of civilians is another matter. In South Africa, generally held to be a case of an elite settlement, the public did respond to civilian atrocities. During the 1992 mass action campaign public response to the loss of life at Boipatong and Bisho served as a catalyst to leaders to redouble efforts at finding a settlement. This probably ranks as the strongest example of a 'bottom-up' drive for peace. These decisive turning points could have gone the other way. In Bosnia, for example, atrocities appear to have served to polarise communities, and to harden the divisions, not to induce the search for compromise.

Finally, much innovation is needed to deal with the culture of violence. Democratic South Africa is still a violent place. Violence has changed from being overtly political to being overtly criminal and/or to reside in that murky middle ground where direct criminal intent (such as financial gain) is intertwined with communal solidarities, issues of collective identities and social obligations. Vigilante groups, criminal gangs and protection rackets occupy this space. The rise of these formations has been attributed, in a large part, to the social dislocations caused by apartheid. The end of apartheid has not led to their decline. This suggests that the peace-making process and the democratic transition have not sufficiently gratified these malcontents. Their deprivation and therefore their continued immersion in the culture and practice of violence persist. There appear to be two sources of post-apartheid deprivation, both of which will have to be overcome in order to break down the culture of violence. The first is material: poverty, unemployment, lack of housing, water, welfare, etc. The second is emotional: the need for identity, esteem, dignity, a sense of purpose, worthiness and social status. Apartheid created social outcasts, but, paradoxically, it also provided young militants with a cause: something to mobilise against, a tangible challenge to overcome, an immense sense of purpose and direction, and with it the emotional rewards of identity and solidarity accorded to warriors. Democratic South Africa can offer them only the bland identity of citizenship. Their need is for stronger rewards, which can only be provided through highly innovative symbolic politics beyond those associated with conventional democratic statecraft.

Notes

1 S. P. Huntington, 'One Soul at a Time: Political Science and Political Reform', *American Political Science Review*, 82 (1988), pp. 3–10 (9).
2 M. van Creveld, *The Transformation of War* (New York: The Free Press, 1991).
3 We take as authoritative the definition used by C. Tilly, 'Reflections on the History of European State-making', in C. Tilly (ed.), *The Formation of National States in Western Europe* (Princeton, NJ: Princeton University Press, 1975), pp. 3–83 (27).
4 The ANC's claim for a 'just war' is found throughout its *ANC Statement to the Truth and Reconciliation Commission*, August 1996, and explicitly so on p. 12.
5 The ANC's Commission on Strategy and Tactics at the National Consultative Conference held at Kabwe, Zambia, resolved that 'We can no longer allow our armed activities to be determined solely by the risk of civilian casualties' (National Consultative Conference of the African National Congress – Main Decisions and Recommendations, Zambia, 16–23 June 1985, University of the Western Cape: Mayibuye Centre, p. 5). Discussion documents relevant to the debate that culminated in this resolution contained various suggestions which argued for the widening of the arena of conflict into civilian life: 'We should liquidate and harass the enemy manpower, puppets and traitors including the rural bourgeoisie (white farmers ...)'; and recommended that they should 'attack the enemy where he list [*sic*] expect us, e.g. in the drinking places like pubs, at the stadiums after thorough reconnaissance has been made in this regard' (ANC, 'Commission on Armed Struggle, Discussion Document D1/II(a)', *Kabwe Papers*, [South Africa: University of the Western Cape, Mayibuye Centre, 1985], p. 4). Examples of attacks on civilians include the 1983 car bomb attack in Pretoria, and the 1986 attacks on the Magoo Bar and Why Not Bar in Durban. Agents of the South African state have engaged in a great number of actions involving the torture and murder of civilians taken into custody during reputed counter-insurgency operations. The best-documented and infamous of these cases are those which led to the conviction of Eugene de Kock, former commander of the Police counter-insurgency unit based at Vlakplaas. The ultimate political responsibility for these policy actions remains a contested issue. The State President during most of the 1980s, P. W. Botha, has denied ordering any such actions, as has F. W. De Klerk, his successor. Umkhonto we Sizwe leadership, in submissions to the TRC, also reiterated that the targeting of civilians was not official policy (*ANC Statement to the Truth and Reconciliation Commission*, p. 56).

6 For the ANC the merging of civilian and military elements was integral to their definition of 'People's War': 'People's War means a war in which a liberation army becomes rooted among the people who progressively participate actively in the armed struggle, both politically and militarily [*sic*], including the possibility of engaging in partial or/and general uprising.' (ANC, 'The Place of Armed Struggle, Discussion Document DI/I', *Kabwe Papers*, [South Africa: University of the Western Cape, Mayibuye Centre, 1985]). The most explicit militarisation of (white) civilian life by the South African state was the system of commandos, comprising non-career reserve military units which consisted of civilians who had undergone basic military training and who were then assigned to a unit within a particular geographic region. See L. H. Gann and P. Duignan, *Why South Africa Will Survive* (Cape Town: Tafelberg, 1981), p. 177.

7 The ANC timed some of its attacks to fall on specific dates, adding symbolic content to the operation. The 14 June 1986 attack on Magoo's Bar, for example, was timed to coincide with, and to commemorate, the 14 June 1985 raid by the SADF on Gaborone, in which 12 people were killed, 5 of them ANC members. See ANC, *ANC Statement to the Truth and Reconciliation Commission*, p. 10. The SADF launched an attack on what they claimed were ANC bases in Gaborone, Lusaka and Harare on the morning of 19 May 1986, the day the Commonwealth's Eminent Persons Group was to meet with Cabinet members on initiating constitutional negotiations. The targets were patently of little military significance, but the attack was intended to demonstrate and symbolise state strength and resolve. See J. Barber and J. Barratt, *South Africa's Foreign Policy – the Search for Status and Security 1945–1988* (Bergvlei: Southern, 1990), pp. 331–3.

8 The coercive aspects of apartheid, such as the huge number of arrests under the pass laws, and the forced removals and resettlement of populations have been aptly described by the ANC as 'bureaucratic terrorism'. See ANC, *ANC Statement to the Truth and Reconciliation Commission*, p. 7. This bureaucratic terrorism had its insurrectionary counterpart in the ANC's strategy of 'ungovernability'. Both strategies aimed at the same target: the social fabric of society. For the coercive element in this aspect of ANC strategy, see J. Kane-Berman, *Political Violence in South Africa* (Johannesburg: South African Institute of Race Relations, 1993).

9 In amnesty submissions before the Truth and Reconciliation Commission members of the PAC admitted to robbing banks and stealing cars as 'fund-raising' efforts to bolster the financing of military projects, *Truth and Reconciliation Commission of South Africa Report*, vol. 2 (Cape Town: Juta, 1998), pp. 209, 210.

10 D. Geldenhuys and H. Kotze, 'Aspects of Decision-making in South Africa', *Politikon*, 10, 1 (June 1983), pp. 33–45; Republic of South Africa, *White Paper on Defence 1977* (Cape Town: Government Printer, 1977); M. Malan, 'Die Aanslag teen Suid-Afrika', *Strategic Review for Southern Africa* (November 1980), pp. 3–16.

11 O. R. Tambo, *Render South Africa Ungovernable*, Message of the National Executive Committee of the African National Congress on the Occasion of the 8th January, 1985, pamphlet (London: ANC, 1985).

12 H. Kotzé and A. Greyling, *Political Organizations in South Africa, A–Z*, 2nd edn (Cape Town: Tafelberg, 1994), p. 53.

13 This section draws heavily on the work of B. W. Kruger, *'Prenegotiation in South Africa (1985–1993): a Phaseological Analysis of the Transitional Negotiations'*, unpublished MA thesis (University of Stellenbosch, 1998).
14 Kotzé and Greyling, *Political Organizations,* pp. 86, 87.
15 Kruger, *Prenegotiation*, p. 93.
16 Ibid., p. 111.
17 P. du Toit, 'Feeling Safe', *Leadership South Africa*, 9, 6 (1990), pp. 74–8 (74).
18 T. D. Sisk, *Democratization in South Africa – the Elusive Social Contract* (Princeton, NJ: Princeton University Press, 1995).
19 S. Friedman (ed.), *The Long Journey – South Africa's Quest for a Negotiated Settlement* (Johannesburg: Ravan Press, 1993), p. 174.
20 Ibid., p. 178.
21 P. Du Toit, *State Building and Democracy in Southern Africa – Botswana, Zimbabwe and South Africa* (Washington, DC: United States Institute of Peace Press, 1995), pp. 238–42.
22 S. Friedman, 'Afterword: the Brief Miracle?', in S. Friedman and D. Atkinson (eds), *South African Review, 7: The Small Miracle, South Africa's Negotiated Settlement* (Johannesburg: Ravan Press, 1994), pp. 331–7 (331, 332).
23 Du Toit, 'Feeling Safe'.
24 Sisk, *Democritization*, p. 87.
25 D. Atkinson, 'Brokering a Miracle? The Multiparty Negotiating Forum', in Friedman and Atkinson, *South African Review*, 7, pp. 13–43 (22).
26 Ibid., p. 24.
27 S. Friedman and L. Stack, 'The Magic Moment – the 1994 Election', in Friedman and Atkinson, *South Africa Review*, pp. 301–30 (310).
28 Ibid., p. 325.
29 Sisk, *Democritization*, p. 286.
30 Friedman, 'Afterword', p. 330.
31 J. Rantete and H. Giliomee, 'Transition to Democracy through Transaction? Bilateral Negotiations between the ANC and the NP in South Africa', *African Affairs*, 91, 365 (October 1992), pp. 515–42 (519).
32 Data on political violence is also a contested terrain. See A. J. Jeffrey, *Spotlight on Disinformation about Violence in South Africa* (Johannesburg: South African Institute of Race Relations, 1992).
33 South African Institute of Race Relations, *Fast Facts*, 4/97 (April 1997), p. 12; E. Sidiropoulos et al., *South Africa Survey 1997/98* (Johannesburg: South African Institute of Race Relations, 1998), p. 51.
34 A. Minnaar, S. Pretorius and M. Wentzel, 'Violent Conflict in South Africa 1990–1995: a Vicious Circle without End?', *In Focus*, 4, 5 (March 1997), pp. 6–9 (6).
35 S. Pretorius and A. Minnaar, 'Loaded Issues! An Analysis of the Proliferation of Weapons in South Africa: 1993–June 1995', unpublished paper (n.d.).
36 South African Institute of Race Relations, *Fast Facts*, 10/96 (October 1996), p. 3, and Institute of Security Studies, *Nedcor ISS Crime Index*, 1 (1997).
37 South African Institute of Race Relations, *Fast Facts*, 1/97 (January 1977), p. 9.
38 E. Sidiropoulos et al., *South Africa Survey 1996/97* (Johannesburg: South African Institute of Race Relations, 1997), pp. 70, 71.
39 Ibid., p. 794.

40 W. Schärf, 'The Resurgence of Urban Street Gangs and Community Responses in Cape Town during the Late Eighties', in D. Hansson and D. van Zyl Smit (eds), *Towards Justice? Crime and State Control in South Africa* (Cape Town: Oxford University Press, 1990), pp. 209–31.
41 Sidiropoulos et al., *South Africa Survey 1996/97*, p. 73.
42 A. Minnaar, 'Violence in Tsolo and Qumbu (Transkei)(1993–1997): Lawlessness, Criminality, Economic Survival and Incipient Democracy at Work', paper presented at the Biennial Conference of the South African Political Studies Association, Mmabatho (8–10 October 1997), p. 2.
43 Ibid., p. 10.
44 E. Sidiropoulos et al., *South Africa Survey 1996/97*, p. 73.
45 I. Oellermann, 'Shock, fear follow Nkabinde verdict', *Cape Times* (1 May 1998).
46 Sidiropoulos et al., *South Africa Survey 1997/98*, p. 32; *Nedcor ISS Crime Index*, 1 (1977), p. D1.
47 A. Minnaar, 'Witchpurging in the Northern Province of South Africa: a Victim Profile and an Assessment of Initiatives to Deal with Witchcraft', paper presented at the 9th International World Symposium on Victimology, Amsterdam, The Netherlands (24–29 August 1997), pp. 6, 7.
48 *Nedcor ISS Crime Index*, 1 (1997), p. D2; Sidiropoulos et al., *South Africa Survey 1996/97*, p. 96.
49 *Nedcor ISS Crime Index*, 1 (1997), p. D37.
50 Sidiropoulos et al., *South Africa Survey 1997/98*, p. 41.
51 Sidiropolous et al., *South Africa Survey, 1996/97*, pp. 74, 75.
52 Ibid., p. 58.
53 Ibid., p. 111.
54 Ibid., pp. 80, 81.
55 Ibid., pp. 93–7.
56 Ibid., pp. 108–10.
57 'Barnard "swindled R1, 4 m"', *Cape Times*, (13 February 1998).
58 C. Goodenough, 'Mystery That Surrounds the Armed Robberies', *KwaZulu-Natal Briefing*, 10 (February 1998), pp. 2–6.
59 Republic of South Africa, *Interpellations, Questions and Replies of the National Assembly*, Second Session, Second Parliament (Cape Town: Government Printer, 18 February 1998), p. 14.
60 Sidiropoulos, et al., *South Africa Survey, 1996/97*, pp. 381, 654, 661, 664.
61 Ibid., p. 359.
62 M. Mokoena, 'A defeated complacency was the mood of June 16 in Soweto this year', *Cape Times* (23 June 1998).
63 T. Bell, 'The Impact of Sanctions on South Africa', *Journal of Contemporary African Studies*, 12, 1 (1993), pp. 1–28 (17).
64 Ibid., p. 375.
65 P. Williams, 'Transnational Organised Crime and International Security: a Global Assessment', in Virginia Gamba (ed.), *Society under Siege: Crime, Violence and Illegal Weapons* (Halfway House: Institute for Security Studies, 1997), pp. 11–42 (27).
66 R. T. Naylor, 'The Rise of the Modern Arms Black Market and the Fall of Supply-Side Control', in Gamba, *Society under Siege*, pp. 43–72.

67 J. Potgieter, 'The Price of War and Peace: a Critical Assessment of the Disarmament Component of United Nations Operations in Southern Africa', in Gamba, *Society under Siege*, pp. 129–68 (148).
68 Sidiropoulos et al., *South Africa Survey 1996/97*, p. 47.
69 H. Kotzé, 'Culture, Ethnicity and Religion: South African Perceptions of Social Identity', *Occasional Papers* (Johannesburg: Konrad Adenauer Stiftung, 1997), pp. 7–10.
70 H. Kotzé and P. du Toit, 'Public Opinion on Security and Democracy in South Africa after Transition: the 1995/96 World Values Survey', *Strategic Review for Southern Africa*, 19, 2 (November 1997), pp. 52–75 (67).
71 *Nedcor ISS Crime Index*, 1 (1997), p. A5.
72 Kotzé and Du Toit, 'Public Opinion', p. 63.
73 *Nedcor ISS Crime Index*, 1 (1997), p. E13.
74 H. Kotzé and L. Hill, 'Emergent Migration Policy in a Democratic South Africa', *International Migration*, 35, 1 (1997), pp. 5–36 (17, 33).
75 Kotzé, 'Culture, Ethnicity and Religion', pp. 11–13.
76 *Nedcor ISS Crime Index*, 1 (1997), p. D22; Sidiropoulos et al., *South Africa Survey, 1996/97*, p. 87.
77 Sidiropoulos et al., ibid., pp. 84, 85.
78 'TRC. The report of the South Africa's Truth and Reconciliation Commission', Extract 4, Supplement to the *Cape Times* (5 November 1998), pp. 1–12.
79 D. L. Horowitz, *Ethnic Groups in Conflict* (Berkeley: University of California Press, 1985), p. 405.

2
Northern Ireland: Long, Cold Peace

John Darby and Roger Mac Ginty

Introduction

There were seven failed attempts to broker an agreement between Northern Ireland's constitutional parties in the years 1972–93. Security-led attempts to 'win' the conflict had a similarly poor success rate. A variation on Georges Clemenceau's observation that 'military justice is to justice what military music is to music' comes to mind. The 1990s, however, were dominated by a lengthy peace process. The peace process followed a 'stop–go' pattern, with long periods of stasis interrupted by concentrated bursts of political activity. Despite paramilitary ceasefires, it was also punctuated by continuing violence. Nevertheless, in April 1998, the Good Friday Agreement was reached.[1]

The Agreement marked the most significant *rapprochement* in Anglo-Irish relations since the partition of the island of Ireland in 1921. It was negotiated and endorsed by most of Northern Ireland's political parties. In a significant break with previous governmental approaches to the Northern Ireland conflict, the main Republican and Loyalist paramilitary organisations were explicitly included in the negotiations. Referendums in Northern Ireland and the Republic of Ireland revealed strong, island-wide, popular support for the Agreement. The Agreement was remarkably comprehensive, covering relations within Northern Ireland, between Northern Ireland and the Republic of Ireland, and within the British Isles. A sophisticated devolution package was established for Northern Ireland, with significant power resting with an inclusive power-sharing assembly. Northern Ireland's position within the United Kingdom was re-affirmed and its future constitutional position was linked to the consent of the people of Northern Ireland. Permanent co-operation on a range of functional issues was to be established between Northern Ireland and the Republic of Ireland. A British-Irish Council, which would enable co-operation between the British and Irish governments, as well as the Scottish parliament and the Welsh and Northern Ireland assemblies, was also to be established. The Council also located the Good Friday Agreement within the wider framework of devolution in the United Kingdom. Finally, the Agreement was complex; a degree in physics rather than English was perhaps more useful in deciphering the 10 000 word text and its evolving and interlocking institutions.

Rethinking the conflict

> Time, events or the unaided individual action of the mind will sometimes undermine or destroy an opinion, without any outward sign of change. It has not been openly assailed, no conspiracy has been formed to make war on it, but its followers one by one noiselessly secede; day by day a few of them abandon it, until at last it is only professed by a minority.[2]

The Northern Ireland peace process did not have a definite starting point. Instead, a number of political, security, economic and perceptual factors came together to form a process and give it a dynamic. There were few 'Road to Damascus' type experiences among political leaders. Nor was a 'solution' suddenly discovered. Rather, over the course of a decade, the main protagonists in the conflict came to rethink their various approaches to the conflict. The essence of the Northern Ireland peace process was a transition from unsustainable approaches to the conflict to more sustainable ones. These strategy reassessments were often slow and usually occurred behind closed doors. Those involved often faced internal dissent. Few of those who embarked on rethinks were cognisant of an end point.

British Government thinking on Northern Ireland changed in three areas. First, the Government developed a more coherent political policy towards Northern Ireland. For much of the 1970s and 1980s, London had approached Northern Ireland as a security problem. Political initiatives were limited in vision. As a result, the development of a strategic political approach to Northern Ireland marked a major change. A second shift in British policy was the development of a permanent and close working relationship with the Government of the Irish Republic on the issue of Northern Ireland. This partnership was to become crucial in the peace process. The signing of the 1985

Anglo-Irish Agreement with the Irish Republic marked the formal and symbolic beginning of a new era of Anglo-Irish co-operation. It took another half decade, however, for this relationship to develop a seriousness able to sustain a peace process. The third major change in British Government policy towards Northern Ireland was the decision to include those on the political extremes in any new political settlement. Until this point, British Government policy had rested on the robust exclusion of those who supported violence for political ends. The new policy position emerged gradually and was not publicly articulated. It was based on a realisation that paramilitary organisations retained the capacity to paralyse any political settlement which excluded them.

For the Irish Government, the major perceptual change had come with the Anglo-Irish Agreement and the recognition that any change in the constitutional status of Northern Ireland was dependent on the consent of the majority of Northern Ireland's citizens. More practically, the Anglo-Irish Agreement secured the long-term policy goal of developing a permanent working relationship with the British Government. The decision to work with, rather than against, paramilitary organisations did not come until the early 1990s and marked a significant change. According to a senior Irish official, 'We really don't see that you can have a stable settlement unless Sinn Féin and the Loyalists are present.'[3]

Militant Irish Republicanism has shaped much of the Northern Ireland conflict. It has been responsible for more deaths than any of the conflict's other protagonists; over 1800. British government policy in Northern Ireland was often a direct response to IRA actions. Ultimately, changes in Republicanism led to changes in the nature of the conflict. Republicanism underwent a number of significant changes from the mid-1980s onwards. An internal debate on the sustainability of the conflict developed. The 'long-war' strategy was little more sophisticated than conflict by attrition, in this case designed to wear down British Government resolve to stay in Northern Ireland. The 'long war' was pursued at enormous cost to the Republican community, in terms of lives, prison sentences and quality-of-life opportunities. Without doubt, this led to a sense of war fatigue. This was compounded by a dramatic increase in Loyalist assassinations of Republicans in the early 1990s. There was also a generational factor; the leadership cadre of Republicans had spent their adult lives in the conflict and their children faced more of the same.[4] More fundamentally, the 'long-war' strategy amounted to an implicit recognition that no unilateral action by any violent actor in the conflict (Republican, Loyalist or British Government) could decisively change the conflict. While the British Government could not win the 'war' neither could Republicans.

Republicans rationalised the use of violence as a legitimate tool for a politically weak community. Yet, rather than an asset, the use of violence was an increasing liability. Civilian casualties from botched operations, such as the Enniskillen bombing on Remembrance Sunday 1987, risked stripping the Republican Movement of its core support, and therefore its legitimacy. Because of their support for violence, Republicans were excluded from elected chambers, civic functions and the airwaves. Republican violence was blamed for a lack of inward investment, high unemployment and the disruption caused by security measures. It was also said to be responsible for Republicanism's failure to make an electoral breakthrough in the Irish Republic.[5] The British and Irish governments, constitutional politicians and the media presented a powerful alliance against paramilitary violence. The end result was that the continued use of violence was increasingly counter-productive for Republicans and resulted in their exclusion and demonisation.

Other, more positive, factors steered Republicans towards a reassessment of the 'long-war' strategy and a more sophisticated, and political, approach. Secret talks with the British Government revealed that it too was suffering from war fatigue.[6] Other peace processes, particularly those in South Africa and Israel–Palestine, encouraged Republicans to pursue the possibility of a peace process in Northern Ireland.[7] The development of a dialogue between the Social Democratic and Labour Party (SDLP) leader John Hume and Sinn Féin leader, Gerry Adams, was also essential. Hume argued that violence was counter-productive and was actually delaying the Republican aim of a united Ireland rather than bringing it closer. Importantly, political argument, rather than moral pleas, characterised Hume's approach to Adams. According to one insider, 'The debate between Sinn Féin and the SDLP was about the efficacy of constitutional politics.'[8] Many Republicans felt that they had won the intellectual argument for a united Ireland and now needed to harness Irish and international goodwill towards that end.[9] A key part of this was the development of a 'Totally Unarmed Strategy' from 1994 onwards. It was based on the idea of developing a coalition of pro-nationalist partners to pursue a united Ireland agenda.[10] This coalition of interests would include Republicans, constitutional Nationalists, the Irish Government, the Irish diaspora, the United States Government and the European Union. In Unionist eyes, this amounted to a 'pan-nationalist front'.[11] For this coalition to come together, however, an IRA ceasefire, and thus a major reassessment of Republican strategy, was required.

For the peace process to become possible Unionism also had to undergo a rethink. First, many Unionists had to re-engage with the political process. Unionists had been so affronted by the 1985 Anglo-Irish Agreement that they withdrew from politics and were acutely suspicious of all political initiatives regarding Northern Ireland.[12] Second, as the parameters of the Northern Ireland peace process took shape, Unionists had to contemplate a comprehensive political settlement. More specifically, this was likely to involve a permanent political relationship with the Irish Republic and power sharing with Nationalists within Northern Ireland. Previously, this had been a step too far. Third, like the other participants in the process, they had to accept the involvement of those on the political extremes. As in other political sectors, this rethink took time, was rarely unanimous, was often painful and required courageous leadership. Much of the leadership came from David Trimble. Elected leader of Northern Ireland's largest political party, the Ulster Unionist Party (UUP) in September 1995, Trimble had a reputation as a hardliner. Over the following years, however, he took a number of decisions which risked his party's unity. The alternative, however, would have been the collapse of the peace process.

Militant Loyalism also underwent a process of critical reassessment from the late 1980s onwards. While Loyalism acquired a greater military capacity, it also developed a more sophisticated and politically aware leadership. According to one senior Loyalist, 'Loyalist paramilitaries had to invent their own parties...' because they felt mainstream Unionist parties were allowing the Unionist case to go by default.[13] Loyalism's entry into mainstream politics was something of a novelty and presented a challenge to the traditional Unionist parties. They also surprised observers with the seeming maturity of their political approach; the Progressive Unionist Party (PUP) and Ulster Democratic Party (UDP) often appeared more pragmatic and willing to compromise than the constitutional parties. Although the Loyalist ceasefire of October 1994 was in direct reciprocation to the August 1994 IRA ceasefire, it was rooted in a fundamental premise. This was the Loyalist understanding that the consent principle would remain inviolable whatever the outcome of the peace process. According to one senior Loyalist, 'What sealed it [the decision to call a ceasefire] for Loyalists was the adoption of the principle of consent by the Irish government.'[14] In other words, Northern Ireland's constitutional position could not change without the consent of a majority of its citizens.

Another rethink was underway in the United States. Traditionally, the official US position had been to regard Northern Ireland as an internal matter for the United Kingdom. This was particularly true in the Cold War era. Under President Clinton this attitude changed. The White House variously acted as friend, guarantor, arbiter and benefactor to the emerging peace process. The emergence of a small group of Irish-Americans, with key political and corporate links, was instrumental in persuading the Clinton White House to become interested in Northern Ireland.[15] The wider Irish-American diaspora, which was traditionally sympathetic towards militant Republicanism, also moderated its attitude and encouraged Irish Republicans to consider the advantages offered by a ceasefire and a peace process.

The peace process

Secret contacts: 1988–94

The strategy rethinks took concrete shape in the form of secret contacts prior to the paramilitary ceasefires. Facilitated by a Catholic priest, Sinn Féin held secret talks with the SDLP and Irish Government. While the IRA campaign was in full swing, the British Government and the IRA also had secret talks. These were concerned with the terms and conditions of a possible ceasefire and the nature of the political process which would follow it. The most significant point about these talks was that the conflict's two main protagonists were, for the first time, engaged in the same task: how to end the conflict. These contacts laid invaluable groundwork for the later peace process and made it clear that the key players in the conflict were serious about working towards a comprehensive settlement. A Presbyterian minister also helped persuade Loyalist paramilitaries of the benefits of calling a ceasefire and engaging in the developing peace process.

Reaction to the ceasefires: autumn 1994

Enormous levels of political activity followed the Republican and Loyalist ceasefires in the autumn of 1994. Issues which had been previously overshadowed by the immediacy of political violence were now raised. Meetings between opponents, which previously would have been regarded as unthinkable, were now held. The simple matter of political debate was aided by the lifting of a broadcasting ban on members of Sinn Féin and the emergence of an articulate leadership for Loyalism.

For Republicans, the main focus of political activity was to push for high-level meetings with the British Government and for negotiations between Northern Ireland's political parties on the constitutional future of the state. The British Government, unconvinced of the permanency of the IRA ceasefire, resisted the pressure for meetings. Northern Ireland's Unionists shared the British Government distrust of Republican motivations. The IRA ceasefire, according to one Unionist MP, was 'more of a comma than a fullstop'.[16] The immediate task for Unionists was to seek assurances from the British Government that a secret deal with the IRA had not been hatched behind their backs. After that, the aim became one of minimising the development of what many saw as an exclusively Nationalist peace process.

For many Unionists, a peace process was a journey into the political unknown. It conformed to few of the norms of British politics. It was prone to outside initiatives, and had no set outcome or timetable. Most fundamentally of all, it would, in the Unionist mind, necessarily lead to a diminution of their position within the United Kingdom. According to one loyalist, 'Unionism ... has never felt any ownership of the peace process ... Change to them can only mean some dilution of the Unionist position.'[17] So, certainly for a year after the ceasefire declaration, most Unionist political engagement with the peace process was defensive. The notion of talking to Sinn Féin was also abhorrent to most Unionists. For many, Republicans were the prime antagonists in the conflict and to involve them in the political process was merely rewarding violence.

British Prime Minister John Major's parliamentary difficulties gave Unionists some leverage. Outright hostility from his Euro-sceptic backbenchers and a series of by-election defeats meant that Major had a dwindling parliamentary majority throughout his stewardship of the peace process. On a number of occasions, Major relied on Unionist votes for political survival. Nationalists complained that this compromised any British Government claim to hold a neutral position in political talks between Unionists and Nationalists.

The Unionist minimalist approach to the peace process contrasted with the Nationalist maximalist approach. For Nationalists, the goal was to broaden the peace process and quicken the pace of developments. It was almost as though a broad cultural difference existed between Unionists and the British Government on the one side, and Nationalists, Republicans and the Irish Government on the other. Despite the critical mass of political activity which followed the ceasefires, there was little substantive political movement. One year on from the paramilitary ceasefires, the main protagonists in the conflict had yet to meet. Formal talks between Northern Ireland's political parties had yet to be convened. Crucially, there was little consensus on the direction, pace, timetable and desired end result of the peace process. Nationalists wanted a Nationalist peace, which entailed a thwarting of a Unionist peace. The reverse held true for Unionists.

The Frameworks Document: February 1995

The British and Irish governments hoped to stamp their imprimatur on the peace process with the joint publication of the *Frameworks for the Future* document in February 1995. The document, they hoped, would form the basis for talks between Northern Ireland's political parties on future political arrangements. According to the British Government view:

> The Government's main political objective in Northern Ireland is to bring about a comprehensive settlement which would both return greater power, authority and responsibility to all the Northern Ireland people, on an agreed basis, and take full account of Northern Ireland's wider relationship with the rest of the United Kingdom and the rest of the island of Ireland...
>
> It is essential that any outcome is acceptable to the people. The Government have already undertaken to submit any outcome from the Talks process to a referendum in Northern Ireland, and the significant implications which any settlement will have for the Republic of Ireland are likely to require a referendum there as well.[18]

The document reaffirmed a three-stranded approach to any Northern Ireland settlement.[19] Strand One would address relationships within Northern Ireland, Strand Two relationships between Northern Ireland and the Republic of Ireland, and Strand Three relationships within the British Isles. The document's greatest import was in signifying that both governments were determined to secure a comprehensive political agreement. It also anchored any emergent political process to a pace and agenda established by the two governments. One Irish official put it simply, 'it was up to the two governments to give guidance'.[20] Unionist political leaders were hostile to the document, but grassroots Unionism, in comparison to reactions against the Anglo-Irish Agreement, didn't seem particularly exercised by the issue. Republicans were also lukewarm about the document. But local political reactions were largely irrelevant. Both governments were adamant that they could control the process as far as was possible and space for alternative processes simply did not exist.

Violence during the peace process

A culture of violence is not easily overturned. 'Paramilitary policing', in the form of punishment attacks, continued within Loyalist and Republican communities.[21] As a concession to the ceasefires, many of these attacks took the form of beatings rather than shootings. Given that the injuries from beatings were often serious, this was of little consolation to the victims. Between April 1995 and January 1996, eight suspected drug dealers were shot dead by the previously unknown organisation, Direct Action Against Drugs.[22] DAAD was widely regarded as a front organisation for the IRA and a means of avoiding an explicit breach of the ceasefire. The main paramilitary organisations were largely successful in policing their own ceasefires, however. The mainstream groups ceased their traditional forms of violence; these included IRA attacks on the British Army, police force and Loyalists, as well as Loyalist assassinations. Splinter groups within Loyalism and Republicanism were also contained in the initial months after the ceasefire announcements. The peace process did herald an increase in non-paramilitary sectarian violence, however. This often took the form of street assaults and arson attacks on identifiably Catholic or Protestant property.[23] Many of these attacks were associated with the parading dispute and were limited to certain periods of the year. They also reflected a deep nervousness in both communities at the prospect of political change and the perception that change would necessarily mean a loss.

The decommissioning of paramilitary weapons

One issue, the decommissioning of paramilitary weapons, dominated all others during the peace process. For the British Government and Unionists, paramilitary organisations could decommission their arsenals as a sign of their commitment to the democratic process. In March 1995, the British Government made paramilitary decommissioning a formal requirement for entry into political talks.[24] For Republicans, and indeed Loyalists, decommissioning was something that could be discussed during a wider talks process, but not before. No side seemed likely to budge on the issue. 'Exploratory dialogue' between British officials, and later ministers, and Sinn Féin representatives failed to break the deadlock.[25] The issue also placed a serious strain on relations between the British and Irish governments, with the Irish Government concerned that a lack of movement towards all-party talks could make Republicans question their commitment to the peace process. In September 1995, the Irish Government called off an Anglo-Irish Inter-Governmental Conference at the last moment.[26] At this stage,

Sinn Féin assessments of the peace process were becoming increasingly desperate. According to Sinn Féin president, Gerry Adams, the process was 'doomed to collapse'.[27]

In late November 1995, on the eve of US President Bill Clinton's visit to Northern Ireland, both governments announced a 'twin-track' approach to the decommissioning impasse. Under this scheme, an independent decommissioning body would consider options on the issue of paramilitary weapons while, in parallel, all-party talks would begin.[28] The International Body on Arms Decommissioning, chaired by former US Senate majority leader George Mitchell, received submissions from both governments and all of Northern Ireland's political parties with the exception of the DUP. Meanwhile, preparatory talks on the ground rules for future political talks were hosted by the Northern Ireland Secretary of State, Sir Patrick Mayhew.[29] In the absence of the decommissioning of paramilitary weapons, this round of talks took place without Sinn Féin and those parties representing the Loyalist paramilitaries.

The International Body on Arms Decommissioning published its report on 24 January 1996.[30] The Mitchell Report's central recommendation was that arms decommissioning and all-party talks should begin in parallel. In effect, this amounted to a rejection of the British position on prior decommissioning. The British Government discounted the central recommendation and instead focused on paragraph 56 of the report which noted, somewhat obliquely, that 'an elective process could contribute to the building of confidence'. The Irish Government, Nationalists and Republicans regarded the idea of elections as an entry mechanism into talks as a diversion. Unionists, however, were broadly supportive of the idea since it drew the peace process into the known political universe.

Although most of the Mitchell Report was placed in abeyance, it was significant in three respects. First, it established George Mitchell as a widely respected figure in the peace process. Second, the model of independent commissions, which sought to take contentious issues temporarily out of the political arena, was established. The model would later be pressed into service for the fraught issues of parades and police reform. Third, the Mitchell Report set out six principles of non-violence as preconditions for entry to negotiations. Known as the 'Mitchell Principles' they soon became a benchmark of a commitment to democratic politics:

1 to democratic and exclusively peaceful means of resolving political issues;
2 to the total disarmament of all paramilitary organisations;

3 to agree that such disarmament must be verifiable to the satisfaction of an independent commission;
4 to renounce for themselves, and to oppose any effort by others, to use force, or threaten to use force, to influence the course or the outcome of all-party negotiations;
5 to abide by the terms of any agreement reached in all-party negotiations and to resort to democratic and exclusively peaceful methods in trying to alter any aspect of that outcome with which they may disagree; and
6 to urge that 'punishment' killings and beatings stop and to take effective steps to prevent such actions.

The principles later became the minimum requirement for entry into political talks. They were also a reflection that the paramilitary ceasefires did not result in a total end to violence.

The collapse of the IRA ceasefire: February 1996

The IRA's formal response to the sidelining of the Mitchell Report came at 6 p.m. on 9 February 1996. A statement announcing the end of the ceasefire accused British Prime Minister John Major and Unionists of 'squandering this unprecedented opportunity to resolve the conflict'.[31] An hour later, a massive bomb exploded at London's Canary Wharf. Planning for the bomb had been underway before the Mitchell Report was published. Hardline elements in the Republican Movement had calculated that John Major's Government was either unwilling, or, because of parliamentary arithmetic, unable to address their agenda of all-party talks leading swiftly to constitutional change in the direction of a united Ireland. Speculation mounted that Gerry Adams had lost control of the Republican Movement. According to one commentator, he was 'a busted flush'.[32] Rallies across Ireland indicated widespread despair at the breakdown of the ceasefire and the apparent collapse of the peace process.[33]

The end of the ceasefire did not mean the end of the peace process. In the words of a senior member of the DUP 'the thing has a life of its own now'.[34] Loyalist paramilitaries calculated that, because of the consent guarantee, Northern Ireland's position within the United Kingdom was safe and so maintained their ceasefire. A senior member of the UUP asked, 'Do we sit around and wait for the next ceasefire ... a peace process should not be solely dependent on the activities of terrorist organisations'.[35] Under its new party leader, David Trimble, the UUP recognised that the peace process was going to deliver a new political arrangement for Northern Ireland and that it was important that they try to shape it from within and arrest developments which they regarded as harmful to the Union. For Unionists this had been the lesson of the Anglo-Irish Agreement.[36] Crucially, while Republicans may have publicly said that the peace process was over (in the words of one, 'It's dead. It's over. It's been a valuable experience all round') they were committed to rebuilding 'peace process mark II'.[37] The resumed IRA campaign was partial and initially restricted to targets in England. A leading member of the DUP shrewdly interpreted the renewed IRA violence as 'not a simple abandonment of the ceasefire'. Instead, he said, it was 'specific and targeted to apply pressure on the British Government to open up all-party talks'.[38] Republican violence was no longer about driving Britain out of Ireland. It was now about entry into a political process in which all of Northern Ireland's parties could discuss political arrangements for the future. This was a remarkable change.

Marking time: spring 1996–spring 1997

In the aftermath of the ceasefire collapse the British and Irish governments announced that multi-party talks would start on 10 June 1996. Without an IRA ceasefire, these talks would not be open to Sinn Féin. Entry to the talks was to be via elections to a Forum for Political Dialogue. Parties would then choose their negotiating team from their Forum members. The Forum itself would have no legislative or administrative functions.

Following much squabbling between the parties, a complex electoral system was designed. A key part of the election formula was a 'top-up' system to allow the smaller parties, particularly those linked with Loyalist paramilitaries, a place at the negotiating table.[39] Despite the debate about the artificial or distorted nature of the electoral system, there was a recognition that the Loyalist parties had to be kept on board. In mid-March 1996 both governments issued their Ground Rules for Substantive All-Party Talks proposals.[40] They contained two proposals which would remain in the various talks processes until the Good Friday Agreement was reached. The first noted that 'Any participant will be free to raise any aspect of the three relationships; including constitutional issues ... which it considers relevant'. In other words, it was legitimate to raise Northern Ireland's constitutional position within the United Kingdom as a matter for debate. The second was that the negotiations would proceed on the principle that nothing would be agreed until everything was agreed. The implication was that both governments were determined that any agreement would be comprehensive.

Electioneering in April and May 1996 precluded any meaningful exchanges between the political parties. Northern Ireland elections tend to be intra-community contests. The elections were significant in that they were the first electoral test for David Trimble as leader of the UUP. Unionists faced a wider choice than usual. The two parties linked with Loyalist paramilitaries, the Progressive Unionist Party and the Ulster Democratic Party, and the more mainstream United Kingdom Unionist Party were competing with the two established Unionist parties, the UUP and DUP.[41] The DUP made significant electoral gains, signalling a strong Unionist distrust of the peace process.[42] In the event, it was Sinn Féin's results which made most headlines. The party increased its share of the vote from 10.0 per cent to 15.5 per cent.[43] According to some, many Nationalists 'lent' their votes to Sinn Féin in order to encourage the IRA to call a ceasefire.[44] Others voted for Sinn Féin to send a message to the British Government that talks should get speedily underway and should include Sinn Féin. Either way, some Nationalists supported the Sinn Féin strategy of simultaneously pursuing entry into peace talks *and* an armed campaign by the IRA.

In the absence of an IRA ceasefire, Sinn Féin was barred from the 10 June talks. Northern Ireland security minister, Sir John Wheeler, spelt out exactly what was required from Sinn Féin: 'first must come the ceasefire ... second must come the signing up to the six Mitchell principles [on non-violence]. Then there must be ... a start towards decommissioning.'[45] The IRA announced that a new ceasefire was 'remote in the extreme' and continued its armed campaign in England.[46] Talks did get underway though, between nine other political parties and the two governments.[47] These talks rapidly became bogged down on procedural issues, particularly over the appointment of George Mitchell as chairman. They were suspended in early July 1996 when tension and violence associated with a contentious Orange Order at Drumcree spread across Northern Ireland. The issue also caused a severe rift between the British and Irish governments. The Irish government quickly formed the view that the Northern Ireland Secretary of State, Sir Patrick Mayhew, 'had run out of steam'.[48] His was a sensitive position, and one which, at such a crucial time, required a figure with more energy. The British Government itself was hamstrung by a dwindling parliamentary majority, and many Nationalists and Republicans saw a British general election as the best chance to re-energise the peace process. An *Irish Times* headline 'Talks process going nowhere as dying government marks time' seemed to sum up the situation.[49]

Yet, despite a tired British Government and parades-related disturbances across Northern Ireland, the talks process survived. By late July the parties agreed on procedural rules.[50] After a summer recess, the two largest parties, the UUP and SDLP, began a series of bilateral meetings, particularly on the issue of where to place decommissioning on the talks agenda.[51] The UUP felt that the SDLP was more interested in securing Sinn Féin's entry into the talks process than reaching a settlement with a fellow constitutional party.[52] As evidence of this, in November 1996, SDLP leader John Hume interceded with John Major on Sinn Féin's behalf.[53] The resumption of the IRA campaign in Northern Ireland itself (from October 1996 onwards), however, made the admission of Sinn Féin into talks even more unpalatable for Unionists and the British Government. The peace process remained stuck at this point until the election of Tony Blair as British Prime Minister in May 1997.

Parades

Although historically contentious, the issue of politico-religious parades became especially sensitised during the peace process. For Unionists the parades were an expression of identity. For many Nationalists they were intimidatory. For both, they were about territory. Nationalist objections to the Orange Order parade at Drumcree in July 1996 led to the police blocking the parade route to stop it passing Nationalist homes. A tense, four-day stand-off developed, with Orangemen and their supporters from across Northern Ireland converging on Drumcree. There was also widespread rioting in Loyalist areas. The police eventually backed down and forced the parade through the Nationalist area.[54] This resulted in rioting in Nationalist areas across Northern Ireland.[55] It was the worst civil disorder for years. Two people were killed and the police fired over six thousand plastic bullets.[56] There was widespread civil disorder and sectarian intimidation. A small but virulent Loyalist paramilitary group broke from the umbrella Combined Loyalist Military Command and embarked on a campaign of sectarian attacks.[57] The SDLP left the Forum for Political Dialogue and did not return. A severe rift also developed between the British and Irish governments.[58] Two observations are worth making. First, the parades issue was left unresolved. Like an open wound, it was ready to flare up each summer. Second, although damaged, the peace process survived.

The Blair administration: May 1997

Elected in May 1997 with a massive parliamentary majority, Tony Blair had more room for manoeuvre than the previous government. The election also benefited Sinn Féin which won two Westminster seats and became Northern Ireland's third largest party by share of vote.[59] Blair's New Labour Government quickly set about drawing Sinn Féin into the political process. Sinn Féin set its stall out. It wanted a start date for inclusive talks, a commitment that the talks would be substantive and address issues other than decommissioning, a time limit on the talks and the implementation of confidence-building measures.[60] The speed with which new Secretary of State, Marjorie (Mo) Mowlam, set about meeting Sinn Féin's entry requirements was startling.[61] The Government gave commitments that it would address issues of police reform, equality in employment and contentious parades. Another 'confidence-building measure' came in the form of the transfer of long-term Republican prisoners in English prisons to jails in the Republic of Ireland.[62] Labour announced that it hoped that the talks could reach a conclusion by May 1998. Crucially, Labour announced that decommissioning, the issue which had effectively held up the peace process for two years and had caused a severe rifts between the British and Irish governments, was 'secondary to actually getting people into talks'.[63] By mid-June, the demand for decommissioning prior to Sinn Féin's entry into talks was dropped.

For Unionists, Labour had embarked on an extraordinary appeasement process. But Blair was careful to reassure Unionists. Significantly, his first trip outside London as Prime Minister was to Northern Ireland. He told a Belfast audience, 'I value the Union', and dampened Republican hopes of a united Ireland by saying, 'none of us in this hall today, even the youngest, is likely to see Northern Ireland as anything but part of the United Kingdom'. He also reassured Unionists that there was no possibility of change in Northern Ireland's constitutional status without the consent of the majority of its people.[64]

The IRA declared another ceasefire on 20 July 1997. The prospect of round-table talks between all of Northern Ireland's political parties was now real. The two governments announced that they wanted substantive talks to proceed from 15 September, by which time the IRA ceasefire could be verified and Sinn Féin would be admitted to the talks.[65] For many Unionists, the prospect of talks with Sinn Féin was abhorrent. According to one commentator:

> All of the main unionist parties have consistently declared that they will not sit at the same table as Sinn Féin, unless decommissioning is ongoing. They see the two governments now acting as conspirators, bringing the representatives of armed republicans into democratic negotiations. Their basic instinct is to kiss the talks goodbye.[66]

For the Democratic Unionists, the issue was straightforward. Party leader Ian Paisley described the talks process as 'madness' and made his exit.[67] The DUP strategy was now to sit back in the hope that the talks would come crashing down around David Trimble. The choice for the UUP was more difficult. The general election had confirmed the Party's dominance within Unionism. Without the UUP, Northern Ireland's largest party, the talks could not hope for a satisfactory outcome.[68] The Party was anxious not to be blamed for the collapse of the talks. At the same time, many members were opposed to entering into talks with Sinn Féin. The Party took the bold step of embarking on a consultation exercise to canvass wider opinion.[69] The consultation was broadly supportive of the UUP taking its place in the talks, and reminded the Party leadership that they wanted them to actively and energetically defend the Union.[70] Sinn Féin also engaged in a series of consultation meetings within its own communities.

Sinn Féin duly entered the talks on 9 September. According to Gerry Adams, Sinn Féin was entering the talks to seek 'an end to British rule on this island'.[71] Not surprisingly, the UUP saw things differently. Throughout the talks, they refused to engage directly with Sinn Féin. The talks continued along the three-stranded approach with few plenary sessions and most of the talking done in subcommittees. Both governments coaxed the participants to reach agreement by May 1998. Such a deadline seemed optimistic in the extreme.

If left to the SDLP and UUP, agreement may have been reached relatively quickly. Both parties had been engaged in a series of talks for most of the 1990s and had reached broad agreement on a number of core issues. Following a series of bilateral meetings, UUP leader David Trimble also developed a working relationship with Irish Taoiseach (Prime Minister) Bertie Ahern.[72] The Irish Government made it clear that it was prepared to remove its territorial claim on Northern Ireland in the event of an overall settlement. The inclusion of those parties on the political extremes, however, led to complexity. Already, Republicans and Loyalists were becoming disillusioned with the talks process. For Loyalists, too many confidence-building measures had been ceded to Republicans, particularly in relation to IRA prisoners.[73] For Republicans, the talks process was moving too slowly.[74] More ominously, it was becoming increasingly clear that the three-stranded framework was incapable of fulfilling the Republican united Ireland agenda. The prospect of a Northern Ireland assembly, the dreaded 'internal settlement' in the Republican lexicon, left Republicans cold. Reports of splits and dissension within both the IRA and Sinn Féin underlined growing nervousness among republicans.[75] There was also dissatisfaction within David Trimble's UUP. Four of his ten MPs made a public call for the party to leave the talks.[76]

For all the political leaders, the task of leadership was twofold. First, party leaders had to manage their parties. The peace process presented parties and communities with new experiences, many of them unpalatable and some open to interpretation as defeat or surrender. For party leaders, managing internal party debates was often as delicate and time-consuming as their involvement in inter-party talks. Second, they had to represent their party position in a talks process aimed at reaching a definitive constitutional agreement for at least a generation. This was no easy feat given that any action or statement risked the censure of the British, Irish and US governments, the paramilitaries and the electorate.

The final straight: spring 1998

On the eve of 1998, Northern Ireland revisited its violent past. Two days after Christmas, a Republican paramilitary group shot dead the leader of a splinter Loyalist paramilitary group inside an apparently 'top security' prison.[77] By the end of January, a wave of revenge and counter-revenge attacks had left ten people dead. Although not formally announcing an end to their ceasefires, it was clear that mainstream paramilitary organisations had been involved in the violence. Under the Mitchell Principles, any party linked with violence would be excluded from the talks. In late January, the Ulster Democratic Party, associated with the Ulster Defence Association and Ulster Freedom Fighters, voluntarily left the talks before it was expelled.[78] Three weeks later, Sinn Féin was expelled from the talks when it became clear that the IRA had been involved in violence. But it was also clear that the British and Irish governments entertained a certain reluctance over expelling both parties. Importantly, both were suspended for relatively short periods and not permanently excluded from the talks. For a senior member of the Democratic Unionist Party, 'Democrats were merely the window dressing', the process was 'terrorist driven'.[79]

In mid-January, the two governments published the broad outline of an agreement which they thought could command popular support in a referendum.[80] They felt that the political parties had sparred for long enough and now had to get down to substantive negotiations. According to a number of talks insiders, George Mitchell's style as chair was indulgent. The result was long party political monologues but little concrete engagement between the parties.[81] The target date for an agreement in order to facilitate a Northern Ireland referendum in May was set as 9 April. In late March, a new phase of more intensive negotiations was initiated. Many issues were outstanding, however. The UUP and SDLP held differing views of how power would be shared in any new Northern Ireland assembly. Sinn Féin was deeply uneasy at the prospect of any new Northern Ireland assembly and, curiously, contributed little to negotiations on this matter.[82] The remit of cross-border bodies and their relationship with the Northern Ireland Assembly and Irish Parliament were also contested. The UUP was anxious to tie the Irish Government down on the precise wording of any proposed changes to its constitutional claim on Northern Ireland's territory.

Three days before the 9 April deadline, talks chairman George Mitchell presented the parties with a draft agreement. It had actually been drafted by the British and Irish governments. Unionist reaction to the document was hostile.[83] UUP deputy leader, John Taylor, announced that he wouldn't touch it with a 40-foot pole. British Prime Minister Tony Blair and his Irish counterpart, Bertie Ahern, arrived in Northern Ireland to mediate the accord personally. After 48 hours of intensive talks, the Good Friday Agreement was reached. The idea that the Ulster Unionist Party and Sinn Féin could consent to the same agreement seemed incredible. The Agreement was not signed. There were no symbolic handshakes between Unionism and Republicanism. The Agreement would be put to the people of Northern Ireland in a referendum. David Trimble left the talks announcing that 'We rise from this table knowing that the Union is stronger than it was when we first sat down.'[84] A noticeably downbeat Gerry Adams left without recommending or rejecting the Agreement: 'when ... we come to a conclusion we will let you know'.[85]

The Agreement: April 1998

A copy of the Good Friday Agreement was delivered to every home in Northern Ireland. It was much more comprehensive than many observers expected. It had five main constitutional provisions. First, Northern Ireland's future constitutional status was to be in the hands of its citizens. Second, if the people of Ireland, north and south, wanted a united Ireland, they could have one. Third, Northern Ireland's current constitutional position was within the United Kingdom. Fourth, Northern Ireland's citizens would have the right to 'identify themselves and be accepted as Irish or British, or both'. Fifth, the Irish state would drop its territorial claim on Northern Ireland and instead define the

Irish nation in terms of people rather than land. The consent principle would also be built into the Irish constitution.

The three sets of relationships which the three-stranded formula attempted to address were dealt with through the proposed establishment of three new interlocking institutions. Relations within Northern Ireland were to be addressed by a power-sharing assembly which would operate on an inclusive basis. All of the main parties would be members of the government. Relations between Northern Ireland and the Republic of Ireland were to be dealt with through the creation of a North–South Ministerial Council which would allow co-operation between the Northern Ireland Assembly and Irish Parliament on certain functional issues. As a safeguard, the Northern Ireland Assembly could only operate if the North–South Ministerial Council was also functioning. Under Strand Three, a British-Irish Council was to be established. This would draw members from the British and Irish governments, and the devolved parliaments in Scotland, Wales and Northern Ireland and 'promote the harmonious and mutually beneficial development of the totality of relationships among peoples on these islands'.

A number of other issues was addressed by the Agreement. A wide range of civil and religious liberties was affirmed, with a Northern Ireland Human Rights Commission to be established. Social, economic and cultural inclusion policies were to be pursued. The needs of victims of violence were also recognised. The British Government pledged itself to a normalisation of security arrangements 'consistent with the level of threat'. Independent commissions were to review the criminal justice system and policing. There was to be 'an accelerated release programme' for paramilitary prisoners. Importantly, the Agreement was reached without the decommissioning of paramilitary weapons. According to one UUP negotiator, the issue 'didn't get mainstream attention in the talks'.[86] A Sinn Féin negotiator concurred, saying that the issue was 'submerged in the subcommittees – literally parked'.[87] Participants in the Agreement did, however, confirm their intention 'to achieve the decommissioning of all paramilitary weapons within two years'.

Post-Agreement

The Agreement was to be put to the people of Northern Ireland in a referendum. 'Yes' and 'No' camps quickly emerged. Strongly in favour of the Agreement were the British and Irish governments, the SDLP, the loyalist parties and the US Presidency. The principal opponent was the DUP. The Agreement posed severe problems for the UUP and Sinn Féin. Many Ulster Unionists, including some who had played a key role in the negotiations, found substantial sections of the Agreement objectionable. On the whole, they found the Agreement's macro-political provisions acceptable. Northern Ireland's conditional place within the United Kingdom, permanent co-operation with the Irish Republic, and power-sharing with nationalists – all of which would have sent the previous generation of Unionists into apoplexy – were now acceptable. Deferred decommissioning, the early release programme for paramilitary prisoners and the prospect of police reform proved to be the real sticking points. David Trimble faced public dissension from within his own party. Finally the party officially endorsed the Agreement. Many Ulster Unionists remained unconvinced however, and supported the 'No' campaign.

Sinn Féin also had problems with the Agreement. A new Northern Ireland Assembly held little attraction for Republicans and risked internalising the conflict. The decision by the Irish Republic to drop its territorial claim to Northern Ireland amounted to an official devaluation of the united Ireland concept. An acceptance of the consent principle (that is, Northern Ireland's future depended on the will of its people) meant that 'armed struggle' could no longer be legitimised. Indeed, the logical extension of the Agreement was that the IRA would 'go out of business'.[88] The Agreement offered prisoner releases and a range of social, economic, cultural and security reforms, however, which would make a real difference to the quality of life in Republican communities. For Republicans the Agreement was not 'the basis for a settlement'.[89] Instead, they saw it as an opportunity or a staging post in the struggle. The task ahead, though, was to be seen to work the Agreement and its institutions, but at the same time attempt to make them transitionary towards a united Ireland. In the words of one senior Sinn Féin member, it was 'a very tall order'.[90] After much debate, and even a morale boosting visit by senior African National Congress figures, Sinn Féin endorsed the Agreement.

The main opposition to the Agreement came from the Democratic Unionist Party and its rejuvenated leader, Ian Paisley. Paisley's party faced much media hostility, with some suggesting the DUP's rejectionist stance amounted to support for violence. The two were not axiomatic. The DUP, and many other Unionists, had sincere objections to the Agreement. The problem for them, however, was that there was no alternative. The success of both governments in establishing the orthodoxy of the three-stranded approach was total. There was no credible alternative. One senior DUP member likened the peace process to a train journey: 'you can quibble about the price of the fare and the type of seats, but you can't change the direction you're going in'.[91]

The referendum campaign had surreal elements, with the Ulster Unionist Party and Sinn Féin both campaigning for a 'Yes' vote. Both held strikingly different interpretations of the Agreement, however. For one, it secured the Union. For the other, it was an opportunity for a further weakening of the Union. The campaign within Unionism was bitter and tested David Trimble's leadership skills. In May, 71 per cent of Northern Ireland's voters supported the Agreement. Virtually all Nationalists backed the Agreement, but Unionism was evenly split between those who supported and rejected the Agreement. It received 94 per cent backing in the Republic of Ireland. The British and Irish government strategy of engineering an agreement with the involvement of the paramilitaries and then having it endorsed by the people had worked. Much remained to be done, however. The new institutions had to be established and the provisions on prisoner releases and police reform, among other things, had to be initiated. Violence by Republican splinter groups left many Unionists convinced that the Republican Movement was simultaneously playing at peace and war. Elections for the new Northern Ireland Assembly were held in late June. UUP leader, David Trimble, and SDLP deputy leader, Seamus Mallon, were confirmed as First Minister and Deputy First Minister. For Unionists, a major sticking point was the prospect of Sinn Féin members assuming ministerial positions without the IRA decommissioning.[92] For Republicans, the Unionist demand for decommissioning was a diversion and masked the real desire to exclude Republicans from government.

Northern Ireland was to have a violent summer. Tensions from the by now annual stand-off between the police and Orange Order at Drumcree spread throughout Northern Ireland. They culminated in an arson attack which killed three Catholic children. This was enough to end most Orange protests, but the issue of Drumcree was left unresolved for another year. In August 1998, a bomb by a Republican splinter group killed 29 people in the market town of Omagh. It was the largest loss of life from a single incident in the modern phase of the Northern Ireland conflict. The scale of the loss, coming as it did after the Agreement and the 'Yes' vote in the referendum, and the profile of the victims, both Catholic and Protestant, stunned many in Northern Ireland. The atrocity allowed political leaders to make gestures which, ordinarily, would have been difficult for them to make. For example,

Sinn Féin condemned the bombing, thus publicly censuring fellow Republicans for the first time. The bomb had another, more profound, effect. It crystallised the division between those supportive or even agnostic on the use of violence for political ends and those committed to peaceful means. Post-Omagh public reaction would accept no equivocation. Political leaders were urged to act more responsibly. Those who were supportive of the Agreement grew more attached to it. This was most significant for Gerry Adams and David Trimble, two figures who, for very different reasons, were luke-warm about the Agreement.

Adams and Trimble had their first face-to-face meeting in September 1998. They did not shake hands. According to Trimble, 'the origin of the handshake is to show that there is no weapon in the person's hand. You offer your hand to show there's nothing in it. He [Adams] doesn't have an open hand to show to people.'[93] This was a reference to the decommissioning of paramilitary weapons which was to dominate the meeting. The UUP was opposed to Sinn Féin entering into the new Northern Ireland government in the absence of decommissioning. According to Sinn Féin, their entry into government was automatic and not dependent on decommissioning. Interventions by the British and Irish Prime Ministers failed to break the deadlock. Both Trimble and Adams were mindful that their positions within their respective parties would be in jeopardy if they were seen to back down on this issue. The issue of decommissioning had been inflated to the extent that it was no longer about weapons.

Much of the Agreement had yet to be implemented. The extent and pace of the implementation were hotly contested. Broadly, the Nationalist 'speedy maximalist' and Unionist 'cautious minimalist' approaches held. First Minister David Trimble and Deputy First Minister Seamus Mallon showed an early understanding of the mutually precarious nature of each other's position. In December, the parties reached agreement on the nature of the power-sharing executive which would govern Northern Ireland. Power would be devolved to ten ministries, although the Secretary of State would retain control over security and justice matters. After much haggling, six implementation bodies were also agreed upon. These bodies would administer cross-border co-operation on certain, limited issues. Six more areas for possible co-operation were identified.

The Agreement's implementation phase reflected its earlier problems; it was dogged by delay, mistrust, petitions by prime ministers, and elements of high farce. The main paramilitary organisations showed no willingness to decommission, despite the Agreement's deadline of

May 2000. A level of violence continued, with paramilitary punishment beatings attracting particular attention. Despite pressure from both governments, First Minister David Trimble and his UUP refused to move towards the establishment of the executive which would give Sinn Féin two ministerial positions. The basic Unionist position of 'no guns, no government' remained solid and a number of target dates for the triggering of the new executive (and other institutions) slipped by in an atmosphere of recrinimation and growing Unionist dissatisfaction with the Agreement.

The sticking points were the refusal of the IRA to decommission and the continuation of violence by paramilitary organisations within both communities. The underlying forces which converted these sticking points into a quagmire were tensions with the UUP.

The Good Friday Agreement, like all peace agreements, was designed to create both a balance of benefits and a balance of concessions. All the major parties accepted it (excepting the DUP), and it was endorsed by a healthy majority in a referendum. So why, within a year of the Agreement, did the Unionist Party, and perhaps the Unionist community in general, feel that the concessions were heavily weighed against them?

The answer lies not in an imbalance between the concessions by the Republicans and Unionists but in the different nature of the concessions made by each side. Consider the changes that were incorporated into and followed the Good Friday Agreement. The two main concessions by the Republican side were concessions of principle, the promise by the Irish Republic to remove its territorial claim for Northern Ireland, and Sinn Féin's acceptance of the 'principle of consent', that Irish unity could not take place without the agreement of a majority in Northern Ireland. However significant they were – and Repulicans regarded the 'principle of consent' especially as a major concession – they were symbolic concessions. They would not be implemented in the immediate future.

The concessions made by the Unionists, on the other hand, were concrete. Most of them had at least started by the end of 1998. Several hundred IRA prisoners had been released. The Irish Republic was centrally involved in directing the peace process; Sinn Féin were not only centrally involved in the negotiations, but had been assigned two cabinet posts when the new executive assumed power; the Pattern Commission concluded in September 1999 that there must be radical restructuring of the Royal Ulster Constabulary, a proposal unanimously rejected by the executive of the Ulster Unionist Party. The DUP's

Peter Robinson seemed to speak for many Unionists when he claimed that, 'There is no point in continuing with the farce of the present Agreement'.[94]

This apparent accumulation of concessions demonstrated to many Unionists, including some who had supported the Agreement, that the balance of benefit had tilted unacceptably towards the Republicans. Republicans felt that the unionists were reneging on the peace accord, and had never intended to share power in the first place. The disjuncture in the nature and timing of concessions had provided Unionist opponents of the Agreement with a persuasive case to threaten the basis of Unionist support for the Agreement.

A March 1999 offer by Gerry Adams that Unionists and Republicans 'jump together', an allusion to a simultaneous formation of the executive and a beginning to paramilitary decommissioning, proved hollow. Instead, Sinn Féin emphasised their distance from the IRA and argued that their electoral mandate gave them a right to ministerial positions regardless of IRA arms and their alleged use. Intensive prime-ministerial mediation failed to produce a compromise. Interestingly though, the notion that the primary onus for resolving the impasse lay with internal actors (the UUP and Sinn Féin) was widely accepted and marked a significant development in Northern Ireland politics. Frustrated, Northern Ireland Secretary Mo Mowlam triggered the establishment of the executive in July 1999. In the absence of paramilitary decommissioning, the UUP stayed away from the ceremonial meeting. In scenes of high farce, an all Nationalist and Republican executive was appointed, only to be deemed invalid because it contravened the Agreement's cross-community criteria. Such was the mood within the UUP that had David Trimble shown any willingness to compromise it was unlikely that he would have retained his Party's leadership. The DUP refused to take part in the nomination procedure, but their presence in the Assembly chamber served to remind David Trimble that the Unionist electorate had other options. The inclusive nature of the new institutions meant that the DUP could assume the position of peaceful spoilers, but spoilers all the same, within Northern Ireland's new government. The day's proceedings ended with the resignation of Deputy First Minister Seamus Mallon who concentrated his criticisims on the absent Trimble for repeated delays in the implementation of the Agreement.

The net result was that the political process was gravely damaged. In little more than a year, the post-Agreement euphoria and optimism had been sapped by problems of implementation and concerns over such security-related issues as the release of prisoners and proposed reform of the police force. The decommissioning issue had grown into the greatest obstacle to the process. Direct Sinn Féin–UUP talks and the energies of the British and Irish Prime Ministers failed to reach a breakthrough. In frustration the parties and governments looked to Senator George Mitchell to conduct a review of the implementation of the Agreement in September 1999.

Progress towards political settlement: Negotiating the Agreement

A number of key political factors shaped the peace process. Four factors relate directly to the strategies adopted by the British and Irish governments. First, the British and Irish governments developed a close, institutionalised working relationship in the years following the 1985 Anglo-Irish Agreement. Over time, this developed into a determination to engineer a political settlement in Northern Ireland which would stabilise the security situation and reach an accommodation on Northern Ireland's constitutional status. Second, by the mid-1990s, both governments were successful in establishing a paradigm hegemony. Through a series of governmental agreements and talks processes among Northern Ireland's political parties, they successfully established the parameters of any future political agreement. The norm of a comprehensive three-stranded approach to talks processes, and the agreements they would lead to, was established.[95] This approach was exclusive and both governments were successful in making it clear that no alternative talks framework was acceptable. Third, and related to the previous point, both governments were successful in elevating themselves to the position of moral and practical guardians of the peace process. They were able to act as gatekeepers to the process (controlling access to the negotiations) and timekeepers (influencing the timetabling of the process). Fourth, the imposition of a deadline for the talks process proved to be crucial. Without this, and pressure from the governments, participants in the talks process (and previous talks processes) showed little willingness to move from the rhetorical to the substantive. Government pressure was required to move the talks from 'the political version of *Groundhog Day*'.[96]

Another key factor in shaping the peace process was the involvement of those political parties linked with paramilitary organisations. This marked a sea change in government policy and was based on a recognition that paramilitaries retained the capacity to bring down any major political agreement which attempted to exclude them. In the case of Loyalism, this required the creation of political parties to represent their views in talks. Indeed, the peace process saw an increase in the number of political parties willing to represent Unionism. A number of these parties were the result of splits or a fear that the established Unionist parties were guilty of selling out the Union. The community that perceives itself to be 'losing' is often prone to splits and defections.

The role of political leadership is worth highlighting. The peace process confronted political leaders with a range of new experiences. The continuation of the peace process, and the eventual Agreement, depended on leadership initiatives at key moments in the process. Leaders often faced their most serious challenges from within their own parties.

Another key political factor in the peace process was vagueness. Rather than risk the collapse of the entire process, certain statements were unmade, questions were left unasked and some difficult issues were deferred. When the Agreement was reached, parties at different ends of the constitutional spectrum made radically different interpretations of the Agreement. Despite rival interpretations, they campaigned for its endorsement. While the deferral of contentious issues may have smoothed the way for the Agreement, it did contribute to a post-Agreement sense of disillusionment when these issues remained unresolved.

The peace process was predicated on the idea of consent: any change in Northern Ireland's constitutional status had to be endorsed by a majority of its citizens.[97] This had a clear democratic rationale. Moreover, if a majority of people supported an agreement then paramilitary organisations could no longer claim a popular mandate for the use of violence.

The peace process was also elongated. With hindsight, the seeds of the process are visible in the decade preceding the Good Friday Agreement. While the longevity of the process introduced complications, it also facilitated a conditioning process. The acclimatisation for possible political change could not take place overnight. Individuals, paramilitary groups, security agencies, political parties and governments needed time to get used to the idea of a major political change. For most that process is on-going and is likely to last for many years. While many participants complained about the pace of the process (Nationalists: too slow; Unionists: too fast), the real concern was direction. The bottom line for Unionists and Nationalists was how the process and subsequent Agreement suited their constitutional goals.

The Northern Ireland peace process followed a broad pattern common in other peace processes. For example, it was preceded by initial secret contacts between governments and paramilitaries. At a later stage, there was debate on the legitimacy of negotiating with those who used political violence. Each side was anxious to test the bona fides of the other side by securing confidence-building measures. The government wanted to make sure that the paramilitary ceasefires were permanent while the paramilitary organisations wanted good faith gestures in the form of security relaxations and the release of prisoners.

Violence and security

The paramilitary ceasefires did not herald an end to all violence in Northern Ireland. Instead, there was a diffusion of the types of violence used, with each type presenting a different threat to the process. With paramilitary punishment attacks, ceasefire breakdowns (announced or unannounced), splinter groups, and an increase in sectarian street violence and arson, Northern Ireland continued to have significant levels of violence. Ceasefires by the mainstream paramilitary organisations, however, did lead to a dramatic decrease in political violence.[98] Reciprocal relaxations in security measures led to a noticeable difference in the quality of life in many parts of Northern Ireland. For example, Belfast in the early 1990s was a city under siege. Paramilitary assassinations and the IRA tactic of using increasingly large bombs in the city's commercial heart resulted in very visible security measures on the city's arterial routes. During the ceasefires, many of the security measures were removed.

When the mainstream paramilitary groups did engage in violence during the ceasefires it differed from previous campaigns in type, intensity and aim. A preliminary point worth making is that the major paramilitary organisations were quite successful in policing their own ceasefires. Both Republican and Loyalist paramilitaries suffered from splits and defections. In both cases, the splinter groups were able to mount significant campaigns and risked destabilising the peace process. The Real IRA and Continuity IRA spawned from Republican dissatisfaction that the peace process amounted to a surrender of the Republican goal of a united Ireland. Both bombed mainly Protestant towns at crucial periods during the peace process in an apparent attempt to goad Unionists into withdrawing from the process and thus prevent a further dilution of the Republican ideal. The campaign culminated disastrously in the Omagh bombing in August 1998 when 29 people were killed. A Loyalist splinter group, the Loyalist Volunteer Force (LVF), pursued a campaign of sectarian assassinations without a clear political rationale. No splinter group was able to sustain a major campaign, however. Censure, or worse, from the main paramilitary organisations played a large role in this.[99] Moreover, the main paramilitary groups succeeded in securing the greater part of their memberships, arsenals and support bases from the splinter groups. This did not happen automatically. Instead, the paramilitary leaderships, and their political associates, invested much energy into consulting with their respective memberships and keeping them abreast of political developments.

Crucial in these consultations was the role of paramilitary prisoners. According to a Sinn Féin leader, 'We visit the prisoners constantly, we discuss the process and involve them, we produce position papers. They have a sense of ownership of the project.'[100] This was mirrored on the Loyalist side, where 'prisoners were very important in getting the ceasefires'.[101] Understanding the key role which prisoners played in arguing for the ceasefires, the British and Irish governments facilitated the Sinn Féin and Loyalist political leadership in entering the prisons to talk to prisoners. In January 1998, at a time of Loyalist dissatisfaction with the peace process, Secretary of State Mo Mowlam held talks with Loyalist prisoners in the Maze prison. For both Loyalists and Republicans, prisoner releases were an essential part of any political agreement. Six months before the Good Friday Agreement was reached, one Sinn Féin negotiator was emphatic: 'prisoners clearly will be getting out of prison as part of the settlement ... that's our bottom line'.[102] But it was an emotive issue and proved to be a major sticking point for those who opposed the Agreement.

As noted, the peace process made a qualitative difference to paramilitary violence which continued after the ceasefires were called. The primary difference was that political violence became more political. The IRA's use of a proxy organisation, DAAD, to kill suspected drug dealers, was motivated by the political desire not to hamper Sinn Féin's entry into talks. When the IRA called off its ceasefire in February 1996, it did not resume its campaign where it had left off in August 1994. Instead, IRA activity was more limited and explicitly linked with Sinn Féin's political ambitions. At first, IRA attacks were limited to targets in England. When attacks resumed in Northern Ireland, the IRA said that its attacks would be limited to the police and British army targets and that it had no wish to draw Loyalist paramilitaries into the violence.[103] The IRA seemed to be 'modulating' its campaign.[104] For example, in November 1996, it seemed to operate an unofficial and undeclared ceasefire while John Hume interceded with John Major on possible conditions for Sinn Féin's entry into talks.[105] Another seemingly undeclared ceasefire came in the two weeks before the 1997 general election, possibly in the hope of maximising Sinn Féin's vote. This ceasefire only extended to Northern Ireland. A deliberate campaign of disruption was mounted in England in the run-up to the general election. Significantly, this seemed to be designed to maximise disruption and headlines while minimising casualties.[106]

The main paramilitary organisations retained a capacity for significant violence throughout the peace process. The Good Friday Agreement was reached in the absence of decommissioning. The paramilitary structures also remained intact. Crucially, however, there was little willingness in either the IRA or those organisations aligned with the Combined Loyalist Military Command to return to war.[107] Nor did the communities which sustained the paramilitaries display much enthusiasm for the ending of ceasefires. It was this factor, rather than security initiatives, which was most effective in limiting paramilitary violence.

While vertical violence by the main paramilitary organisations seemed to become more controlled, incidents of horizontal violence increased. This took the form of sectarian rioting, arson and street assaults. Much of the street politics was linked to marching disputes. In the absence of large-scale paramilitary violence, many deemed it 'safer' to engage in street protests and demonstrations. The greater numbers prepared to take to the streets also reflected an increased unease, in both communities, at the direction and possible outcomes of the peace process. The paramilitary ceasefires heralded much speculation on rising crime rates. Alarming increases in crime rates had followed the South African transition. In Northern Ireland, an increase in drug-related crime was noticeable after the ceasefires were announced, but there were no dramatic increases in crime rates generally. Recorded crime fell by 9.2 per cent in 1997.[108] The relatively low levels of 'ordinary decent crime' may be partially explained by a large police force with a strong surveillance capability. 'Paramilitary policing' or punishment attacks may offer another explanation.

External factors

The only external actor to make a significant political contribution to the Northern Ireland peace process was the United States. The European Union contributed money, but little else. South Africa, Israel–Palestine and other peace processes contributed by example. The United States contributed political clout. The extent of US involvement in the Northern Ireland peace process from 1994 onwards is startling; particularly given the traditional US approach of regarding Northern Ireland as an internal matter for the United Kingdom. Crucial to the new US interest in Northern Ireland was Bill Clinton's election to the White House and the development of the powerful Irish-American lobby with key links in politics and corporate America. Clinton had little natural interest in Northern Ireland. He was courted. The Irish-American lobby sought to engage him on the Irish issue when he was a presidential hopeful. Once he had been elected, the Irish Government sought to interest him in the possibilities of a developing peace process. Irish Republicans also regarded an activist White House as a member of the 'pan-nationalist front' coalition of interests.

The Clinton White House made a number of vital interventions in the peace process. The decision to grant Gerry Adams a US entry visa before an IRA ceasefire was called was crucial in helping Adams persuade the hawks in the Republican Movement of the benefits which constitutional legitimacy offered. In this decision, Clinton overruled advice from the State Department and FBI. He also risked damaging Anglo-American relations. In general, however, the US position was to support the approach of the British and Irish governments. The Clinton White House also worked hard to overcome the notion that the United States was pro-Nationalist.[109] The US role was pragmatic, helping where the opportunity presented itself, rather than intervening and banging heads together. According to Clinton, 'the United States had no ulterior motive, no particular political design in mind'.[110] As the peace process developed, US intervention became regularised (rather than institutionalised). In the assessment of one key Irish government negotiator, US intermediaries waited until they were asked before intervening.[111] Clinton did stress, however, that 'people who take risks for peace will always be welcome in the White House'.[112] The offer was taken up repeatedly by Northern Ireland's political leaders and the two governments, all of whom wanted US intercession on their behalf.

Following the common pattern that diaspora communities are often more radical than the home population, many Irish-Americans were strong supporters of militant Republicanism. With time, and much persuasion by Irish governments and constitutional Nationalists, these attitudes changed. The Irish-American community became particularly important in persuading the Republican Movement of the opportunities offered by an IRA ceasefire and a peace process.

Economics: a peace dividend?

A peace dividend, so goes the 'conventional wisdom', follows a peace process.[113] The existence of a Northern Ireland peace dividend is open to debate. Certainly, evidence supporting the argument is more readily available in the Northern Ireland case than in other peace processes. The new South African government set high economic targets for itself which were left unfulfilled. In 1997, the standard of living for black South Africans was comparable to the world's 124th wealthy state, Congo, while for white South Africans it was comparable to the 24th, Spain.[114] Palestinian living standards in the 'Occupied Territories' have also declined during the Arab–Israeli peace process. In Northern Ireland, the ceasefires did have a positive impact on the tourism and retail sectors, and helped attract inward investment.[115] They also brought a £240m Special Peace and Reconciliation package from the European Union, £40m from the International Fund for Ireland, and various private sector investment initiatives.[116] It is more difficult to estimate the level of delivery on the prospect of external investment emphasised during President Clinton's visits to Northern Ireland, in 1995 and 1998, and the hopes that the Irish diaspora in North America would swing in behind the peace process.

Peace dividends are accompanied by peace deficits. A substantial security industry of police, prison officers, security officers and part-time soldiers grew during the years of the Troubles and played an increasingly significant part in Northern Ireland's economy. The return of peace meant inevitable reductions in all these posts. Economic opinion in Northern Ireland was surprisingly sanguine about the prospect, however, suggesting that it would be accompanied by well-funded redundancy packages and pensions, which would remain in the local economy.[117]

The expectation that public funding is available for such payments arises from one of Northern Ireland's advantages over other contemporary peace processes. It is a small region within a rich nation state, itself part of a prosperous economic union. Indeed Northern Ireland's economic revival had started during the years of violence.[118] It was heavily dependent on support from the UK exchequer, and was partly fuelled by the need to redress the economic disadvantages of the Catholic community. Northern Ireland's housing stock had improved dramatically since the 1960s, when it had been one of the major grievances of the civil rights campaign. Infant mortality rates and life expectancy had moved from the worst position within the United Kingdom into the group of average regions. Even the unemployment rate, which had historically been more than double British levels, had moved to a position of greater equality.

These improvements amounted to a form of anticipatory peace process before the peace process began. They also left, as an inheritance, serious structural deficiencies which would remain unaffected by the peace process. Indeed, the peace process even threatened some sectors of the economy. Northern Ireland relies on an annual British Government subvention approaching £4bn, which approximates to one-third of Gross Domestic Product.[119] Just over 46 per cent of the working population are employed in the public sector, many in the security-related positions. A sustained peace would put many of these in jeopardy. Economic growth was very much dependent on wider political development. For example, tourist revenue, which grew spectacularly in the first year after the ceasefire announcement, fell back sharply when violence resumed. The British government went to pains to make clear that the costs of disturbances, such as those connected with the Drumcree parade, would come from existing budgets. The linkage between political stability and economic growth was a constant refrain from the British, Irish and American governments. The issue failed to catch the local political or public imagination. The peace process and Good Friday Agreement were rarely discussed in terms of economics.

Popular responses

The most significant popular input into the Northern Ireland peace process came in the form of the 71 per cent endorsement of the Good Friday Agreement in the May 1998 referendum. The people of the whole island had the opportunity to vote on their political future and relationship with each other. Much of the peace process was elite-led, however, and insulated from direct popular pressure. Opportunities for popular input were limited, particularly during the early stages of the process. Key peace process players operated behind closed doors. The Downing Street Declaration and Frameworks for the Future documents were formulated at the elite governmental level, often between prime ministers. Both documents were to form much of the basis of the peace process and subsequent Good Friday Agreement. Neither was offered to the people of Northern Ireland in a referendum. Paramilitary organisations were also largely insulated from popular input. So were most political parties, although the Ulster Unionist Party was something of an exception in holding public consultations in the summer of 1997 on whether or not it should enter into a talks process which included Sinn Féin.

The talks process itself was semi-confidential. Politicians gave regular media briefings outside of the talks venue but rarely went into detail on the text of a possible agreement. Five elections during the peace process did offer the opportunity for popular input.[120] The intra-community nature of Northern Ireland elections meant that each election was a mini-referendum within each community. In the Unionist community, the question revolved around whether or not Unionist politicians should engage with the peace process, and, if so, to what extent. Since most Nationalists were supportive of the peace process, the Nationalist community was less fractured. As a result, support for political violence was often the key issue which divided SDLP and Sinn Féin voters.

Apart from parades-related disturbances, the peace process did see a number of more positive public demonstrations of popular will. President Bill Clinton's visits to Northern Ireland, in November 1995 and September 1998, were public celebrations of the peace process. Both visits attracted large crowds. The Northern Ireland Office attempted to garner post-ceasefire, and subsequently post-Agreement, goodwill by staging a number of public events.[121] The collapse of the IRA ceasefire in February 1996 prompted mass peace rallies throughout Ireland. At a minimum the rallies indicated a strong popular attachment to an absence of violence. While the rallies reflected a heartfelt frustration, they were not linked to a particular political programme and so their impact was negligible. Few were prepared to accept peace at any price. Unionists protested in favour of a Unionist peace, while Nationalists protested in favour of a Nationalist peace. A number of civil society initiatives did make a significant contribution to the peace process. The most notable was the Northern Ireland Women's Coalition which was established in the run-up to the May 1996 Forum elections. The party deliberately avoided taking a position on constitutional issues. As a result it was free to perform a brokerage and bridge-building role in the political negotiations. The media was also almost universally in favour of the peace process and subsequent Agreement. No significant media outlet opposed the Agreement.

Civil society played a key role in the Pro-Agreement referendum campaign. An argument can be made, however, that questions of whether the peace process was primarily 'top down' or 'bottom up' are not strictly relevant in the Northern Ireland case. Much of Northern

Ireland's civil society was a construct of the political elite. From the late 1980s onwards, a range of legislation, best practice and new statutory agencies was introduced with the aim of encouraging equality in employment and provision of government services. It also aimed to bolster minority faith in the protection of cultural rights and the administration of justice. Put bluntly, it was an attempt to co-opt the Catholic middle class into the administration of Northern Ireland.[122] Added to this, much of the EU funds which followed the autumn 1994 ceasefires were channelled towards think-tanks and pressure and community groups. The result was that a critical mass of activities and thinking developed which was broadly supportive of a political accommodation. Northern Ireland-wide disturbances sparked by the July 1996 Drumcree parade were a reminder that community divisions would not be easily overcome.

Symbolism

Political symbols have a negative and positive potential, particularly in a divided society. Northern Ireland seemed more willing to make use of symbols in a negative way. No single symbolic image captures the Northern Ireland peace process.[123] Other peace processes have produced memorable images. For example, the Rabin–Arafat handshake on the White House lawn or Nelson Mandela's attendance at the 1995 Rugby World Cup. There was no signing ceremony for the Good Friday Agreement. But symbols and rituals played an immense role in the Northern Ireland peace process. Indeed, heightened sensitivities during the peace process attached greater significance to symbolic events and issues. Religious, political, cultural and community symbols which had been previously regarded as peripheral to core political issues became concretised. They were credited with absolute value and adopted a political reality.[124] Symbols abounded in the peace process: in the parading dispute, in meetings between former protagonists, in handshakes, in debates over policing reform, prisoner releases or the treatment of victims of violence. They were employed in two main ways. First, in the allegorical sense, to illustrate how a particular community thought it might be treated under a new political dispensation. Second, as a deliberate political technique. Given the ambiguity of symbols, particularly in a deeply divided society, they often became contentious. Seemingly the other community could interpret innocent symbols of group identity as offensive.

An often overlooked point is that symbolic politics usually amounts to a low-cost political activity. Nationalists and Unionists invested immense energy into maximising the import of their own 'symbolic inventories' and denying the legitimacy of the other's symbols.[125] The message was often conveyed at the emotive level, requiring a minimum of articulation and intellectual engagement. It was deflective, switching attention away from substantive issues. This was aided by the structure of the Northern Ireland peace process. The absence of formal talks for extended periods during the process, together with the expectations and fears which the process aroused, meant that many issues were discussed at the symbolic rather than substantive level. The issue of police reform, for example, was often discussed in terms of proposed changes to the name of the Royal Ulster Constabulary and the colour of its uniform.[126] The overall impact of a superficial discussion of a series of issues, often discussed in terms of symbolism, resulted in their sensitisation in advance of real political negotiations.

Symbolism was perhaps most visible through the parading issue. The issue came to represent something much more than the right to march along a particular stretch of road. For the Orange Order and other institutions, the right to march was a basic and fundamental freedom. They interpreted their right to march as an indicator of how they would be treated in a post-agreement Northern Ireland. According to Jeffrey Donaldson, Assistant Grand Master of the Orange Order, 'if nationalists cannot tolerate the culture and tradition of the Orange Order for 15 minutes in one year then I think we are entitled to ask what hope there is for the future?'[127] Equally, many Nationalist protesters saw a direct linkage between the willingness of the British Government to 'tackle' the marching issue and its willingness to treat Nationalists fairly on broader political issues.[128]

The parades issue, more so than many other issues in the peace process, was particularly amenable to the use of symbolism as a political technique. It was one of the few opportunities for face-to-face sectarian confrontation, particularly in periods in which there were no formal political talks. It was played out in public, on streets and in villages rather than in conference rooms. It was participative, with marching organisations and residents' groups often relying on sheer force of numbers. It was heavily ritualised. A 'marching season', with most marches concentrated in the summer months in which they followed certain routes on certain dates, injected an element of predictability into the issue. For the organisers of set-piece confrontations, it was an issue from Heaven. According to one commentator, the marching dispute risked 'the biggest riot ever – the biggest land battle on the island of Ireland since 1798'.[129] Furthermore, the parades and protests were highly televisual. This factor was not lost on either the marching organisations or the residents' groups. Both employed visually strong images in an attempt to raise support for their cause. Residents' groups, for example, often lined the routes of contentious parades with anti-marching murals and posters. In one case, an anti-parades protest used Ku Klux Klan and Nazi imagery to represent the Orange Order.[130] It was often elderly, sober-suited Orangemen who handed over letters of protest at the lines of riot police when marches were being re-routed. Both sides sought to emphasise their victim-hood and communicate their fears to their supporters in other areas within Northern Ireland and the wider media.

The peace process saw an increase in the deliberate targeting of symbols for attack. Arson and vandalism attacks on identifiably Protestant or Catholic properties increased sharply.[131] Most of the attacks were carried out during the marching season or at times of political tension.[132] They constituted soft targets and were chosen to maximise offence. More subtle forms of symbolic conflict were used as well. A common method was the appropriation of symbols associated with political opponents. For example, in the run-up to the Good Friday Agreement, Republican sympathisers, in mockery of the state, distributed fake banknotes bearing Gerry Adams's face.[133] Loyalists incorporated Cuchulain, a figure from Irish mythology, into their wall murals.[134] Indeed, the invocation of cultural rights by Unionists and Loyalists strengthened during the peace process. For much of the Troubles it had been Nationalists who had pursued a cultural equality agenda. Many Unionists and Loyalists, perhaps regarding the peace process as a threat to their cultural heritage, launched themselves into a cultural mini-renaissance. There was, for example, a renewed interest in the Scots-Irish dialect.

States and institutions were also keen to appropriate sensitive anniversaries lest they became the political property of Nationalism or Unionism.[135] Museums and statutory bodies charged with the guardianship of heritage and culture attempted to promote neutral versions of a fraught past. The result was often poor history, but good politics. A neutral approach to cultural heritage had been institutionalised in Northern Ireland since the early 1990s.[136] The peace process gave renewed impetus to Northern Ireland Office attempts to re-brand Northern Ireland and they mounted a number of massive advertisement campaigns aimed at encouraging support for political accommodation. The British and Irish governments were also careful to project an image of intergovernmental unity. This was crucial to their position of moral guardians of the process. Despite differences, there were regular intergovernmental conferences and summits and joint press statements. The symbolic unity stretched to the British and Irish prime ministers going to the pub together.[137] One can only sympathise with the regular clientele.

Perhaps the most symbolic part of the peace process was the fact that an agreement was reached at all. A loyalist negotiator in the talks process reflected the opinion of many in stating that, 'right up to the last fortnight [of the talks], the consensus of opinion throughout Northern Ireland, and throughout both sections of the community, was that there was little or no possibility of the parties reaching agreement'.[138] Yet an agreement was reached. The August 1998 Omagh bombing allowed political leaders to make gestures which, ordinarily, would have been difficult for them to make. The atmosphere following the bomb also contributed to Gerry Adams's decision to make a statement that violence was 'a thing of the past'.[139] Days before the bombing, Adams had vehemently rejected speculation that he would make such a statement.[140] In the aftermath of the bomb, First Minister David Trimble travelled to Dublin to discuss security responses with the Irish Government. Also in the Irish Republic, he attended the funerals of three Catholic victims of the bombing. All of these were significant gestures. All were, to a certain extent, made more acceptable by the post-Omagh public mood.

Conclusion

Two main themes are worth highlighting in conclusion. The first is some of the political factors which shaped and sustained the process. The key roles played by the British and Irish governments in establishing an exclusive framework for the peace process were essential. Much in the process was deliberately and artificially engineered by the governments to guarantee their overall objective: a comprehensive political settlement, backed by popular support, and reinforced by an end to the campaigns by the main paramilitary organisations. Both governments made a point of acting together as much as was possible and controlled access to the process and its timetabling. Also important was the involvement of those paramilitaries who were capable of bringing down any settlement if excluded. All previous attempts at reaching a settlement which had excluded the paramilitaries had foundered. The process also reinforced the importance of political leadership, a clear lesson being that leadership skills are often most needed within parties rather than in engagements between parties. While issues of the pace of political developments (the Northern Ireland peace process was elongated) were a constant refrain, a more crucial issue was the direction of political change.

The other important theme is the relationship between violence and the peace process. The paramilitary ceasefires did not mark an end to political violence. They did herald a greater diffusion of the types of violence used. Surprisingly, there was little use of violence in the strategic sense, that is, the mainstream paramilitary groups who were party to the process attempting to influence events inside the negotiation chamber by the carefully targeted use of violence outside of it. The Mitchell Principles and other schemes to penalise the use of violence may have kept a control on this strategic violence. But, as with other peace processes, there was an increase in the use of spoiler violence, by splinter elements eager to derail the wider process. Although significant, spoiler violence did not derail the process; in large part, this was due to the efforts of the mainstream paramilitary organisations to minimise splinter group activity within their own camps. Also worth mentioning was the increase in horizontal violence during the peace process. Sectarian street confrontations and mob violence, common in the early years of the Troubles, had given way to more organised violence by paramilitary groups by the mid-1970s. There was a resurgence in this street violence during the peace process, however, probably reflective of an increased nervousness among both communities at the direction of the peace process.

The Good Friday Agreement notwithstanding, Northern Ireland remains a deeply divided society. The causes of the conflict are unaffected. The major change, however, is that the conflict's main protagonists reached an agreement on how to manage their differences. Central to the new management technique is a control on violence. For paramilitary groups, killing people was no longer the most effective way of pursuing their agendas. For Republicans in particular acceptance of the Good Friday Agreement was a recognition that the Provisional project of the previous quarter of a century had failed. What had once been about revolution was now about reform. Republicans would, for the first time, have the opportunity to hold, or more accurately share, power. But the price of power was recognition of the state of Northern Ireland, a state that they had attempted to destroy. For Loyalists, the peace process was a means of ending a violent campaign which had no political or military rationale. The principle of consent – that Northern

Ireland's constitutional status would not change unless a majority of its population wanted it – was in place before the Good Friday Agreement was reached. The Agreement merely reaffirmed this.

The Agreement meant that Unionists had to share power with Nationalists. The imposition of direct rule from London in 1972 meant that the holding of power, shared or otherwise, was a novel experience for many Unionists. There was little outrage over this. Unionism's psychological defeat had come with the 1985 Anglo-Irish Agreement. The vigour of rejectionist Unionists aside, many Unionists accepted the notion of power-sharing and functional co-operation with the Irish Republic with equanimity. Most Unionist opposition to the Agreement stemmed not from constitutional issues but from the reform agenda on practical matters such as prisoner releases, reform of policing and the treatment of victims. These are emotive issues and still retain the capacity to destabilise the wider Agreement. They underscore the fact that the conflict requires careful and constant management in future years. The Good Friday Agreement is a significant stage, but only a stage, in a continuing peace process.

Notes

1 Because of the sensitivity over language, the official title of the Agreement reached on 10 April 1998 is 'The Agreement' although it has been referred to, among other things, as 'The Good Friday Agreement' and 'The Belfast Agreement'.
2 Alexis de Tocqueville, *Democracy in America* (Hertfordshire, UK: Wordsworth Editions Limited, 1998), pp. 330–1.
3 Author interview with a senior member of the Irish Department of Foreign Affairs (13 March 1996).
4 This is the assessment of a senior official from the Irish Department of Foreign Affairs. Author interview (13 March 1996).
5 Author interview with a senior member of Fianna Fáil (6 June 1996).
6 E. Mallie and D. McKittrick, *The Fight for Peace: the Secret Story behind the Irish Peace Process* (London: Heinemann, 1996), pp. 99–107.
7 Author interview with a senior member of Sinn Féin (23 July 1996).
8 Ibid.
9 Author interview with a senior member of Sinn Féin (25 February 1997).
10 The document is reprinted in Appendix 3 of Mallie and McKittrick, *Fight for Peace*, pp. 381–4.
11 Author interview with a senior member of the UUP (26 March 1996).
12 One senior Orangeman's view of political initiatives was 'Every time something comes along it is worse than what came before' (Author interview [31 January 1998]).

13 Author interview with a senior member of the UDP (26 March 1996). The UDP is linked with the Ulster Defence Association and Ulster Freedom Fighters paramilitary groups. The PUP is linked with the Ulster Volunteer Force.
14 Author interview with a senior member of the UDP (26 March 1996).
15 See, 'Chasing the Yankee Dollar: the Americans behind the Peace Process', *Business and Finance*, 35, 4 (26 November 1998), pp. 20–1; A. Guelke, 'The United States, Irish Americans and the Northern Ireland Peace Process', *International Affairs*, 72, 3 (July 1996), pp. 521–36; and R. Mac Ginty, 'American Influences on the Northern Ireland Peace Process', *Journal of Conflict Studies*, 17, 2 (Fall 1997), pp. 31–50.
16 P. Robinson, deputy leader of the DUP, quoted in 'Security pledges', *Newsletter* (28 October 1994).
17 Author interview with a senior member of the UDP (12 March 1997).
18 *Frameworks for the Future* (Belfast: HMSO, 1995), p. v.
19 The three-strands approach dates from talks initiatives from the early 1990s.
20 Author interview with senior official from the Irish Department of Foreign Affairs (13 March 1996).
21 According to police figures, in the first nine months of 1996, there were 100 assaults by Loyalist paramilitaries and 140 by Republicans. See 'Casualties as a Result of Paramilitary Assaults' on the RUC website: http: www.ruc.police.uk/index.htm, 1997.
22 See, for example, 'IRA is blamed for killing of alleged drug dealer' and 'Northern politicians condemn Sinn Féin silence on latest Belfast killing', *Irish Times* (9 and 29 December 1995).
23 See, for example, 'Arsonists hit churches, halls and cars in North', 'Concern at number of arson attacks in North', 'Church, Orange hall damaged in arson attacks', 'Orange hall arson attack investigated', 'Church fears IRA organised attacks', 'Orange hall in Cavan damaged', 'Appeal for calm after arson attacks on Catholic homes', 'Arson attack on Harryville church', 'Woman hit with stone at church peace vigil', 'Arson attack wrecks sacristy of Catholic church in Co Down', 'Antrim Orange hall attacked', 'Protests at Harryville set to start again', and 'Harryville gates rammed', all from *Irish Times* (22, 23 and 25 August 1995; 24 July 1996; 13 and 25 September 1996; 6 and 10 December 1996; 10 March 1997; 17 and 24 April 1997; 15 September 1997; and 5 January 1998).
24 Paramilitary groups would have to abide by the so-called 'Washington Three' criteria: 1. commit themselves to disarm in principle; 2. agree on the modalities of disarmament; and 3. engage in some actual disarmament to test the modalities and demonstrate good faith.
25 'Talks part of larger process – Ancram', *Irish Times* (10 May 1995).
26 'Bruton postpones summit in arms deal deadlock', *Irish Times* (6 September 1995). See also, F. Finlay, *Snakes and Ladders* (Dublin: New Island Books, 1998), pp. 289–94.
27 'Adams at odds with Dublin, London on doom remarks', *Irish Times* (25 September 1995).
28 'Snap summit sees all parties invited to talks about talks with firm aim of results by March', *Irish Times* (29 November 1995).
29 'New phase of political contacts on North to begin', *Irish Times* (4 December 1995).

30 The full text of the 'Mitchell Report' is available at http://www.nio.gov.uk/mitchrpt.htm, 1996.
31 IRA statement contained in 'Truce lies in tatters', *Belfast Telegraph* (10 February 1996).
32 D. McKittrick, 'What are the options for peace?' *Independent* (14 February 1996).
33 'Ulster citizens implore IRA to give peace a chance', *International Herald Tribune* (21 March 1996).
34 Author interview (23 February 1996).
35 Author interview (26 February 1996).
36 This point was made by Reg Empey, a key negotiator for the UUP, in an address to a 'Yes' campaign meeting in Enniskillen in April 1998. He said that Unionism gained its first knowledge of what was in the Anglo-Irish Agreement when a copy was passed to protesters through the gates of Hillsborough Castle.
37 Author interview with a senior member of Sinn Féin (23 July 1996).
38 Author interview with a senior member of the DUP (23 February 1996).
39 F. Millar, 'Election Bill for North makes history amid fear of unreality', *Irish Times* (24 April 1996).
40 Text published in *Irish Times* (18 March 1996).
41 'Loyalist parties bring element of class politics into the campaign' and 'UK Unionists predicting "significant" electoral gains', both from *Irish Times* (23 and 27 May 1996).
42 The DUP secured 18.8 per cent of the vote in the Forum election, against a 1992 General Election result of 13.1 per cent. A table of Northern Ireland election results from 1968 can be found on the Conflict Archive on the INternet (CAIN) website: http://cain.ulst.ac.uk/issues/politics/election/electsum.htm, 1998.
43 The 10 per cent figure comes from the 1992 general election. A full breakdown of the election results can be found in *Irish Times* (1 June 1996).
44 J. Stephenson, Chairman of the SDLP, used the term 'lend'. Cited in 'Sinn Féin describes SDLP claim of five to seven seats as arrogant', *Irish Times* (2 April 1997). D. Coughlan, 'IRA left with fewer and fewer options as pressure for ceasefire builds up', *Irish Times* (8 June 1996).
45 Quoted in 'British again emphasise the need for decommissioning', *Irish Times* (14 June 1996).
46 'IRA statement dismisses possibility of ceasefire and rules out decommissioning' and 'Dublin ultimatum to SF after bomb outrage', both from *Irish Times* (6 and 17 June 1996).
47 The parties were: UUP, DUP, SDLP, PUP, UDP, Alliance, UKUP, Women's Coalition, and Northern Ireland Labour.
48 Author interview with a senior adviser to the Bruton/Spring coalition government in the Irish Republic (31 July 1996).
49 F. Millar, *Irish Times* (2 August 1996).
50 'Mitchell plan may propel talks out of procedural deadlock' and 'NI parties adjourn to September with parties agreeing rules of procedure', *Irish Times* (24 and 30 July 1996).
51 'SDLP, UUP set to deal with impasse over arms', *Irish Times* (9 September 1996).

52 Author interview with a senior member of the UUP (26 February 1996).
53 'Search for formula to allow SF into talks intensifies' and 'Hume to step up his efforts to persuade Major on IRA ceasefire', *Irish Times* (4 and 18 November 1996).
54 'Fury lined the route as 1300 marched along Garvaghy Road', *Irish Times* (12 July 1996).
55 'Violence spreads in northern nationalist areas', *Irish Times* (13 July 1996).
56 '6000 plastic bullets fired since Drumcree stand-off', *Irish Times* (16 July 1996).
57 'Brutal murder raises question of whether loyalist paramilitary ceasefire has any chance of holding', *Irish Times* (9 July 1996).
58 'Taoiseach tells Major of anger, deep concern over march', *Irish Times* (12 July 1996).
59 Sinn Féin was actually surprised by the strength of its vote in May 1996 and did not expect to do as well in the May 1997 General Election. Author interview with a senior member of Sinn Féin (25 February 1997). The SDLP remained the largest nationalist party with 24.1 per cent of the vote, and the UUP the largest party overall with 32.7 per cent. Sinn Féin reached 16.1 per cent and the DUP 13.6 per cent. Full election results can be found in *Irish News* (3 May 1997).
60 See Martin McGuinness's comments in 'Sinn Féin calls for British to authorise talks with officials', *Irish Times* (10 May 1997).
61 According to a senior member of the SDLP, much of the preparation work had been completed in the run-up to the British general election before Labour were in power. Blair dispatched Paul Murphy (subsequently political development minister in Northern Ireland) to meet the parties and discuss decommissioning and Sinn Féin's entry into the talks. Author interview (10 October 1997).
62 'Straw agrees transfer of IRA prisoners', *Irish Times* (21 May 1997).
63 'Decommissioning is secondary to inclusive talks – Mowlam', *Irish Times* (10 May 1997).
64 'Blair insists time is right to forget past and find peace', *Irish Times* (21 May 1997).
65 'Governments stand firm on talks deadline', *Irish Times* (24 July 1997).
66 G. Martin, 'Defence of the Union needs united approach', *Irish Times* (6 August 1997).
67 'Talks process is madness, Paisley tells Mowlam', *Irish Times* (8 August 1997).
68 Martin, 'Defence of the Union'.
69 See, 'Take your seat Trimble urged', *Newsletter* (3 September 1997).
70 'UUP body backs Trimble approach to Stormont talks' and 'A win for silent majority as Trimble walks into talks', *Irish Times* (15 and 20 September 1997).
71 G. Moriarty, 'Adams, Mowlam pave way for talks', *Irish Times* (7 August 1997).
72 'Ahern, Trimble agree on usefulness of talks', *Irish Times* (21 November 1997).
73 'PUP waiting for British response on talks issue', *Irish Times* (23 December 1997).
74 'Britain must show greater urgency on NI – Adams', *Irish Times* (28 November 1997).
75 S. Breen, 'Conflicting claims on defections cause confusion for IRA', *Irish Times* (15 November 1997).

76 In the words of UUP MP William Thompson, 'The talks are going nowhere'. Cited in 'Four UUP MPs tell Trimble that party should withdraw from Stormont talks', *Irish Times* (23 December 1997).
77 'Security stepped up in North after Wright funeral for fear of backlash', *Irish Times* (31 December 1997).
78 According to one senior member of the UDP, 'We obviously knew what the probable repercussions would be as far as a political party was concerned. We were prepared to face up to that.' Author interview (28 April 1998). 'UDP walks as governments agonise and shuffle', *Irish Times* (27 January 1998).
79 Author interview (1 May 1998). A senior member of the UUP dismissively referred to the government censure of Sinn Féin as 'two weeks in the sin bin'. Author interview (18 May 1998).
80 'Sinn Féin expresses unease at NI talks proposals', *Irish Times* (15 January 1998).
81 Author interview with a senior member of the UUP (18 May 1998).
82 Author interview with a senior member of the SDLP (23 April 1998). This view was disputed by a senior member of Sinn Féin (author interview, [27 April 1998]).
83 'UUP rejects "unacceptable" draft paper', *Irish Times* (8 April 1998).
84 'Trimble says "great opportunity" to start healing process promises stability for all in North', *Irish Times* (11 April 1998).
85 'Time to draw breath, assess the agreement and decide if it answers the questions, says Adams', *Irish Times* (11 April 1998).
86 Author interview with a senior member of the UUP (18 May 1998).
87 Author interview with a senior member of Sinn Féin (27 April 1998).
88 Author interview with a senior member of Sinn Féin (27 April 1998).
89 Ibid.
90 Ibid.
91 Author interview with a senior member of the DUP (1 May 1998).
92 Author interview with a senior member of the UUP (18 May 1998).
93 UUP leader, David Trimble, cited in G. Younge, 'Whole world in their hands', *Guardian* (8 September 1998).
94 'Statement by DUP Deputy Leader, Peter Robinson MP, 19 July 1999', DUP website:
http://www.dup.org.uk/scripts/dup_s/electiondetails.ide?article ID=387, 1999.
95 Under the three-stranded approach, strand one related to relations within Northern Ireland, strand two to relations between Northern Ireland and the Republic of Ireland, and strand three to relations within the British Isles.
96 Author interview with a senior member of the SDLP (12 March 1997).
97 Referendums on the Good Friday Agreement were held in Northern Ireland *and* the Republic of Ireland.
98 'Mainstream paramilitary groups' refer to the IRA on the Republican side and those groups under the Combined Loyalist Military Command umbrella on the Loyalist side, namely, the Ulster Volunteer Force (UVF) and the Ulster Defence Association/Ulster Freedom Fighters (UDA/UFF).
99 There is some evidence to suggest that the main Republican and Loyalist paramilitaries 'policed' other splinter paramilitary groups within their communities. See, for example, 'Attack on bar may signal beginning of loyalist

feud', *Irish Times* (22 August 1997), and 'UVF will "wipe out" rival loyalists', *Irish News* (25 August 1997).

100 Author interview with a senior member of Sinn Féin (23 July 1996).

101 Author interview with a senior member of the UDP (27 February 1997). Loyalist prisoners withdrew their support for the peace process in the summer of 1996. See, 'Loyalist ceasefire strained as prisoners reject process', *Irish Times* (1 October 1996).

102 Author interview with a senior member of Sinn Féin (30 September 1997).

103 'Bombers strike at Army's heart', *Independent* (8 October 1996). See also, the IRA statement in 'IRA admits planting bombs at barracks', *Irish Times* (9 October 1996).

104 Author interview with a senior member of Sinn Féin (25 February 1997).

105 E. Maloney, 'IRA holds fire to help secret peace talks', *Sunday Tribune* (17 November 1996).

106 D. McKittrick, 'IRA bombs its way into the election', *Independent* (27 March 1997). See also 'Motorway chaos after morning bomb alerts', 'Bombs and bomb warnings that cripple UK transport condemned', 'Massive security ordered to stop IRA disrupting British election' and 'British refuse to be cowed by IRA after bomb alerts', *Irish Times* (4, 19, 26 and 30 April 1997).

107 According to a senior member of the UDP, 'There is no appetite whatsoever for loyalism to go back to conflict.' Author interview (27 February 1997).

108 See RUC Chief Constable's Annual Report for 1997, http://www.ruc.police.uk/, 1998.

109 Author interviews with a senior member of the UDP (26 February 1996) and a senior member of the UUP (26 March 1996) seemed to bear this out.

110 Clinton interview, *Irish Times* (9 December 1995).

111 Author interview with a senior adviser to the Bruton–Spring Irish government (31 July 1996).

112 President's address to White House Investment Conference, *Irish Times* (25 May 1995).

113 See J. K. Galbraith's comments on the 'conventional wisdom' in *The Affluent Society* (London: Hamish Hamilton, 1958), pp. 5–6. Certainly a peace dividend was predicted: see, for example, 'Global chains plan Ulster hotels', '10,000 jobs in peace balance' and 'Jobs on the up and up', *Newsletter* (7, 9, 12 September 1994). See also, 'Markets show first flicker of positive response' and 'Development fund stands to gain new cash', *Financial Times* (1 September 1994).

114 Figures cited in B. Hamber, 'Who Pays for Peace?', paper presented at the Catholic Institute for International Relations (30 October 1998). The South African government aimed to achieve 6 per cent growth rates per year, but growth in 1996 was below 3 per cent. 'S Africa: Mandela confident on economic strategy', *Financial Times* (8 February 1997).

115 J. Michie and M. Sheehan, 'The Political Economy of a Divided Ireland', *Cambridge Journal of Economics*, 22 (1998), pp. 243–59; 'City store tills ring to the ceasefire', *Newsletter* (21 September 1994).

116 See *Irish Times* supplement for the White House Investment Conference (24 May 1995).

117 Author interview with senior economist (30 March 1999).

118 Growth rates in the 1990–6 period averaged at 2.4 per cent p.a. in Northern Ireland, compared with the United Kingdom average of 1.5 per cent. From 'Economic Uncertainties', *Business and Finance*, 34, 31 (11 June 1998), p. 20.

119 'Economic Uncertainties'.

120 The elections were: Forum for Political Dialogue (May 1996), British General Election (May 1997), Northern Ireland Local Government elections (May 1997), Referendum on Good Friday Agreement (May 1998) and Northern Ireland Assembly (June 1998).

121 For example, a pop concert was held in the Stormont grounds in May 1998.

122 See T. Hadden and K. Boyle, *The Anglo Irish Agreement: Commentary, Text and Official Review* (London: Sweet & Maxwell, 1989), p. 70; J. Ruane and K. Todd, *The Dynamics of Conflict in Northern Ireland: Power, Conflict and Emancipation* (Cambridge: Cambridge University Press, 1996), pp. 187–8; J. Morison and S. Livingstone, *Reshaping Public Power: Northern Ireland and the British Constitutional Crisis* (London: Sweet & Maxwell, 1995), pp. 137–43, 156–68; and R. J. Cormack and R. D. Osborne, 'The Evolution of the Catholic Middle Class', in A. Guelke (ed.) *New Perspectives on the Northern Ireland Conflict* (Aldershot: Avebury, 1994), pp. 65–85 (70).

123 The joint appearance of SDLP John Hume and UUP leader David Trimble on stage with pop group U2 as part of the 'Yes' referendum campaign ('Leaders unite in peace poll push', *Newsletter* [20 May 1998]) or their collection of the Nobel Peace Prize may be the closest to a defining symbolic image.

124 For general accounts for the role of symbolism in politics and conflict, see, R. Firth, *Symbols Public and Private* (London: Allen & Unwin, 1973), or S. Harrison, 'Four Types of Symbolic Conflict', *Journal of the Royal Anthropological Institution*, 1, 2 (1995), pp. 255–72. For the case of Northern Ireland, see J. A. Sluka, 'The Writing's on the Wall: Peace Process Images, Symbols and Murals in Northern Ireland', *Critique of Anthropology*, 16, 4 (1996), pp. 381–94, or B. Rolston, 'Culture as a Battlefield: Political identity and the State in the North of Ireland', *Race and Class*, 39, 4 (1998), pp. 23–35.

125 The term 'symbolic inventory' is quoted by Harrison, 'Four Types of Symbolic Conflict', p. 255, from I. Kopytoff, 'The Cultural Biography of Things: Commoditization in Process', in A. Appadurai (ed.) *The Social Life of Things: Commodities in Cultural Perspective* (Cambridge: Cambridge University Press, 1986), pp. 64–91.

126 This point was made in an author interview with a member of the British Labour Party front bench on Northern Ireland (3 April 1996). See also, 'RUC recruits no longer to swear oath to the Queen', *Irish Times* (2 December 1997).

127 *Irish Times* (4 July 1996).

128 Author interview with leader of a residents' group (2 June 1997).

129 Author interview with leading media commentator (21 October 1997).

130 See photographs accompanying 'RUC may seal roads before Drumcree march', *Irish Times* (23 June 1997), 'Ulster stares into abyss', *Guardian* (5 July 1997), and 'Street theatre with a cutting edge', *Irish Times* (18 July 1997). See also the photograph of Orange protesters holding placards

reading 'Stop Talking, Start Walking' and 'Ulster's Protestants Demand Civil Rights' accompanying 'Orangemen reject brokered compromise on Dunloy marches', *Irish Times* (10 April 1998).

131 See table marked 'Attacks on Orange Halls, Churches, Chapels, GAA Premises and Schools, 1994–2 July 1998', on the RUC website: http://www.ruc.police.uk/index.htm, 1998.

132 On a single night in 1998, ten Catholic churches were damaged or destroyed by fire. It followed the British Government decision forbidding an Orange Order parade along a mainly Nationalist road and the appointment of David Trimble and Seamus Mallon as the First Minister and Deputy First Minister of the Northern Ireland Assembly. 'Blair rushes to Ulster after 10 church fires', *International Herald Tribune* (3 July 1998).

133 'New face of northern cash', *Irish News* (27 March 1998).

134 See Harrison, 'Four Types of Symbolic Conflict', pp. 258–9.

135 See, for example, M. Holland, 'Why Blair deserves bouquets for famine apology' (5 June 1997), and 'Republicans and FF criticised by Quinn as house remembers 1798' (4 July 1998), both *Irish Times*.

136 Morison and Livingstone, *Reshaping Public Power*, pp. 142–3.

137 'Major and Bruton slip away to sample the life of Reilly's', *Irish Times* (22 December 1995).

138 Author interview with a senior member of the Ulster Democratic Party (28 April 1998).

139 Quoted in 'Trimble invites Sinn Fein leader to meeting', *Irish Times* (2 September 1998).

140 'Adams rejects calls to say "war is over"', *Irish News* (10 August 1998).

3
A Path Strewn with Thorns: Along the Difficult Road of Israeli–Palestinian Peacemaking

Tamar Hermann and David Newman

Introduction

Five years down the road from the signing of the first Oslo Declaration of Principles (September 1993), the Israeli–Palestinian peace process had considerably slowed down, even if it was still alive, as the optimists maintained.[1] The immediate post-Oslo Accords euphoria of autumn 1993 had long since dissipated in the wake of the near breakdown of the negotiations, confirming that much more than the signing of formal documents was needed for a state of war to be transformed into a state of peace.

The setback in the peace process was seen by each side as being the fault of the other. The Palestinians attributed the setback to the rise to power of the Netanyahu Government in Israel in May 1996, the continued expansion of West Bank settlements and the provocative actions undertaken by many of the settlers themselves. Israel argued that the refusal of some Palestinian organisations to abandon terror as a means of managing the Israeli–Palestinian conflict, together with the reluctance of the Palestinian Authority to undertake the necessary measures to prevent further terrorist attacks, was responsible for the cessation of the peace talks.

While these reasons reflect the daily realities of the perceptual environment in which the peace process was managed, it is maintained in this essay that in order to understand why the process had taken such a backward turn it is necessary to deal with the deeper roots of the conflict in general, in particular the way in which each side perceived the intentions and deeply rooted beliefs of the other side. This, we will argue, is even more important when dealing with the perceptions of the public at large, as contrasted with those of the political elites and negotiators who were responsible for the management of the peace talks and whose understanding of the other side did not necessarily correspond with the views prevalent at the grass-roots level.

We maintain that, for a legal peace treaty to be translated into a reality of mutual accommodation, the nation's leaders and political elites who are responsible for promoting such a political reorientation[2] must ensure that it attains 'cognitive legitimacy' at the grass-roots level.[3] As peacemaking is a 'course', or 'basic' sort of decision which, unlike 'crisis' decisions, is implemented over a lengthy period of time, attaining broad cognitive legitimacy plays a crucial role in the progress of the peace process. This is not only because it reflects what society feels but it also feeds back and influences the next rounds of formal decision-making.[4] However, when a general reorientation in favour of peace negotiations follows years of extensive mobilisation of the citizens in accepting continuous and intense conflict as constituting the normative condition, the mustering of public support for a peace process is particularly difficult. If the implementation of the peace process is to be sustained and is to attain widespread support, alternative mobilisation of the public in favour of the new political realities has to be undertaken during the early stages of the process, particularly if it is to retain support when obstacles, such as the continuation of violence, the expansion of settlements, and other sorts of offensive behaviour by anti-peace forces, continue to take place. This would also assume that there is a real culture of change which takes place, as populations are prepared to think in terms of peace rather than conflict, and are prepared to see the 'Other' as potential partners rather than as enemies.

Our second argument is that the Arab–Israeli conflict is replete with political symbolism, not least because of the very deep emotional attachments displayed by both sides to the notions of land, statehood, security and survival. It is the symbolic and historic elements of the conflict, rather than the practical features of conflict resolution, which are zero-sum, as each side focuses on its own exclusive interpretation of the conflict. The roots of the failure of Israeli and Palestinian leaders to make a breakthrough in the peace negotiations must be understood against the background of the symbolic dimensions of the decisions and developments comprising the peace process, as well as the reactions to these decisions at the grass-roots level.

Third, we will argue that certain political leaders and negotiators on both sides are ready to reach quick solutions concerning the tangible elements of the conflict, be it due to their sincere conviction that reality justifies such a move, or (perhaps cynically) motivated by their expectation of cashing in on such an external achievement at home in the next elections. However, this disposition of the elite is often incompatible with that of the general public hindered by deep-rooted fears and long-held definitions of the situation as zero-sum. Both sides still see themselves as the victims of the injustices inflicted by the 'Other' – either as victims of terror (Israelis) or as victims of uprooting (Palestinians). This self-image results in a strong belief in the majority on both sides that genuine resolution of the conflict, as contrasted with its technical regulation, is very difficult to be achieved, if at all possible. Therefore, a much longer time scale is required for the general public to join the peace process bandwagon, endorsing the course of reconciliation with the former enemy. This gap between the politicians' time span for such strategic transformations and that of the ordinary citizens results in the former being unable to mobilise the necessary support for the peace process to strike roots. Technical solutions to conflict resolution are simply not sufficient if they are unable to be translated into genuine resolution of the conflict which includes the changing of attitudes as part of a long-term culture of change.

This chapter attempts, therefore, to elucidate the centrality of the following dimensions of conflict resolution: cognitive legitimacy, political symbolism and discrepancies between the adaptability of leaders and public opinion. We suggest that they reflect fundamental feelings and attitudes that lie at the very heart of the way in which the relations between the two sides are perceived at the grass-roots level. When cognitive legitimacy is not attained, the situation is depleted as contrasting perceptions of the symbolic elements result in the development of a large gap in the way that the new situation is understood by the political elites and the general public respectively. In such cases, one could expect reserved, sometimes even negative, reactions from the general public to the objective events and developments that constitute the peace process. In the Israeli–Palestinian case, such attitudes have proved to be major stumbling blocs in the way of conflict resolution.[5]

We would assume that many of these attitudes and reactions were reflected in public opinion surveys which covered a wide range of issues relating to the conflict resolution. These surveys mirrored the gut feelings of the public and the reasons why Israelis and Palestinians were, or were not, prepared to support the continuation of the peace process.

The political processs

The commencement of the Israel–Arab peace negotiations in Madrid (1991) marked the beginning of a fundamental political reorientation for both sides. As such, it involved redefining the overall situation, the major actors and the acceptable rules of conduct within this specific context.[6] Madrid involved fundamental cognitive and practical changes concerning basic issues, such as the ability to reach a mutually accepted political solution to what had traditionally been perceived as an essentially military, zero-sum, Middle-Eastern conflict.

The most significant structural change in the nature of Israeli–Palestinian negotiations came about as a result of the signing of the Oslo Accords, two years after the Madrid conference at which the Palestinians had still not had any independent standing.[7] In Oslo, for the first time in the history of the Israeli–Palestinian conflict, direct negotiations between the leaders of both sides were conducted face-to-face and on eye-to-eye level, regardless of the fact that one party represented a sovereign state while the other was no more than a stateless liberation movement. This change was all the more remarkable given the fact that for over forty years each side had continually refused to recognise the other as constituting a legitimate independent political entity. Thus, the most important change manifested by the Oslo negotiations was the replacement of a politics of mutual denial with a politics of mutual legitimation. The implementation of the various agreements reached in the framework of the Oslo process was therefore important not only in terms of the limited Israeli withdrawal from parts of the occupied territories and their transfer to the Palestinian Authority but also – and perhaps even more importantly – in terms of the creating of a new, more favourable geopolitical context in which the ensuing peace dialogue and negotiation took place.

Notwithstanding, the Israeli–Palestinian peace process has been deadlocked since 1996, not because one or another leader has come to power, but because the two sides have failed to transcend their particularistic interests and one-sided cognitions and to develop a basic sense of a mutual interest in the resolution of the conflict. While much of the conflict resolution politics has been devoted to tedious negotiations over practical and technical issues, it has not addressed the cognitive aspects of the process. Not only have many of the deeper-rooted fears and reservations of the two peoples been neglected by the pro-peace leaders, they have equally been manipulated for their own purposes by the anti-peace elites. Each side to the conflict has continued to see the 'Other' as being the sole recipient of all the benefits, while not offering anything in return. The lack of concern for adequate confidence-building measures was unhelpful in that it did nothing to rectify this perceptual discord. Furthermore, due to the asymmetrical power relations between the conflict protagonists, such impediments cannot be compensated for even by excessive war fatigue and an apparently genuine desire for peace of the majority of both Israelis and Palestinians.

This argument will be examined in the following four thematic sections of this paper: (a) agreements; (b) security/violence; (c) territory discourse; and (d) external actors. Each section will include a brief factual description of the developments in that particular sphere during the five years since the Oslo Accords, followed by an analysis of the symbolic dimensions of these political changes and the way in which these are expressed in public opinion surveys.

Agreements

The resolution process of the Israeli–Palestinian conflict has been accompanied by the signing of several agreements. In this section, we discuss briefly the main points of three major agreements/documents: the Madrid Framework (1991), the Oslo A, Israeli-Palestinian Declaration of Principles (1993), and the Oslo B Interim Agreement (1995), as well as a number of supplementary agreements which have been completed since the launch of the peace process. It should be noted that these agreements were not uniform in structure or content. Some of them, such as the declaration which concluded the Madrid conference were no more than a general statement of intent, while others such as the Oslo A and B agreements provided a more concrete framework for the implementation of the first and interim stages of the peace process. Others still, such as the Gaza and Jericho First (Cairo) Agreement and the revised Hebron Protocol were replete with practical details concerning the implementation of the agreement on the ground. Furthermore, some marked a dramatic change of relations, for example, Oslo A, while others were mainly of incremental significance, for example, the Paris Protocol on Economic Relations. Naturally, their respective symbolic significance and public reactions to them were different.

The Madrid Framework

The Madrid international conference was designed to serve as an opening forum for future regional peace dialogue, having no power to impose solutions or veto agreements. Yet, the protagonists to the

Middle-Eastern conflict, Israel and the Arab States, were both disinclined, although for different reasons, to take part in it and were urged to do so by the insistent Bush Administration (see external actors section below). The Palestinian delegation was not yet formally recognised as a legitimate, independent negotiating partner by Israel and was forced to take its place at the conference table as part of the Jordanian delegation.

The Madrid conference resulted in the commencement of two separate yet parallel negotiating tracks – the bilateral and the multilateral tracks. The bilateral negotiations were meant to resolve the conflicts of the past. Direct talks between Israel and its immediate Arab neighbours opened in Madrid on 3 November 1991, immediately following the international conference. Over a dozen formal rounds of bilateral talks were subsequently hosted by the US Department of State in Washington, DC, based on a two-stage formula: 5-year interim self-government arrangements, to be followed by negotiations on the permanent status issues. The multilateral negotiations, in conrast, were intended to help construct the Middle East of the future, while building confidence among the regional parties. These talks, which opened in Moscow in January 1992, included five separate working groups attended by delegations from countries in the region as well as representatives of the international community. The negotiations focused on key issues that concern the entire Middle East – water, environment, arms control, refugees and economic development.[8]

The Oslo A Agreement (Declaration of Principles)

The Oslo A Agreement was the major groundbreaking agreement of the Israel–Palestine conflict. The Agreement was drawn up in a round of secret talks between Israeli and Palestinian diplomats and academics in Norway during 1993, with the assistance of Norwegian politicians. On the basis of these talks on 9 September 1993, PLO Chairman Yasser Arafat sent a letter to Israeli Prime Minister Rabin, in which he stated that the PLO:

- recognised the right of Israel to exist in peace and security;
- accepted UN Security Council Resolutions 242 and 338;
- committed itself to a peaceful resolution of the conflict;
- renounced the use of terrorism and other acts of violence;
- assumed responsibility over all PLO elements to ensure their compliance, prevent violations and discipline violators;
- affirmed that those articles of the PLO Covenant which deny Israel's right to exist were now inoperative and no longer valid; and

- undertook to submit to the Palestinian National Council for formal approval of the necessary changes to the Covenant.

In reply, Israel recognised the PLO as the legitimate representative of the Palestinians in the peace negotiations and the Palestinians' right to national self-determination.

On 13 September 1993, a joint Israeli–Palestinian Declaration of Principles (DOP), based on the agreement worked out in Oslo, was signed by the two leaders – Arafat for the Palestinian people and Rabin for the State of Israel – on the lawn of the White House in Washington, DC. The DOP outlined the proposed interim self-government arrangements, as envisioned and agreed by both sides. The arrangements contained in the DOP included immediate transfer of the Gaza Strip (excepting the Israeli settlements) and the town of Jericho on the West Bank from Israeli control to Palestinian self-rule, early empowerment for the Palestinians in West Bank, and an agreement on self-government and the election of a Palestinian council shortly afterwards. Additionally, extensive economic co-operation between Israel and the Palestinians played an important role in the DOP.

Shortly after the signing of the Declaration of Principles, negotiations commenced between Israeli and PLO delegations on the implementation of the DOP and resulted in three further agreements dealing with the practical aspects of the implementation process:

1 The Paris Protocol on Economic Relations was signed on 29 April 1994. This protocol defined the future economic relationship between Israel and the Palestinian Authority. They reached agreements on import policy, monetary policy, taxation, labour, agriculture, manufacturing and tourism, fuel and insurance.
2 The Gaza–Jericho First Agreement was signed in Cairo on 4 May 1994, and applied to the Gaza Strip and to a defined area of about 65 square kilometres, including Jericho and its environs (Figure 3.1). The document included agreement to a withdrawal of Israeli military forces from these two areas, a transfer of authority from the Israeli Civil (practically military) Administration to Palestinian self-rule, the structure and composition of the Palestinian Authority, its jurisdiction and legislative powers, a Palestinian police force, and relations between Israel and the Palestinian Authority.
3 On 29 August 1994, the Agreement on Preparatory Transfer of Powers and Responsibilities was signed by Israel and the Palestinians. In accordance with the DOP, this agreement provided for the

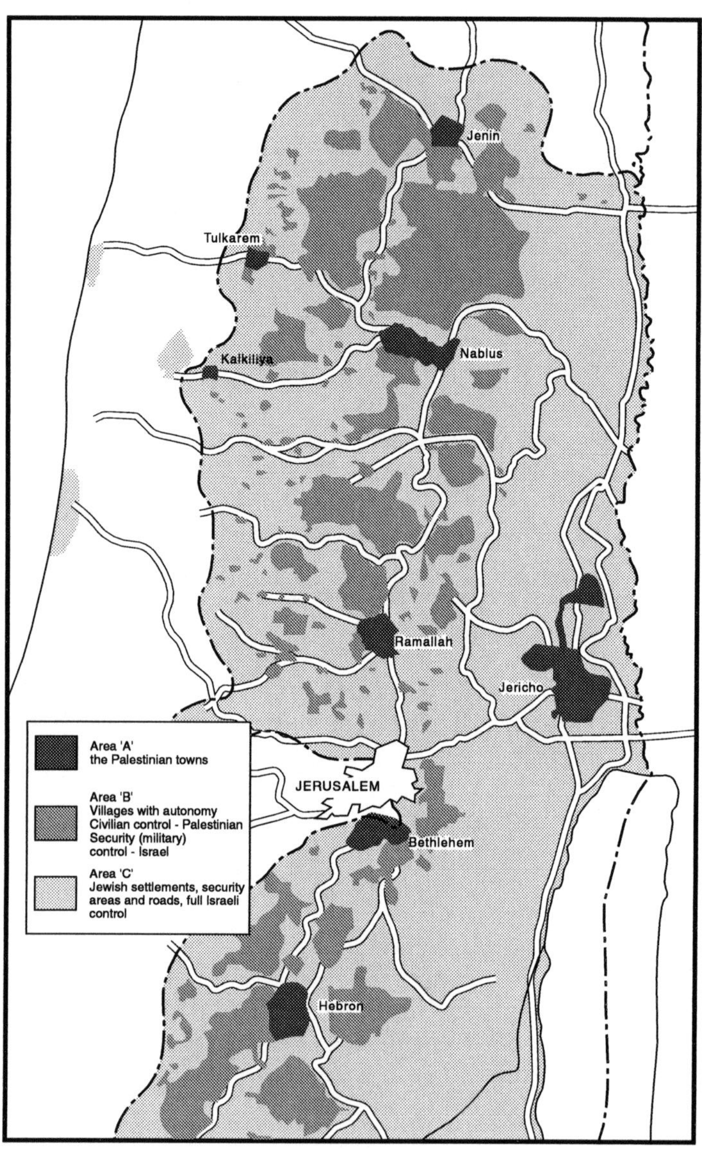

Figure 3.1 The Gaza–Jericho First Agreement
Source: D. Newman, 'Creating the Fences of Separation: the Territorial Discourse of Israeli-Palestinian Conflict Resolution', *Geopolitics and International Boundaries*, 3,1 (1998), p. 6.

transfer of powers to the Palestinian Authority in five specified spheres: education and culture, social welfare, tourism, health, and taxation. On 27 August 1995, a further protocol was signed transferring additional spheres to the Palestinian Authority: labour, trade and industry, gas and gasoline, insurance, postal services, statistics, agriculture, and local government.

The Oslo B Interim Agreement

On 28 September 1995, the Israeli-Palestinian Interim Agreement on the West Bank and the Gaza Strip was signed, again in Washington, DC. While still perceived by both sides as being no more than a transitional agreement on the path to full autonomy and/or statehood, this was more far reaching than the Oslo I Agreement, both in terms of the nature of autonomy and the amount of territory to be included.

The main object of the Interim Agreement was to broaden Palestinian self-government in the West Bank by means of an elected self-governing authority – the Palestinian Council – for an interim period not to exceed five years from the signing of the Gaza–Jericho Agreement (that is, no later than May 1999). This was intended to enable the Palestinians to conduct their own internal affairs, reduce points of friction between them and the Israelis, and open a new era of co-operation and coexistence. At the same time it was designed to protect Israel's vital interests, and in particular its security interests, both with regard to external security as well as the personal security of its citizens in the West Bank. The Oslo B Agreement divided the West Bank into three areas: Areas 'A', 'B' and 'C'. Areas 'A', including all of the major Palestinian towns, with the exception of East Jerusalem and parts of Hebron, were to be transferred to full Palestinian autonomy. Areas 'B' included most of the Palestinian villages, in which partial autonomy, including all matters relating to civil society, would be transferred to the Palestinians, but Israel would retain certain defence and security functions. The remainder of the West Bank, including all of the Israeli settlements and their inhabitants, were designated as Areas 'C', to remain under full Israeli control/occupation.

In effect, the implementation of the Oslo B Agreement resulted in the transfer of over 90 per cent of the Palestinian population to Palestinian autonomy, but on an area covering less than 30 per cent of the West Bank. The Agreement was implemented in a series of rapid Israeli military withdrawals from the Palestinian towns. However, the town of Hebron had not been evacuated by the time of the 1996 elections, in which the Labour Party failed to get re-elected. Rather than immediately implement the final parts of the Oslo B Agreement, the new Netanyahu administration insisted on renegotiating the Hebron redeployment. The revised Hebron Protocol signed and implemented early in 1997 was only marginally different to that which had been drawn up in the original Oslo B Agreement. Yet, while the new Israeli government insisted on better security arrangements for the Israeli settlers in Hebron, the Palestinians demanded that Israel commit itself to a clear timetable for the holding of permanent solution talks and also raised the issue of the Dehaniyah air field in the Gaza Strip. Beyond these and some other more technical details, this agreement was of major significance as it was seen as a test of the intentions of the Netanyahu administration regarding the continuation of the peace talks with the Palestinians. In retrospect, this was an erroneous judgement, as Netanyahu was honour bound to implement the Agreement which had been signed by the previous Israeli government, but was not equally obliged to undertake the next round of negotiations beyond what had already been signed and sealed.

The Wye Agreement

In October 1998, ten days of intensive, direct negotiations between Israeli and Palestinian leaders were held, under American supervision, at the Wye Plantation. This resulted in the signing of a further agreement. The 'Wye River Memorandum' ploughs and re-ploughs familiar ground. Israeli demands for Palestinian action on security issues were embodied in a specific timetable of actions that was supposed to imprison wanted terrorists in Palestinian Authority (PA) jails, reduce the rolls of PA police from 40 000 to the Oslo-authorised 30 000, act against the Hamas 'infrastructure', collect unauthorised weapons, and take other measures specified in a secret US-brokered security plan. The Israelis would also at last have the public spectacle of a mass Palestinian gathering to renounce the Palestinian Charter's anti-Israel provisions, presided over by President Clinton.

In return, the Israelis agreed to re-deploy from 13 per cent of their exclusively controlled territory. Three per cent was to become a 'nature preserve' on which no new building was allowed, thereby preventing Palestinian obstruction of Israeli security requirements. All in all, the Palestinians would have control or mixed control over 40 per cent of the West Bank. Israel would relocate several military bases and construct access routes to newly isolated settlements. Finally, the Palestinians obtained long-sought rights to operate an airport and safe passage between Gaza and the West Bank. Both sides also expected fresh financial assistance, said to be at the $500 million level. Economic co-operation committees were also to be revived. Wye broke fresh ground primarily through the mechanism for carrying out the reciprocal obligations. A five-stage timeline attached to the Memorandum indicated that Israeli re-deployments over 12 weeks were to occur only as the Palestinians fulfilled their security pledges, as certified by various US-chaired committees. Both sides would also commence 'accelerated' final-status negotiations.

The signing of the agreement in yet another public ceremony in the White House did little to dissipate the atmosphere of mutual mistrust between the two sides and the feeling that this agreement had been imposed by strong-arm tactics on the part of the United States. Netanyahu insisted on emphasising the 'reciprocity' factor, continually stating that further territorial withdrawal would only take place if terror was combated and if the Palestinian Charter was annulled. Immediately following the signing of the agreement and the return of both leaders to their own countries, it was clear that both sides interpreted the implementation of the Wye Agreement differently, and that it was unclear whether or not it would actually be implemented on schedule.

Permanent status negotiations

The Israeli–Palestinian negotiations on the permanent status arrangements commenced in Taba, on the Israel–Egypt boundary on the Red Sea on 5 May 1996. These negotiations were meant to deal with the remaining issues to be resolved, including Jerusalem, refugees, settlements, security arrangements, borders, relations and co-operation with neighbouring countries. Notwithstanding these negotiations, the changed political climate in 1995–6 resulted in a breakdown of the Israeli–Palestinian dialogue. The move towards the resolution of all outstanding issues did not progress, while the Israeli government offered to withdraw from only a relatively small part of the West Bank, and even this only if a long list of contraventions by the other side were rectified. The Palestinians saw the permanent status negotiations as eventually resulting in a Palestinian state on all, or most, of the West Bank territory and, as such, were not prepared to accept the minimal offers of the Israeli government.

While the various agreements presented above were full of legal and technical details, both Israelis and Palestinians attributed extreme importance to their symbolic aspects. Paradoxically, despite the differences in both sides' symbolic understanding of the agreements, there was a great deal of symmetry in the way that each side minimised the significance of the concessions made by the other. Each also perceived its own concessions as constituting far-reaching manifestations of good will, not sufficiently appreciated by the other. Thus, the PLO recognition of the State of Israel, after the Palestinians had denied its legitimate existence since 1948 was not seen by most Israelis as being a major ideological concession. Instead, it was ascribed to the fact that the Palestinians were left with no other option but to admit the reality of Israel's existence and the fact that Israel constituted a military and regional power. Similarly, Israel's decision to transfer some parts of the West Bank to the Palestinians was not considered by the latter as a major compromise, not least because Israel continued to control the majority of the area directly and also because, from a Palestinian perspective, this was occupied territory which Israel had no right to control in the first place.

There was also much symbolism concerning the highly contested topics which were not discussed and which, by the request of one side or the other, were left out of the negotiating agenda in the early stages of the peace process. The emotion-laden issues were to be discussed at a later, undefined, stage of the peace process. These included such issues as East Jerusalem, Palestinian refugees, Israeli settlements and the establishment of a Palestinian state.

Yet, despite the leaders' unwillingness to touch upon them, some of these issues have gained saliency in the public discourse as a result of actions on the ground. For example, the declarations made by the Netanyahu administration regarding its intention to expand settlements and to construct new neighbourhoods in East Jerusalem led to the issue of Jerusalem being pushed forward to the centre of the domestic and international debate, resulting not only in condemnation of Israel but also in certain cases to a cessation of the activity due to internal and external pressures.

The cognitive dimensions of the way in which the public perceived the agreements were reflected in the findings of public surveys amongst both Israelis and Palestinians. Contrary to the theories which characterise public opinion as either indifferent or 'moody', Israeli and Palestinian public opinion regarding the Oslo process appeared to be fairly stable both in structure and in content. Neither the ups and downs in the negotiations between 1993 and 1995, nor the prolonged standstill since mid-1996 seemed to have dramatically changed these basic traits. The graph below presents the calculated scores of support for and belief in the Oslo process amongst Israeli Jews from June 1994 to January 1998.[9]

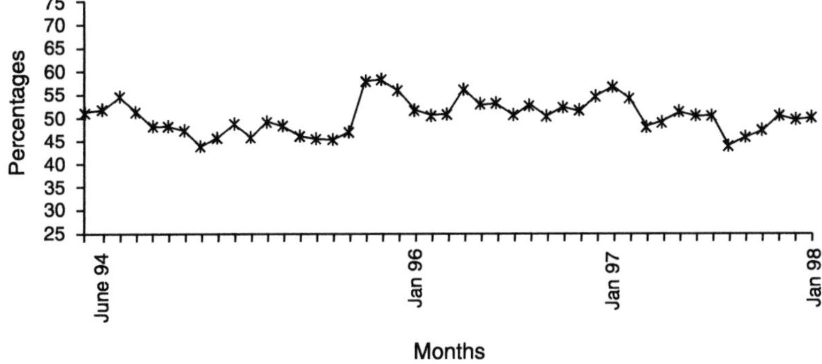

Figure 3.2 Calculated scores of support and belief in the Oslo process 1994–8

Figure 3.2 indicates that from June 1994 to January 1998, the Israeli Jewish public was almost equally split between those who supported and those who opposed the Oslo process. The support for Oslo hit the lowest point in April 1995, after a series of fatal Palestinian attacks on Israelis within the Green Line (pre-1967) borders, and peaked later on, in November of the same year, immediately after Prime Minister Rabin was assassinated by a right-wing Jewish extremist who was opposed to the continuation of the Oslo peace process. However, this peak was apparently part of a transitory shock effect, and did not indicate a genuine accumulation of support and hope in the process *per se*, as suggested by the fairly rapid decrease of the public support for the process in the ensuing months almost back to its pre-assassination level.

The surveys also show that the belief of Israeli Jews in the Oslo process has been continually lower and more oscillating than the support for it. In other words, those who supported the agreements with the Palestinians often did not believe that the agreements would bring about a real change in relations between Israel and the Palestinians.

Furthermore, the data on Israeli Jewish public opinion supports the argument that the acceleration of peace talks at the decision-makers' level in 1995–6, the last phase of the Labour government term, was not translated into a parallel increase in the public's support for the process.[10] By and large the public was either slow in supporting the new policy of the Labour leaders or were reluctant to do so altogether. Apparently, the spirit of *rapprochement* which developed at the elite's level did not diffuse deep down into the grass roots. When asked whether, from Israel's point of view, the Oslo process entailed more prospects or more dangers, 46.0 per cent of the respondents considered

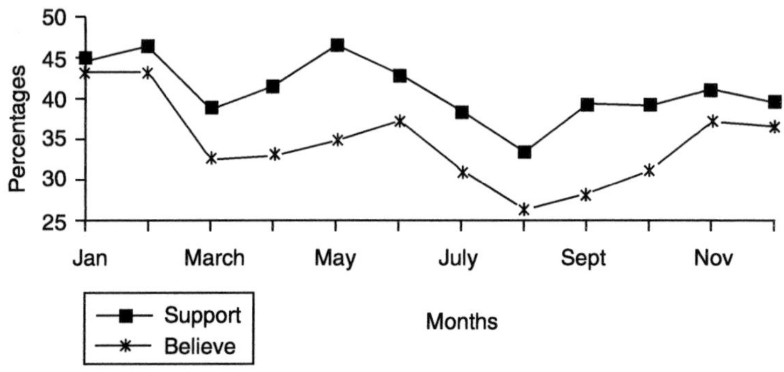

Figure 3.3 Support vs belief in the Oslo process, 1997

it more dangerous and only 22.5 per cent as having more prospects (the remainder had no clear opinion).[11] Interestingly, following the 1996 elections, that is after Netanyahu took over and slowed down the negotiations, the Oslo process looked less dangerous to many Israelis than when Rabin was in power: in August 1996 only 27.0 per cent saw it as more dangerous while about 38.0 per cent attributed more prospects to it.

However, there were some positive developments in Israeli public opinion, which were clearly related to the spirit of the agreements signed. For example, all surveys indicated greater readiness to accept the idea of a Palestinian state.[12] In 1998, more than half of Israeli Jews said that they could live with this compared to less than a third just ten years before. Increasing numbers of Israelis recognised the Palestinians' right for an independent state and above 70 per cent believed that this would be achieved in the foreseeable future. Another development was the slight improvement in the Palestinians' image in the eyes of many Israeli Jews. For example, while in mid-1995 only 5 per cent of the respondents said that the Palestinians fulfilled their obligations according to the Oslo DOP, this figure rose to 27 per cent by summer 1996.[13]

Arab citizens of Israel have continually displayed higher support for the Oslo process than their Jewish counterparts.[14] (See Table 3.1.) Arab-Palestinian citizens of Israel did not share Israeli Jews' security concerns or the latters' religious attachment to the vision of a Greater Israel. For them, the Oslo process entailed neither significant risks nor real costs. The Oslo process was perceived by the Israeli–Arab sector as a window of opportunity for a fundamental positive change in both the

Table 3.1 Support for the Oslo process among Israeli Arabs and Israeli Jews, 1995–7

	Israeli Arabs			*Israeli Jews*		
	Support	*Oppose*	*So-so/Don't know*	*Support*	*Oppose*	*So-so/Don't know*
March 1995	67.6	9.6	22.8	33.1	37.5	29.4
August 1996	63.0	13.5	23.5	51.8	17.4	30.8
November 1997*	79.5	17.5	3.0	56.3	34.7	9.0

*In this survey the So-so option was not offered to the respondents. Thus the comparison of the three different in time measurements is somewhat problematic. However, the Jewish–Arab comparison within the 1997 measurement, the one relevant for the discussion here, is methodologically solid.
Source: Peace Index public opinion surveys (March 1995; August 1996; November 1997).

external and domestic systems. They believed that a stable and genuine peace with the Arab world in general, and the Palestinians in particular, would enable them to move towards greater equality as Israeli citizens and, at the same time, openly display their national identity.[15]

Surveys indicated strong, even if declining, support for the Oslo Agreements among the Palestinian residents of the Occupied Territories. The Center for Palestine Studies and Research (CPSR) in Nablus reported that in January 1995 about half of the respondents expressed support for the Oslo negotiations and Agreements. This support increased to 65 per cent in March and May 1995, to 71 per cent in September 1995 and peaked (78 per cent) in March 1996. Following the change of government in Israel in 1996 and the subsequent policy changes, the Palestinians' support for the process slightly decreased to 70 per cent by the Fall of 1996.[16] A poll conducted by another Palestinian research institute, The Jerusalem Media and Communication Center (JMCC)[17] in late November 1997 indicated that 60 per cent of the Palestinians supported the Oslo process. This relatively high Palestinian support for the Oslo Agreements, somewhat surprising in the light of their minimal political achievements, can be explained by their recognition that, imperfect as they were, the Oslo Agreements were the best which could be attained under the circumstances and that the only feasible alternative to them was the continuation of Israeli military occupation.

Security and violence

Notwithstanding their different interpretations by, and implications for, Israel and the Palestinians the various agreements signed in the framework of the Oslo process still function as a shared point of reference. The issues of security and violence, in contrast, are addressed by Israelis and Palestinians from entirely different, in fact opposite, objective and subjective perspectives, thus serving as a dividing rather than coalescing factor. Israeli and Palestinian antithetical perceptions of security and violence reflect first and foremost the unbalanced power relations between them – the powerful occupier versus the much weaker occupied. This can be contrasted with the geopolitical realities of the Middle East, with Israel as a small and isolated Jewish state in the region, surrounded by a number of much larger and antagonistic Arab nations, despite the fact that Israel maintains superior conventional and non-conventional military capabilities. This did not prevent, however, the infliction of fatalities on Israeli citizens during the period of the Intifada during the late 1980s and early 1990s, the weapons mainly being stones and knives rather than the conventional armed forces of a foreign country. Neither did the military capability provide an effective defence against the suicide bombings in the post-Oslo period, further eroding Israelis' sense of personal and thus national security. In other words, the military superiority displayed by Israel at the level of the state does not necessarily translate into greater security at the personal level.

Israeli security discourse

The issue of security underlies much of Israeli strategic thinking and dominates the internal debate concerning the acceptable nature – territorial configuration, military status, etc. – of the Palestinian entity/state to be established. The Israeli security debate has two distinct, although inseparable, dimensions: (a) national security relating to Israel's relative position in the regional and global power structures; (b) domestic security, relating mainly to Arab violence against Israeli civilians and its effects.

National security. National security is perhaps the issue in which the gaps between outsiders' and insiders' perceptions regarding Israel's position are the widest. While outsiders tend to see Israel as a regional middle-power of highly skilled and well-equipped military with conventional and non-conventional capabilities, the Israeli security outlook is based on the deep conviction that it operates under a permanent existential threat and that this threat is not going to disappear in the foreseeable future, even if and when peace agreements with all Arab neighbours are signed. This perceptual gap is critical in order to understand Israel's positions and moves in the context of the peace process.

The core notion of Israeli thinking on national security issues is the asymmetry with the Arab world, in terms of both population and territory. This is often displayed visually by the Foreign Ministry by showing maps of a small Israel superimposed upon a single state or province of the United States or Canada respectively, or a map of Israel and the Middle East in which a small Israel is located alongside 15 Arab neighbouring countries, each of which (besides Lebanon) is larger than Israel. No wonder then that the constitution of a Palestinian state, even if demilitarised, is perceived by many in Israel as an additional and threatening security liability.

Although all surveys indicate that a growing number of Israelis display a greater readiness to agree with the establishment of an independent (but demilitarised) Palestinian state it appears that this greater readiness is explained more by the respondents' assessment that this is already a *fait accompli*, rather than by their conviction that such a state will not pose a threat to Israeli national security interests. In fact, many Israelis see an independent Palestinian state as being no more than a springboard from which to attack Israel in an attempt to destroy the country. They therefore view such a state as resulting in the worsening, rather than improvement, of the general security situation.

Within this cognitive context, any step taken by Israel's neighbours is almost reflexively seen as offensive and not open to any other explanation, whereas each measure adopted by Israel is self-perceived as purely defensive.[18] Furthermore, the protracted violent strife between Israel and the Arab world is commonly perceived as the sole responsibility of the latter. This is also reflected in the name of the Israeli army, the IDF – Israel Defense Forces – defining it as a protecting, rather than an offensive, force. Wars, such as the Six Day War, in which Israel struck the first blow are seen as 'wars of no choice', in which the first strike served a basic preventive purpose. The notion of an aggressive, expansionist, Israel is rejected almost unanimously by Israeli policymakers as well as by the public.[19]

Developments on the regional level seem in the eyes of many in Israel to sustain the strategic imperatives derived from this basic security perception. Two conflicting forces struggle in the Middle East of the 1990s – moderation and accommodation on the one side and extremism and fundamentalism on the other. Observers from the outside may attribute similar weight to both forces, particularly those who question the extent to which Israel's existence is still under objective external threat, after the territorial advantages achieved by the military victory of the Six Day War in 1967 and the exclusion of major military threats by the signing of the Israel–Egypt peace accords at the end of the 1970s and the peace agreement with Jordan in 1994. Israeli strategic thinking, however, places greater emphasis on the second development, which is seen as constituting a new collective threat to Israel's existence, the only non-Islamic state in the region. This factor is evidently of major importance when decisions regarding territorial compromises are made.

Rooted in the common perception of Israeli geopolitical and demographic inferiority *vis-à-vis* the Arab world, the mainstream security doctrine puts forward the need to: establish accumulative deterrence, including the development of nuclear capabilities, wage only short wars, deliver the battle outside of Israeli territory, and achieve a qualitative edge, by developing high-technology weapons. The strategic shift apparently manifested by the Oslo process is in fact widely seen as the successful result of this multi-faceted strategy. This, in turn, lies behind the uncompromising Israeli demand to retain control of defensible boundaries and the strategic hilltops overlooking the Israeli metropolitan centres, even when peace is established.[20] This security-based demand carries, in fact, much more public support for the retention of territory than the religious or historical arguments. Thus, for example, there is greater consensus within Israel concerning the need to retain control of the strategic Golan Heights than over the religiously and historically cherished West Bank. As could be expected, then, the transition to strategic modes of thinking based on terms of mutual, collective or co-operative security instead of unilateral national security required in the context of peace talks is difficult to achieve.

The apparent difficulty of the Israeli collective to transform its way of thinking on security matters is due to a number of reasons: the long national traumatic historical experience, the reoccurring manifestations of Arab hostility (Israel's self-image of weakness and vulnerability has been enhanced in the 1990s by the susceptibility of the Israeli population to the Iraqi missile attacks during the Gulf crises) or the territorial and demographic objective inferiority of Israel *vis-à-vis* the Arab states. Yet, it seems that the Israelis' adherence to the existential threat caveat is at least in part the outcome of an ongoing process of social construction of the threat, often used by the political elite both as a means of rallying the increasingly heterogeneous population around a single national ethos and as a means of justifying some questionable military actions to the outside world, particularly the United States.

Whether from a rational reading of the political map or the outcome of the elite's manipulation, the Israeli public's sense of threat to their national security has remained unchanged despite the launch of the peace process. A suggestive analysis of the Israeli Jewish public's view of the external conditions under which Israel was operating, carried out in 1994, just a few months after the signing of the Oslo DOP, indicated that most Israelis were political realists,[21] in that: they regarded their regional and international environment as a self-help anarchic system; they viewed their Arab neighbours as extremely hostile and as posing an existential threat to the state; and they emphasised the need for self-reliance and looking out for their own interests, as they could not identify any external power able and willing to assume responsibility for their security and survival.[22] A survey conducted in 1995 showed that about 68 per cent of Israeli Jews (compared to 22 per cent of Israeli Arabs) still believed that the Palestinians had not come to terms with Israel's existence and would have destroyed it if they could. The results were not much different in summer 1996, three years after the signing of the first Oslo DOP. Approximately 60 per cent of the Jews (23 per cent of the Arabs) attributed such intentions to the Arabs in general. Almost the same results were attained in the 1997 survey.[23] At the same time, Israelis seemed to be quite confident of the State's ability to defend itself against the external military threats. When asked immediately after the second Gulf crisis of early 1998 'how do you assess Israel's ability to prevail if a war were to break out today?' 43.0 per cent responded that Israel's ability to withstand a war was very strong, and 43.9 per cent said it was fairly strong, while only 7.0 per cent believed it was fairly weak and 2.6 per cent that it was very weak (3.5 per cent didn't know).[24]

Terror and domestic security. Anti-peace groups on both sides of the conflict have acted as 'spoilers' in their attempts to derail the peace process. This has normally taken the form of acts which have undermined the security of the other side, thus reducing even further grassroots support for the leaders in their attempt to move ahead with further negotiations. In particular, 'spoiler' groups, such as the Hamas and Islamic Jihad on one side and the West Bank settler militias on the other side, are spurred on by fundamentalist religious ideologies which negate all form of compromise over those elements which, to their own way of thinking, are pure and cannot be invalidated. Each sees their rights to the land as being part of a divine plan, entitling them to undertake actions which work against any form of territorial partition, and favouring the exclusive dominance of one group at the expense of the other.

Continued violence on the part of the Hamas and Islamic Jihad has meant that, since the peace talks were launched in the early 1990s until late 1997, Israeli's sense of personal security has, understandably, gradually declined. Such attacks were not a new phenomenon. Those carried out from the early 1990s onwards were seen by Israelis, however, as different to those of the 1960s, 1970s and 1980s, because they occurred against the background of the peace dialogue, rather than in the context of armed conflict. The first large-scale violent act occurred in October 1994 when a bus was blown up in Tel Aviv in a suicide operation (22 dead and 48 wounded). In its wake the first cracks appeared in the fragile Israeli belief in the other side's sincere desire for peace. The signing of the Israeli-Jordanian peace agreement a few days later partially counterbalanced this negative input as did the successful Casablanca economic summit which took place in the following week. The wave of terror against civilians increased further, however, in early 1995. On 22 January two Islamic Jihad members from Gaza detonated themselves at the Bet Lid junction bus stop killing a total of 22 Israelis and wounding 61. Israel blamed the Palestinian Authority for these actions, the general feeling in Israel being that Arafat was not doing enough to prevent terrorism from the anti-peace groups. This could be contrasted with the almost universal condemnation of the Omagh bombing in Northern Ireland, when even the IRA strongly condemned the continuation of violence now that a peace agreement had been signed. In general, Israelis were looking for a similar sort of condemnation of Hamas bombings on the part of the Palestinian Authority.

In 1995, Rabin's government was rapidly losing public support for being allegedly too appeasing towards the Palestinians. Suicide bombings in March, April and July of that year in Jerusalem, Tel Aviv and in other locations further weakened this support. To bridge the widening gap between the accelerating peace talks on the one hand and the growing fear of terror on the other, Rabin and Peres referred to the terrible outcomes of the Palestinian violent attacks as 'the price to be paid for peace', thereby trying to convince the general public to maintain its support of the peace process. What could be termed 'normal violence' has also been reflected in the increase in crime, especially car thefts, much of which has been attributed by Israeli authorities to Palestinians from the Autonomy Areas. Stolen cars were taken to the self-rule area to evade the Israeli authorities. Between 1993 (the signing of the Oslo A Agreement) and 1997, the number of stolen cars increased from 23 000 to 46 000, and the issue was even raised in Israeli Cabinet meetings as part of the discussions concerning the implementation of the Oslo Accords. Israeli decision-makers realised that practical solutions to the rising wave of violence and the decreasing sense of personal security it brought in its wake should be found. Thus the immediate reaction of the government to each terror event from then on was to put the West Bank and Gaza under a tight closure. This move was designed at reducing the probability of further attacks, as well as keeping Palestinian workers out of sight. Yet, a more fundamental solution to the security problem was sought. The idea of separation between Israelis and Palestinians in the short run and between Israel and the Palestinian entity/state in the longer term was developed by the political and military decision-makers.[25] Rabin went as far as saying that the goal of the entire peace process was the territorial separation of Israelis and Palestinians which, he said, would make Israelis safer.

Israelis' sense of personal security did not recover: in July 1995 only a small minority (21 per cent) felt an improvement in their personal security as a result of the peace process, as against 48 per cent who felt less secure.[26] The Israeli Jewish public was and remained highly sceptical concerning the possibility that terror will totally disappear even if and when all relevant peace agreements are signed. In 1994, just one year after the Oslo A Agreement, only 8 per cent of the respondents believed that should peace prevail terror would stop, while by July 1997, three years into the process, this had only increased to 13 per cent of the respondents. Even in 1998, five years after the famous handshake with Rabin on the White House lawn, 42 per cent of the Israelis still perceived Arafat as a terrorist, as against 26 per cent only who considered him a statesman.[27] An absolute majority (about 75 per cent) of Israeli Jewish respondents still favoured the separation option. The surveys also indicated that most Israelis prefered the influx of hundreds of thousands of foreign workers into the Israeli labour market, rather than allowing the Palestinian workers to return to their jobs within the Green Line. This attitude was based on the common belief that the majority of the Palestinians supported violent attacks on Israeli civilians.

The violent Palestinian attacks on Israeli civilians were manipulated extensively and successfully by the right-wing Likud Party in its election campaign, focusing on exposing Labour's impotence in dealing with domestic security matters. This was demonstrated most effectively by Netanyahu in his election campaign and in many of his public statements concerning the peace process on his coming to power. By emphasising the security element as a condition for progressing on the peace front, Netanyahu successfully played to the basic and innermost fears of the Israeli population. The results of 29 May 1996 general election proved that the growing sense of insecurity made Israeli voters a captive audience of Netanyahu who promised them 'peace with security'. It is this which has to be understood as the background to Netanyahu's election, despite the signing of both Oslo Accords and the assassination of the Israeli Prime Minister, acts which would, so it would be logical to assume, have resulted in a victory for the Labour government at the polls. The issue here is not the fact that Netanyahu defeated Peres by just 1 percentage point, but rather the reality in which 50 per cent of the Israeli population voted for a change in government.

Terror did not disappear after Netanyahu's election. Yet, when such actions occurred, they were met by forceful rhetoric by the incumbent Likud government. This was positively seen by many Israelis: the number of those who believed one year after the elections that their personal security had improved under the new government (42 per cent) exceeded by far the number of those who responded negatively to this question (25 per cent).[28] The slowing down of the peace process was perceived by many as the proper response to terrorism and the public support for tough, even tougher, policies towards the Palestinians was fairly widespread.[29] The Likud-led government that was opposed to the Oslo Agreements from the outset made no real effort to contest this cognitive linkage between crime and punishment. On the contrary, it reinforced it by emphasising the alleged responsibility of the Palestinian Authority for the recurring acts of violence against Israelis, local and sporadic as they might be. This policy was explicitly expressed in a document published on 9 September 1997 by the Israel Government Press Office in Jerusalem, summarising Israeli views on Palestinian security commitments:

> The Palestinian Authority's (PA) commitment to fight terror must be constant and absolute. It constitutes a sine qua non to the integrity of the peace process. The PA must fulfil the following measures to comply with its basic obligation under the Oslo Accords and the Hebron Protocol:
>
> 1 Full and unconditional security co-operation;
> 2 Deterrence and punishment of terror;

3 Dismissal of terrorist elements from police;
4 Fulfilment of Hebron security commitments;
5 Confiscation of illegal weapons;
6 Cessation of incitement to violence;
7 Limitations on police weapons;
8 Reducing size of Palestinian police;
9 Transfer of wanted terrorists to Israel;
10 Dismantling the terror infrastructure.[30]

Subsequently, the main focus of Israel's negotiating stance at the Wye Plantation talks in October 1998 was on the Palestinian commitment to fight terror and to ensure greater security for the Israeli population. Immediately following the signing of the Wye Agreements, further attacks were carried out, notably at the Mahane Yehuda market in Jerusalem. This led to the Israeli Cabinet temporarily suspending their meeting which was supposed to have ratified the Wye Accords, as a clear indication that Israel would not undertake any further territorial withdrawal and would not implement their side of the deal, if attacks on their civilians did not cease altogether.

The Palestinian refusal in 1996–7 to co-operate with Israeli security forces, due to what they saw as Israel's repeated violations of the Interim Agreement, appeared to sustain Netanyahu's argument that the other side had no real interest in preventing terror which, in turn, posed serious questions concerning their genuine wish for peace. The opposition leader, former IDF Chief of Staff, Ehud Barak, expressed similar views, thereby sustaining the cross-partisan validity of this argument. The fact that both Rabin and Barak had been former Chiefs of Staff of the Israeli army was influential in lending security credence to the Labour Party, pro-peace, platform. It is possible to surmise that without this security-oriented political presence, the security fears could have been played up even more strongly by the right-wing parties than they were.

While most Israeli Jews were concerned about the slowing down of the peace negotiations (about 80 per cent in January 1998)[31] only a minority saw Netanyahu and his government as responsible for this unfavourable situation while many (about 40 per cent) saw the Israeli government's policy as a major reason for the decline in the level of Palestinian terrorism.[32] Public opinion resonated the motif of the PA's responsibility for, but not necessarily genuine interest in, preventing Palestinian violent attacks on Israelis, an argument which was central to Netanyahu's rhetoric and his politics of delaying the negotiations.[33]

Palestinian security discourse

The Palestinian security discourse is of a totally different nature than the Israeli one. Still at the pre-state phase, with no army, and with much of the West Bank still under Israeli military occupation, the Palestinian Authority does not yet play any role in the regional power equation. Nor does it have, for the same reason, a full-fledged security doctrine. If, and when, a sovereign Palestinian state is finally established, Israel is likely to argue forcefully that such a state should be demilitarised or, at the very least, be limited to light weapons with some form of joint control over the military hardware allowed to enter the country.

Five years after the signing of the Oslo DOP only 10 per cent of the Palestinians believed that the Palestinian Authority was fully capable of meeting Israel's security threats while 44 per cent expressed the belief that it had no such capability.[34] Aware of their inferior power position, the Palestinians could not, or refused to, see why a military regional power such as Israel still endorsed the notion of existential threat, and continued to take far-reaching security precautions in the peace negotiations. From the Palestinian point of view, security related to the level of their susceptibility to, or protection from, violent and other detrimental measures taken against them by Israeli political authorities, armed forces and sometimes by the Jewish vigilantes from the settlements. Much like the Israelis, they saw themselves as innocent victims of the rancorous acts taken by the other side and therefore made little or no effort to understand its motivations. For example, in 1995, after the above-mentioned series of fatal suicide attacks executed by Palestinian extremists in Israel had taken place, most Palestinians interviewed by the pollsters expressed their belief that the idea and policy of separation fostered by Israeli decision-makers in response to these attacks was just a form of retaliatory and vindictive collective punishment against them.[35]

In particular, the Palestinians security dilemma is related to the presence of the Jewish settlers in the West Bank. West Bank settlers are allowed to move freely with arms, allegedly designated for their own safety. On some occasions these arms have been used in vindictive actions against Palestinians, while this came to a climax with the murder of dozens of innocent Moslem worshippers in a mosque in Hebron in 1994 by a Jewish resident of the Kiryat Arba settlement on the outskirts of Hebron. No wonder then that the re-deployment of the Israeli army in the West Bank and the establishment of Palestinian self-rule over most Palestinian cities was reflected in a growing sense of security in these places. Most Palestinians (64 per cent) sensed an improvement in this regard while only 12 per cent felt that their situation had worsened.[36] Thus the security fears are mutual, despite the fact that they figured much more prominently in the Israeli discourse than that of the Palestinians, somewhat paradoxically given the respective strengths of each side.

The continued expansion and consolidation of Israeli settlements is another factor which greatly weakens the feeling of security amongst Palestinians. Not only is this seen as an infringement of the Peace Accords, the expansion of civilian settlements is perceived as an action which effectively reduces even further the limited amount of land available for a future Palestinian state. This has both economic and political implications. It is little wonder that sporadic renewals of violence have often broken out as a direct result of Israeli settlement expansion, not least in East Jerusalem. For Palestinians the issue of land ownership is tied up with their feelings of economic security which, in turn, are an integral part of their aspirations for independence and statehood, not least owing to their current low levels of economic development when compared with Israel.

Another issue which Palestinians see as central to their national security while Israelis tend to deal with it separately is the economic issue. The almost total economic dependence of Palestinians on Israel exposes them to excessive pressures and increases their sense of national insecurity. The frequent and prolonged closures which prevented the impoverished Palestinian workers from entering Israel for long periods of time, together with unfavourable economic arrangements set by the Cairo Agreement are seen by Palestinians as a sort of non-violent but highly damaging warfare used by Israel against them. Even as late as 1998, only 29 per cent of Palestinians believed that the Palestinian Authority could fully or partly meet Israeli economic threats while the rest did not believe that it was capable of undertaking any action in this respect.[37]

Palestinian public opinion exhibits certain features which are highly dysfunctional as far as building confidence in the Israeli side is concerned. For example, the Palestinians' overt alignment with Iraq during the Gulf crises of both 1990 and 1998, or their public delight when the Scud missiles hit Tel Aviv in 1990, were highly negative inputs to the process of *rapprochement* with Israel, as was the support of many Palestinians for the deadly attacks carried out by Hamas and the Islamic Jihad organisations on Israeli civilians in 1994–5. Indeed, the support for violence and suicide attacks dropped from around 57 per cent in 1993 to only 20 per cent in the aftermath of the February–March 1996 suicide attacks,[38] but this was reversed in 1997, with the attacks in Tel Aviv receiving the support of 40 per cent of the respondents, thus sustaining the Israelis' assessment of the basic antagonistic attitude of the Palestinian people.

The increasing Israeli pressure on the Palestinian Authority to deal with the Hamas and Islamic Jihad violence has resulted in internal violence amongst the Palestinians themselves. Many Palestinians see Arafat's attempts at arresting the Hamas activists as being no more than carrying out Israeli policy. Moreover, during the first five years of Palestinian autonomy, the Palestinian police and security forces acted in such a way as to reduce, as far as possible, any opposition to Arafat's leadership, resulting in the emergence of an added dimension of internal security fears within the Palestinian community. Given the combination of settlement expansion, a downturn in economic activity as a result of closures, and the imposition of a stringent police rule, the overall security felt by many grass-roots Palestinians decreased significantly during the five years after Oslo. This did not mean that the Palestinians would prefer a return to Israeli rule, but rather that they desired the evacuation of the settlements on the one hand and an increase in internal Palestinian democratisation on the other.

The territorial discourse

Together with security, the territorial issue has occupied the centre of Israeli domestic political discourse ever since the 1967 War. It is only since the launching of the Oslo process, however, that the territorial debate concerning the West Bank and Gaza Strip has become one of practical significance. The question as to whether territorial compromises should be made in return for peace has been transformed from an abstract question into a matter of practical policy-making, in a way similar to that which took place during the Camp David Peace negotiations between Israel and Egypt, which resulted in Israel's withdrawal from the whole of the Sinai peninsula.

The competition for land between Palestinians and Jews is particularly fierce given the small piece of real estate in question. The real extent of Israel is no more than 20 000 sqkm, while the Occupied Territories – the whole of the West Bank, Gaza Strip and Golan Heights – adds approximately 5000 sqkm. Under the Oslo A and B Agreements, approximately 27 per cent of the West Bank was handed over to Palestinian autonomy, although this included some 90 per cent of the Palestinian population, concentrated in the main urban centres. The only urban areas of significance which remained under direct Israeli control were East Jerusalem and parts of Hebron.

The Oslo A Agreement resulted in the Israeli withdrawal from the Gaza Strip and the town of Jericho, while this was extended to include further towns and some Palestinian villages under the terms of the Oslo B Agreement. The implementation of the Oslo B Agreement resulted in the creation of a disconnected Palestinian territory, geographically discontinuous and dissected into numerous exclaves and enclaves, requiring access to each other on roads passing through Israeli-controlled areas. It was clear, at the time of the signing of the Oslo B Agreement, that this was no more than another transitional stage on the way to even further territorial changes, which would eventually create a single territorially contiguous territory on which Palestinian autonomy/statehood would be implemented.

For Palestinians, accepting a Palestinian state in the West Bank and Gaza Strip is a major concession in that it signals the abandoning of claims to the whole of pre-1948 Palestine, accepting less than 30 per cent of the total land. From the Israeli perspective, Palestinian claims to the whole of the West Bank reflect a maximal claim which cannot be met. The semantic difference between 'just' the West Bank (Palestinian) or the 'whole' of the West Bank (Israeli) reflects the major territorial differences posited by each side.[39] Many Israelis view the Palestinian claim for the 'whole' of the region as indicative of the fact that they will not cede one centimetre to Israel, and that they only see the West Bank as a springboard for future territorial claims within Israel itself. For their part, the Palestinians see Israel's attempt to retain control over some parts of the West Bank as indicating that they are not even prepared to compromise over a small part of Palestine, even after the Palestinians have given up their claims to the rest of the territory.

The Labour government were prepared to discuss most of the region with the Palestinians, but this decreased considerably to no more than an additional 13 per cent of the area under the Netanyahu government, justifying this territorial posture on the grounds that the remainder of the territory was necessary for Israel's strategic posture, the control of scarce water resources, and their desire to leave all Israeli settlements *in situ*. The Netanyahu proposals for further territorial withdrawals included Israeli retention of east–west routes linking metropolitan Israel with the eastern border along the Jordan valley. The implementation of such a proposal would mean that the Palestinian autonomy areas would remain geographically disconnected and dissected into numerous territorial islands and exclaves. Various proposals aimed at increasing the amount of territory available to the Palestinians while, at the same time, ensuring maximum Israeli retention of the settlements, have been proposed, but none of these has been acceptable to the Palestinian side.[40] These proposals varied from the Israeli retention of over half of the region and all of the settlements to just 10 per cent of the West Bank and about 60 per cent of the settlements. Some of the proposals demanded that Israel retain control of the Jordan valley and various lateral roads for 'security considerations', while others suggested that this was no longer necessary and that it was possible to withdraw from the strip of land along the Jordan river.

As aforementioned in the Wye Agreement of October 1998, Israel declared its intention to withdraw from a further 13 per cent of the West Bank. This included expanding some of the existing autonomy areas into a more compact territorial entity, but did not include any part of the Jordan valley or the evacuation of even the smallest and most isolated Israeli settlement. New bypass roads were to be constructed as a means of ensuring safe passage for all Israeli settlers only through territory controlled by Israel, even where such routes were indirect and longer than travelling through Palestinian-held territory. Implementation of this agreement would mean further territorial separation between the two populations, but would still leave over 50 per cent of the West Bank under direct Israeli control.

Despite the differences in terms of the eventual territorial configurations of Palestinian autonomy/statehood, there was a number of common themes. In the first place, each attempted to retain Israeli control over as large a number of settlements as possible, as a means of reducing internal opposition within Israel, while at the same time maximising the amount of territory to be transferred to the Palestinian Authority, in order to reduce Palestinian opposition to the proposal. A second dimension which figured in many of the proposals was the need to retain control over those areas which were perceived by Israeli policymakers as being essential for security purposes, such as the Jordan valley or lateral east–west access roads, as well as key water resources and underground aquifers.[41]

In terms of the demographic makeup of the region, the Israeli settlers account for no more than from 7 to 8 per cent of the region's population (in the Gaza Strip they are less than 1 per cent), and this is decreasing as the Palestinian natural growth rates far outstrip the migration of new settlers from Israel into the West Bank. But the settlements are widely dispersed, with some of the more rabid centres of political activity being situated in those settlements which are to be found in the mountain interior and/or in the Kiryat Arba suburb of Hebron. It is precisely these settlements which would have to be evacuated if an agreement was reached enabling the Palestinian entity/state to control a contiguous, compact piece of territory, unless, that is, the settlers agreed to remain under Palestinian sovereignty, a highly unlikely scenario.

Palestinians see the West Bank and Gaza Strip, their future state, as the place to which Palestinian refugees will return. In accepting the notion of a West Bank–Gaza Strip state, they are, effectively, giving up on the notion of refugees returning to their former homes and villages within Israel itself. They demand, in return, that all Israeli settlements in the West Bank be totally evacuated and that the entire area remains at the disposal of the Palestinian Authority. From an Israeli perspective, the return of refugees to the West Bank and Gaza Strip would, given the already difficult economic and housing conditions of the Palestinian residents of the region, create new social and economic pressures which would eventually break out into political unrest and which would lead to renewed claims by the Palestinian entity/state for additional land and/or a return to their former homes in Israel. For this reason, Israel is opposed to uncontrolled refugee return even to areas no longer under direct Israeli control. Thus, the demographic and territorial dimensions of the conflict resolution process are closely entangled one within the other.

Symbolic and metaphysical attachment to territory, defined as intangible or relational values by others, can often be the most critical forms of attachment in determining actual policy decisions with respect to territorial claims.[42] It is the settlers who, more than any other group, stress the symbolic and emotional dimensions of the territorial discourse. While the concrete manifestation of territory, either as an economic resource or as a strategic asset, can be quantified by each side to the conflict, this is not the case with the symbolic dimension. In other words, as a tangible asset, territory is a pawn which can be traded for concrete benefits. But as a symbolic asset, territory is an intangible object, one which cannot be traded or exchanged for any form of peace agreement. For both peoples, the territory of Israel/Palestine is part of an ancestral homeland, filled with sites, locations and myths which form an integral part of national identity formation. Just as the Jewish population trace their ancestry in this area back to Abraham and, later, to the conquest of the land by Joshua following the exodus from Egypt, so too do the Palestinians trace their own residence in this area back to Abraham and the Canaanite peoples. Each side uses historical sources and archaeological evidence to back up their claims, both in terms of 'priority' (having been the first people to reside in the region) and 'duration' (having experienced uninterrupted residence over long periods of time).[43] Each side continues to see its ultimate right to control land exclusively as irrefutable, meaning that any further progress over re-partition of the territory has to negate the argument which is at the ideological core of the mutual claims to control.

In the Israeli–Palestinian case symbolic attachments to land have been influential in determining territorial policies, especially in the post-1967 era. But when faced with the possibility of achieving immediate political gains, it has normally been the pragmatic, rather than the symbolic, factors which have proved to be the key factors influencing the decision-makers. This was as true of the decision to accept partition in the 1930s and 1940s as it was of the decision to withdraw from Sinai as part of the Camp David Accords, and the handing over of territory to the Palestinian Autonomy areas as part of the Oslo Accords in the 1990s. But the rise to power of a government that drew on its political and electoral support from, amongst others, the settler population and their supporters meant that the symbolic factors played a major role in the slow down in the negotiations over further territorial withdrawals.

The rhetoric of territorial symbolism is an effective tool for stating one's case under conditions of heightened conflict, but it is relegated to secondary significance under conditions of conflict resolution. The concrete arguments, especially those relating to security and strategic issues, carry far greater public consensus than do the historic/religious arguments, explaining to a great extent why public opinion is far more divided over the West Bank issue, much of which is couched in the language of symbolic territory, as contrasted with the Golan Heights and/or South Lebanon, both of which are perceived as being straightforward strategic issues.

At the same time, where the symbolic attachment to territory comes to the forefront of political decision-making, the issues are much harder to resolve. This is clearly evident with respect to the ideological opposition to any withdrawal from the West Bank – Judea/Samaria, and even more so with respect to the sensitive issue of Jerusalem. The emotional attachment to this city extends beyond any other piece of micro-territory within Israel/Palestine. Its choice as the capital city of the state in 1948 was based on the symbolic attachment, while the rhetoric of a post-1967 'unified' city, forever to be the eternal capital of the Jewish people, never again to be divided, is a political rhetoric which derives its roots from the symbolic and emotional attachment displayed by a large majority of the Jewish residents of the country to this city. Conflict resolution only begins to take place when there is a conscious decision to compromise over the tangible elements and an understanding that the symbolic attachment to land will remain unresolved or, as has been the case with the Oslo Accords, struck off the negotiating agenda until a future time.

Despite the symbolic importance attached to territory, surveys of public opinion show that during the last two decades Israeli Jews' readiness to give up parts of the territories occupied in 1967 has significantly increased. In the early 1990s the majority of Israelis, Israeli Jews and Arabs alike, supported Israel's withdrawal from the turbulent Gaza Strip. Almost half of the Jewish population was apparently ready to give up considerable parts of the West Bank in return for full peace with the Palestinians (the figures regarding the Golan Heights were considerably lower). The other half of the Jewish public either totally opposed giving up the territories or was only ready to make minor territorial concessions.

Why would people agree to withdraw from the territories? This question has been included in the annual surveys conducted by the Jaffee Center of Strategic Studies, at Tel Aviv University, since 1986. At the outset, the ideological argument 'We have a right to the land' to explain why not to pull out of the territories was by far the most prevalent response and reached about 50 per cent. At much lower rates people said that returning the territories would prevent the establishment of a Palestinian state (28 per cent in 1986), that it would provide strategic depth for the military (17 per cent in 1986) and that it would be a useful bargaining chip in future peace negotiations (9 per cent in 1986). The percentage shifted drastically over the years. By 1993 each of the four answers received from 22 to 30 per cent of the responses. By 1995, with negotiations under way and the domestic controversy over this matter at its peak, the percentage which cited the territories as a bargaining chip fell back to 9 per cent while the ideological right to the land reason revived and was mentioned by 42 per cent of the respondents.

The structure of opinion among Israeli Arab citizens on the question of territorial withdrawal is totally different. Israeli Arabs overwhelmingly supported the removal of all settlements or most of them (80 per cent).[44] At that time, about a quarter of the Jewish respondents said that no settlement should be removed and another quarter was prepared to support the removal of all or most settlements in the context of the final settlement with the Palestinians. The remainder (50 per cent) was only willing to remove those settlements that were located within or next to densely populated Palestinian areas. Also twice as many of Israeli Arabs (65 per cent compared to 33 per cent of the Jewish respondents) maintained that should the settlers refuse to leave their homes they should be forcibly removed, if necessary.

From a Palestinian perspective, the most severe violations of the various Oslo Agreements have to do with the expansion of the settlements and the construction of new Jewish neighbourhoods by the Israeli government, particularly in symbolic sites such as Jabel Abu Ghnaim (Har). When asked to state what is the greatest impediment in the way to peace, the second largest group of interviewees (17 per cent), in the survey conducted in December 1997, named the settlements.[45]

External actors

The history of the Israeli–Arab conflict is laden with numerous examples of external intervention. External actors have been present in almost every large-scale eruption of violence or, alternatively, as mediators in all significant attempts at conflict resolution. Britain's divide-and-rule policy of the pre-1948 era played a major role in the escalation of the Jewish-Arab confrontation. During the Cold War era, the intensive involvement of the USA and the USSR in Middle East affairs was a major factor in the conflict. All Israeli–Arab wars (1948, 1956, 1967, 1970, 1973, 1982) were brought to an end by external mediation.

The USA is the external actor most involved in, and committed to, the peace process since its inception. The Madrid conference was hosted by the Government of Spain and co-sponsored by the US and Russia (then the USSR). In the aftermath of the Cold War, together with America's dominant role in the Gulf War, the USA occupied an almost hegemonic position in terms of its influence in the Middle East. This meant that none of the invitees could actually refuse their invitation, or summons, to the conference table. The initial step of the process, the Madrid conference, was a part of President Bush's 'New World Order' plan. Between March and October 1991 US Secretary of State James Baker made eight visits to the region, in a tireless effort to convince Arab and Israeli leaders to attend an international peace conference. Israel gave its reluctant consent in April, following a crisis over the issue of US loan guarantees, earmarked to help Israel absorb half a million Jewish immigrants from the former USSR.

The hesitant Arab leaders were also finally convinced to take part in the conference, that is, in direct peace negotiations with Israel, an idea which they had rejected for years. This was to a great extent due to Bush and Baker's consecutive condemnations of Israeli settlements as a major impediment to peace. This public expression of American dissatisfaction with Israel's policies in the territories was a critical factor in bringing Syria and the PLO to the negotiation table. These actors had to be persuaded that the US could indeed serve as a mediator, despite its negative image in the Arab world following the Gulf War and its historically closer relations with Israel.[46] Although, then as now, Arab leaders generally preferred a UN peace initiative for the region, the circumstances of the early 1990s left no option other than US steerage of the negotiations.

Despite its unchallenged international status during this period, the US considered it important to maintain the façade of equal co-operation with its Western allies, mainly Britain and France and to a lesser extent Germany, Italy, Spain, etc. The leaders of these European powers were afforded all the symbolic status as senior partners to the American mediation effort from Madrid onwards. For their part, the European partners saw this as a means of regaining a foothold in the region. Aware of their inability to contend with the predominant American influence in the global arena, the Europeans have concentrated their efforts in the Middle East in the economic, rather than direct political or diplomatic, sphere of activity. Their involvement in this or any other capacity has been highly welcomed by the Arab participants who see the Europeans not only as allies but also as a counterbalance to the American domineering role.

Another partner to the process, officially equal but in reality of much less significance, was the Soviet Union, now Russia. The Soviet motives in the Middle East in the past, as well as Russia's present motives, are traditional ones of *realpolitik*. However, their re-entry into the Middle East in the framework of the present peace process cannot be understood only as a reassertion of national interests but also as an attempt to deter Islamic assertiveness by intimidating Turkey, co-opting Iran and exploiting Washington's failure to create a viable peace in the region.

The intensive involvement of the USA in the process continued in the ensuing 11 rounds of talks which took place immediately after Madrid. These discussions ended in the first of many deadlocks, in mid-1992. Besides its contribution to the advancement of the peace process in general, the victory of the Labour party in the Israeli general elections in 1992 reinforced the US position. Rabin's highly positive attitudes towards the Americans and his experience in productively communicating with Washington's statesmen were widely regarded. Thus, although the Washington sponsored track-one negotiations failed short of achieving any significant breakthrough, the situation did not revert to square one.

The breakthrough was, however, eventually achieved due to the intervention of another, quite unexpected, external actor. Norwegian political figures played a crucial role in encouraging the Israeli-Palestinian negotiations in Oslo in the summer of 1993. Once the Palestinians and Israelis, with the Norwegians' assistance, but without any overt active participation on the part of the US, agreed on a draft peace agreement, the USA regained its status as the prime peace broker. This was evident in the ceremonial signing of the (Oslo) Declaration of Principles on the White House lawn on 13 September 1993. On 14 December, the UN General Assembly, wishing to leave its own mark on the progressing peace process, passed an eight-point resolution, 48/58, expressing full support for the Israeli-Palestinian DOP.

In the five years after the signing of the Oslo Accords, neither the configuration of external involvement nor the order of importance between the different external actors changed. On a number of occasions, Egypt attempted to act as a go-between for Israel and the Palestinians, either through their own initiative or because they had been urged to do so by the US. However, in every case, Egyptian influence proved to be limited. Egypt's relations with Israel have deteriorated since the 1996 elections, and the chances of Egypt exerting its unquestionable influence in the Arab world to create a New Middle East seems unlikely.

Another external actor was Jordan's King Hussein. Of all the Arab leaders in the region, Israelis looked more favourably on Hussein. Since the formal implementation of the Israel–Jordan peace agreement, Israeli leaders have become constant visitors to Amman. Hussein's sympathy for the parents of Israeli schoolchildren that were killed by a Jordanian border guard was viewed very positively in Israel. The fact that there is a great deal of tension between the Hussein regime and the Palestinians within Jordan itself is another factor which made the King more acceptable as a go-between amongst Israel's Arab neighbours. Hussein's role was clearly evident in the tough negotiations which took place at the Wye Plantation in October 1998, resulting in his being a co-signatory to the Agreement when it was signed at the White House. Hussein's death in February 1999 added an element of uncertainty to Israeli–Jordanian relations.

With the Europeans rejected by Israel and disappointed by the poor standards of administration displayed by the Palestinian Authority under Arafat, with Egypt virtually out of the game, with UN incompetence and with Russia too busy with its domestic troubles, the US has remained the only external actor of importance and of interest in the Middle East peace process. However, despite the State Department's unequivocal statements that Washington is deeply disappointed with the two side's stubbornness (Israel) and failure to forestall terror (Palestinians), it would appear that even the US administration is rather sceptical now of its ability to bring about peace to this region in the foreseeable future.

From an Israeli perspective, the role of external powers, particularly that of the USA, is a double-edged sword. On the one hand, Israel is eager to present its case to the international community and to receive support for its fight to survive. On the other hand, an important part of the state survival ethos is that Israel must make its own decisions regarding its conduct of the Arab–Israel conflict, especially concerning its own definition of what constitutes a vital security and/or strategic interest. Many Israelis objected to what they perceived as the strong-arm tactics of the American administration during the Wye Plantation talks, with strong pressure exerted on both Netanyahu and Arafat to come up with an agreement. Many of the clauses in this agreement were backed up by accompanying letters on the part of the American administration to undertake such acts as would ensure the compliance by both sides of the reciprocal nature of the agreement.

Despite the fact that Israel's sovereignty is based on the 1947 United Nations Resolution, Israel is suspicious of the UN as a mediator. This dates back to the unilateral withdrawal of United Nations peacekeeping forces from the Sinai peninsula prior to the Six Day War in 1967 and the many subsequent anti-Israel resolutions which have been passed with large majorities by this international organisation. The multi-national peacekeeping force in the Sinai peninsula today is an American, not UN, led force, while Israel has already intimated that any agreement concerning withdrawal from all, or part, of the Golan Heights would also necessitate an American-led peacekeeping presence.

Unlike the Western Europeans, let alone the Russians, only the Americans have been perceived by Israelis as being sympathetic to, and supportive of, Israel's basic security needs. The common explanation in Israel to this exceptional caring for its fate is twofold: (a) the democratic values both countries allegedly share, and (b) the strong Jewish influence in American public life. During the Cold War era the American strategic need for reliable allies in the Middle East to hinder Soviet expansionism was also viewed as a reason for the consistent American support and constant provision of military and other assistance. At that time it was widely believed that the USA was in real need of Israel's services in the region and was in fact returning a debt by assisting its only ally there. Given the demise of the Soviet Union and the Cold War, this explanation is no longer relevant.

Consequently, the large majority of Israeli Jews are highly supportive of American involvement in the peace process. In a Peace Index survey conducted in April 1997 about 80 per cent of the respondents wished to see deeper American active participation, compared to 42 per cent who wanted to see the UN more involved and 40 per cent who favoured a greater European role in the Middle East. Egypt came fourth in this survey with only 34 per cent of the Israeli respondents favouring its higher engagement in the process. Notwithstanding, when Egyptian President Mubarak publicly offered his services as a mediator, 44 per cent of Israeli Jews saw it as a positive sign and maintained that it might be of some help in breaking the ice between Israel and the Palestinians.[47]

Palestinian public opinion on external involvement is different to that of the Israelis. The Palestinians see Egypt as their main Arab benefactor, thus desiring increased involvement on their part. The Europeans are perceived as impartial arbitrators in the Israeli-Palestinian disputes. The Palestinians do not view the Americans as a non-partisan actor. Their involvement is nevertheless accepted, not least because the Palestinians have no other option, but also because some of them hope that the strong US relations with Israel will enable it to exert effective pressure on Israel to undertake policy changes.

Although both Israel and the Palestinians have become disillusioned with the present peace process, the disparity between their respective positions on the external actors issue and, in particular, on the American role has apparently broadened during the last few years. When asked before the signing of the first Oslo Accord, 'Do you think that the US can play the role of mediator in the negotiations?'[48] a somewhat larger group of the Palestinian respondents said 'no' (53.3 per cent) while 40.8 per cent said 'yes' (5.9 per cent didn't know). Four years later, however, the Palestinian disappointment with the American functioning seemed to be extremely high. When asked in 1997, 'The US is acting as the sponsor and broker in the peace process. Do you believe that the US is siding with the Palestinians, acting as a neutral side, or biased towards Israel?' only 0.8 per cent thought that the Americans were siding with the Palestinians, 4.1 per cent considered them neutral while the majority of the Palestinian respondents (91.2 per cent) believed that the US was biased towards Israel (3.9 per cent didn't know).[49]

Conclusions

This chapter has attempted to show that the slow down of the Israel–Palestine peace process has much deeper roots than the change in government in Israel or, alternatively, the violence against civilians exerted by the Palestinian extremists. In the five years after the signing of the

Oslo DOP concrete – albeit partial – progress was made in terms of the Israeli withdrawal from the Occupied Territories and the constitution of Palestinian National Autonomy. However, this was not accompanied by parallel perceptual changes on the part of Israelis and Palestinians concerning their own individual and collective security as well as in their mutual images and assessment of basic intentions. Neither did it change the deeply rooted beliefs held by many people on both sides that the territory, in its entirety, 'belongs' to them and that it should not be divided, even if there are practical considerations for doing so. Thus, it is important to differentiate between the tangible negotiable aspects of peace and the deeper rooted perceptions of the 'Other' as constituting a long-term threat, when attempting to understand the changes which have, or have not, taken place. In other words, there has not been any discernible culture of change which has taken place, over and beyond the general support for peace as contrasted with violence.

Apparently, the signing of formal agreements has not been enough for the transition of both peoples from a conflict-oriented mentality to a conflict-resolution oriented state of mind. Thus, when the formal negotiations did not progress smoothly or reached a dead end, no significant pressures from below were exerted on the decision-makers to make greater concessions in order to push the process forwards. On the contrary, the leaders of both sides have had to invest great efforts in sustaining grass-roots support for the process, while at the same time often being blamed by their followers for being too compliant towards the other side. Furthermore, manifestations of greater toughness by the negotiators were often preferred and applauded by the two publics. As has recently been evidenced in Israel, the promotion of a tough stance, such as that displayed by Netanyahu, may be a greater electoral asset than the pro-peace compromise stance promoted by Rabin and the Labour party. Despite the downturn in the progress of the peace process, domestic support for Netanyahu had after two years of his government and despite a difficult first year in power, increased rather than decreased, although this was not necessarily reflected in the composition of the government itself. Following the signing of the Wye Agreements in October 1998, many of his traditional right-wing supporters threatened to withdraw their support from Netanyahu and bring the government down. Paradoxically, it was the left-wing opposition parties who offered him a short-term lifeline for as long as it took him to implement the latest agreement. Despite renewed right-wing opposition to the Wye Agreement, especially on the part of the settlers and their supporters, public surveys showed that over 70 per cent of the Israeli population supported this latest attempt at furthering the shaky peace process. Given this reality, we could argue that not only has the political leadership been unable to affect a top-down process of infiltration of pro-peace attitudes, but, to a certain extent, it has been the opposite process – a bottom-up feeling of dissatisfaction with the tangible gains of the peace process which brought Netanyahu to power in the first place and influenced his policy-making.[50]

It would also appear that the ability of the leaders to discuss and negotiate directly with their counterparts was not met in any way by a similar *rapprochement* taking place amongst the populations at large. This could be attributed at least in part to the fact that while Palestinian and Israeli politicians (of both the left and right) and academics constantly meet, the vast majority of both populations do not have any contact and remain ignorant of the feelings and aspirations of the 'Other'. A prominent Israeli political analyst recently described it as a situation in which 'The Palestinians lost hope while the Israelis lost interest'.[51] A Palestinian journalist has explained in an open letter to his Israeli colleagues why, in the present state of affairs, genuine communication between the two sides is practically impossible: 'For communication to succeed, and in order to avoid miscommunication across boundaries, [it] must be seen as a way of learning rather than a way of jamming thoughts from the other side. It can't, and shouldn't be, a reflection of the balance of power'.[52]

It is particularly at the level of symbolic politics where the mutual feelings of mistrust are instigated and felt. Practical questions, such as how much territory, which roads, how many police and how many arms, who controls the water, and so on, have been at the centre of the negotiation dialogue. For the population at large, however, as well as in the rhetoric of some leaders, a formal agreement on these issues has been only secondary to the demand to see some overt change in public sentiment expressed by the other. Thus, while Israeli statements and activities concerning the permanent nature of the settlements and the indivisibility of Jerusalem as Israel's capital are a red rag to the Palestinians, so too are Palestinian statements concerning the future establishment of a Palestinian state with its capital in East Jerusalem and the ambiguity surrounding the annulment of the Palestinian Charter. It is no longer an issue of whether the Palestinian Charter calling for the destruction of the state of Israel is practical or not. Judged from this perspective, there is little likelihood of the Palestinians being in a position to destroy the State of Israel. But from an Israeli perspective, their refusal publicly to reject the whole Charter is a symbolic indication that the Palestinian desire to destroy the Jewish State still exists and that there is no point in making any further concessions until such a Palestinian statement is made.

The asymmetry between the symbolic and concrete dimensions of the conflict resolution dialogue is partly due to the often incompatible messages which have been disseminated by the political leaders to their external and domestic audiences. The messages which constitute part of the negotiation process with the other side to the conflict are not, and cannot be, the same as those used as a means of gaining the support of the domestic audience. For example, while symbolic sentiments such as Jewish historical attachment to the entire Land of Israel and Zionist aspirations are downplayed in the context of the Israeli-Palestinian strategic dialogue, they form the very core of the domestic discourse between the elite and the public in Israel. This tactic is understandable as, for much of the Israeli population, the question of maintaining a Jewish state or retaining control of the biblical Land of Israel are the key objectives which take precedence over political negotiations and which are considered to be more important than an uncertain peace. Likewise, the Palestinian leaders prefer to highlight the Israeli reluctance to comply with the course and timetable outlined in the various Oslo Agreements, while downplaying the fact that, by concentrating on the future of the West Bank, they have virtually given up their symbolic demand for the entire Palestine in its pre-1948 War borders, as well as for the right of return of all refugees to Haifa, Jaffa and other places within Israel, populated by Arabs in the pre-State era.

The lack of active support for the Oslo process presently displayed by large segments of both the Israeli and Palestinian publics can also be explained as an outcome of the frustration felt by both sides with the results of the first stages of the process. While the Israelis have been highly disappointed with the decrease in their personal security, the Palestinians have suffered from the sharp downturn in their economic situation, a situation which is exacerbated when the Palestinian autonomy exclaves are sealed by the Israeli army, thus preventing freedom of movement in, or out, of these areas. Besides its objective sources, this frustration is also rooted in the elite grass-roots gap mentioned above. In order to get the cognitive legitimacy needed to launch the peace process, the leaders of both sides had emphasised its long-term advantages, such as the 'New Middle East' vision in the Israeli case and the extensive economic peace dividends for the Palestinians, rather than focusing on expected difficulties to be encountered during the first stages of conflict resolution. Therefore, the respective populations expected too much to take place in too short a period of time. The fact that the transfer of territory and the establishment of Palestinian autonomy was still greeted by suicide and terrorist bombs on one side and the expansion of settlements on the other meant that for many the peace process had not brought about any tangible benefits in terms of reduced violence and fear on the part of Israelis, or less confiscation of land or dismal economic conditions on the part of the Palestinians. Having expected so much, and having achieved so little in the short term, it would be reasonable to argue that this was translated into deep feelings of mutual frustration and a tendency not to support any further concessions on the peace front.

There is a clear relationship between the implementation of the peace agreements and economic growth. In the immediate aftermath of the Oslo Accords, there was a significant growth in the number of major international corporations and governments who were prepared to invest in the region. Major economic summits took place in Casablanca, Jordan and Oman, places which were previously off-limits to Israeli businessmen and industrialists. The idea of a 'New Middle East' which would become a new economic superpower in the global economy was floated around during the heady days of 1994 and 1995. However, this underwent a severe downturn as the peace process slowed down in 1996 and 1997, with potential investors no longer prepared to commit themselves to a region which, once again, appeared to be on the brink of renewed conflict. While the Israeli economy was unable to exploit the potential widening of its regional and global links, it remained a fairly stable and buoyant economy. The situation in the Palestinian Autonomy areas was much worse, with GDP falling dramatically in the wake of poor economic management, on the one hand, and the constant closures of the autonomy areas by the Israeli authorities following terror attacks inside Israel, on the other.

Furthermore, in both societies the domestic debate of the peace process has severely deepened internal cleavages and intensified domestic tensions. On the Israeli side it led to bitter, and in some cases, violent opposition from the right wing, culminating in the assassination of Prime Minister Rabin. On the Palestinian side, it brought about persecution of those groups which oppose the process and/or the continued leadership of Yasser Arafat. In both cases, some of the most vehement opposition has come from religious groups (Gush Emunim or the Hamas) which have the tendency to emphasise the symbolic, rather than the tangible, factors which govern their respective world-views.

Paradoxically, the opposition of these extreme groups, and their emphasis on the religious and symbolic factors, comes about precisely when the leaders have reached an initial compromise over the tangible and practical factors of conflict resolution. The much cherished internal unity displayed by both Israelis and Palestinians in their respective struggles has been sacrificed for a contested and uncertain peace which may, or may not, come about in the future. Thus, there is a form of cost-benefit analysis practised by both sides, in which the internal disintegration and fragmentation of a national unity has to be weighed against the potential benefits from future external peace with the historic enemy.

Thus the prospects for the resolution of the Israeli-Palestinian conflict would appear to be slim. Despite the discouraging state of affairs on the perceptual level, this does not have to be inevitable, provided that realistic goals and expectations are set. The mutual legitimisation and recognition resulting from the very peace negotiations, even if only partly successful thus far, are apparently irreversible. They are expected to lead to somewhat greater sensitivity to the other side's demands and feelings as indicated, for example, by the growing number of Israelis who have come to terms with the Palestinian demand for self-determination and even for a state. The fact that even the hawkish right-wing government of Israel, headed by Netanyahu, which opposed the signing of the agreements with the Palestinians by the previous Labour government, openly endorsed the Oslo process, albeit with far greater restrictions and conditions, cannot be easily dismissed and neither can the Palestinian leaders' practical ongoing efforts to push the process ahead despite their vociferous reproach of the Likud government and its policies of settlement expansion. The apparent recognition by the politicians on both sides that the resolution of the conflict is going to be a considerably longer and more complicated process than expected, not least because of the difficulty of mobilising public support, could also prove to be positive – in the long term – if more realistic objectives and timetables for the strategic transformation of Israeli-Palestinian relations are set.

There are some general lessons to learn from the limited success of the Oslo process concerning the chances of transforming protracted violent conflicts into peaceful coexistence. First, desirable as it may be, the total cessation of violence and the immediate constitution of benevolent modes of co-operation immediately after, or just because, formal peace agreements are signed should not be promised or expected. Peace processes are not necessarily linear – rather, they tend to fluctuate, progressing at one point and freezing at another. The consequential stages theory does not always hold up, not least because of unexpected political events taking place which had not been foreseen in the initial stages of the process.

Second, the Israel/Palestine case brings into question the concept of 'borrowing' from one conflict resolution process to another. Social and political discourse in Israel has always focused on the unique, rather than the universal, explanatory factors. While the Irish and South African peace processes may be held up as indications of what could be achieved in the future, most Israelis and Palestinians see their own conflict as being too unique to warrant any borrowing of concepts or ideas for conflict resolution from other *milieux*. Given the down turn in the nature of the Israel/Palestinian peace process, there is also much scepticism in Israel concerning the long-term future of the other peace processes, with much attention being given to incidents of sporadic violence in these places, rather than focusing on the long-term structural changes which have taken place elsewhere.

Finally, the timetable for the implementation of the agreement should take into consideration the deep-rooted difficulties involved in transforming a conflict-oriented public into a new mode of thinking. This is particularly true today, when the public's level of confidence in its leaders is relatively low and, therefore, automatic support for their decisions is not guaranteed. The setting of too tight a timetable, which does not allow for the necessary cognitive process of adaptation to take place and for the symbolic aspects of the new situation to replace those of the blood-soaked past could lead to the total collapse of the process, leaving in its wake even deeper antagonism, violence and destruction.

One of the common characteristics of most peace processes is their non-linear character. A change in the domestic political context, an increase in outside intervention, a sudden breakthrough in the negotiations or alternatively an eruption of violence by 'spoilers', can being about a reversal – positive or negative – in the development of a peace process. This is most apparent in the Israel/Palestine context. Between the time of writing the original version of this chapter and the publication of the book, significant changes have taken place within Israeli politics which have, at least at the time of writing this postscript, brought about a renewed phase of optimism that the process may, after three years of stalemate, once again be moving ahead. The change in government which took place in Israel in May 1999, with the election of Ehud Barak as Prime Minister in place of Benjamin Netanyahu, has resulted in a renewal of negotiations between Israel and the Palestinian

Authority. The short-term outcome has been the signing of the Sharm-el-Sheik memorandum in September 1999 (revising the Wye Agreement), and the opening of the next round of negotiations, destined to bring about a final-stage agreement between the two sides.

In effect, Barak does not occupy a position far to the left of Netanyahu. Both of these leaders, as well as Rabin in 1992, won their respective elections by appealing to the centre of the Israeli electorate, a centre which, so the survey material in this chapter has shown, desires to move ahead with the peace process, is prepared to make certain territorial concessions for the sake of peace, but wants to be ensured that their security – personal and collective – is not at risk. Barak, like Rabin before him, came to the political stage as an ex-military hero and commander-in-chief, and was able to portray a personality that would not put the security of the country at risk.

The postscript is indicative of the inherent problem in writing about these processes while they are still in the process of implementation. Notwithstanding, the detailed analysis of the ups and downs of the Israel/Palestine process, from Oslo through the Rabin assassination, the rise to power of Netanyahu and his eventual replacement by Barak cannot remove the basic structural and long-term change in this conflict which was brought about by the onset of the Oslo process. This is reflected in public opinion and the general increase in support for the peace process in general, providing that security needs (as defined by the domestic audience) are met, and the fact that an increasing percentage of the Israeli population recognises, and even accepts, the inevitability of a two-state solution, including the establishment of an independent and sovereign Palestinian state in all, or part, of the West Bank.

Notes

1 For example, R. Pundik, *Is Oslo Alive? The Security Dimension. Is Oslo Alive? Panel Deliberations* (Jerusalem: The Konrad Adenauer Foundation, the Harry S. Truman Institute and the Palestinian Consultancy Group, 1998), pp. 25–30.

2 For a definition and discussion of this term, see K. J. Holsti, *Peace and War: Armed Conflicts and International Order, 1648–1989* (Cambridge: Cambridge University Press, 1991).

3 For both the importance and difficulty in attaining such legitimacy, see A. George, 'Domestic Constraints on Regime Change in US Foreign Policy: the Need for Political Legitimacy', in O. Holsti, R. Siverson and A. George (eds), *Change in the International System* (Boulder, CO: Westview Press, 1980), pp. 233–62.

4 T. Hermann and E. Yuchtman-Yaar, 'Two People Apart: Israeli Jews' and Arabs' Attitudes towards the Peace Process', in Peleg, *Middle East Process*, pp. 61–86.
5 This accounts at least in part for the fact that external rather than domestic constraints were responsible for initiating conflict resolution or reduction in the Israeli–Arab conflict as indicated. Furthermore, domestic constraints became very important once the process got under way (Y. Bar-Siman-Tov, *Peace Policy as Domestic and as Foreign Policy: the Israeli Case*, Davis Occasional Papers, 58 [Jerusalem: The Leonard David Institute, 1998]).
6 For an account of the Madrid conference as a political breakthrough see E. Ben Tzur, *The Road to Peace Goes through Madrid* (Tel Aviv: Yediot Aharonot, 1998) [Hebrew].
7 For a view from an insider of the Oslo negotiations, see U. Savir, *The Process* (Tel Aviv: Yediot Aharonot, 1998) [Hebrew].
8 For a discussion of the multilateral talks, see J. Peters, *Pathways to Peace: the Multilateral Arab-Israeli Peace Talks* (Chatham House, London: Royal institute of International Affairs, 1996).
9 Based on the findings of the Peace Index Project, executed by Prof. Ephraim Yuchtman-Yaar and Dr Tamar Hermann of the Tami Steinmetz Center for Peace Research, Tel Aviv University. The measure presented here was composed of the answers to the following two questions: 'Do you support or oppose the DOP signed by Israel and the Palestinians in Oslo?' and 'Do you believe that the Oslo Process will bear fruit in the foreseeable future?' Should all respondents both support and have faith in the Oslo process the index score would have been 100 points. Were all opposing it and disbelieving in its prospects the score would have been 0. The results of all surveys since June 1994 can be found at the Center's home page:
http://www.tau.ac.il/peace or upon request by email: steinmet@ccsg.tau.ac.il.
10 D. Makovsky, *Making Peace with the PLO: the Rabin Government's Road to the Oslo Accord* (Washington DC: Washington Institute for Near East Policy; Boulder, CO: Westview Press, 1996), pp. 40, 41.
11 Peace Index public opinion survey (March 1995).
12 See, e.g., J. Shamir and M. Shamir, *The Dynamics of Israeli Public Opinion on Peace and the Territories*, Research Report Series, no. 1 (Tel Aviv: The Tami Steinmetz Center for Peace Research, 1993).
13 Peace Index public opinion survey (March 1995; August 1996).
14 Peace Index public opinion survey (March 1995; August 1996; and November 1997).
15 For a discussion of the relationship between the national identity of the Arab-Palestinian citizens of Israel and the peace process, see Y. Peled and G. Shafir, 'The Roots of Peacemaking: the Dynamic of Citizenship in Israel, 1948–93', *International Journal of Middle Eastern Studies*, 28, 3 (1994), pp. 391–413.
16 The entire set of CPSR findings can be found at
http://www.cprs-palestine.org.
17 The entire set of JMCC findings can be found at http://www.JMCC.org.
18 S. Feldman, 'Israel's Changing Environment: Implications for Arms Control', in Feldman, *Confidence Building and Verification*, pp. 195–206 (196).
19 For an alternative discussion of the security threat, and the way in which this is related to the growth of the militarism ethos in Israel,

see U. Ben-Eliezer, *The Making of Israeli Militarism* (Bloomington: Indiana University Press, 1998). The changing territorial dimension of this threat is discussed in D. Newman, 'The Geographical and Territorial Imprint on the Security Discourse', in D. Bartal, D. Jacobson and A. Klieman (eds), *Concerned with Security: Learning from the Experience of Israeli Society* (Connecticut: JAI Press, 1998), pp. 73–94.

20 The Israeli concept of 'defensible boundaries' along the Jordan river was part of the post-1967 Allon Plan, and is outlined in D. L. Horowitz, *Israel's Concept of Defensible Borders*, Jerusalem Papers on Peace Problems, no. 16 (Jerusalem: Hebrew University of Jerusalem, Leonard David Institute for International Relations, 1975). For a discussion of the territorial dimensions of the security discourse, and the extent to which this discourse is part of a social construction of threat, see, D. Newman, 'The Geographical and Territorial Imprint on the Security Discourse', in D. Bartal, D. Jacobson and A. Klieman (eds), *Concerned with Security: Learning from the Experience of Israeli Society* (Connecticut: JAI Press, 1998), pp. 73–94.

21 This follows notions of Political Realism, as developed by Kenneth Waltz, *Man, the State and War* (New York: Colombia University Press, 1952).

22 Feldman, 'Israel's Changing Environment', p. 195.

23 Peace Index public opinion surveys (May 1995; August 1996; December 1997).

24 Peace Index public opinion survey (February 1998).

25 For a discussion of the significance of territorial separation, see D. Newman, 'Shared Spaces – Separate Spaces: the Israeli–Palestine Peace Process', *Geojournal*, 39 (1996), pp. 363–76. For Israeli's attitudes towards this idea, see T. Hermann and E. Yuchtman-Yaar, 'Do They Lend It Their Consent? Israeli Public Opinion and the Political Process', in D. Capsi (ed.), *Communication and Democracy in Israel* (Jerusalem: Hakibbutz Hameuhad, 1997), pp. 191–222.

26 Peace Index public opinion survey (July 1995).

27 Peace Index public opinion survey (July 1998).

28 Peace Index public opinion survey (June 1997).

29 Peace Index public opinion survey (July 1998).

30 http://www.israel-mfa.gov.il, 1995.

31 Peace Index public opinion survey (January 1998).

32 Peace Index public opinion survey (July 1998).

33 Peace Index public opinion survey (July 1998).

34 CPRC public opinion survey (July 1998).

35 CPRS public opinion survey (February 1995).

36 JMCC public opinion survey (November 1997).

37 CPRS public opinion survey (July 1998).

38 H. Shikaki, 'Palestinian Public Opinion, the Peace Process and Political Violence', MERIA on-line journal, www.biu.ac.il/SOC/besa/meria.htm, 1998.

39 The contrasting claims to the territory of the West Bank by Israelis and Palestinians is discussed in D. Newman and G. Falah, 'Bridging the Gap: Palestinian and Israeli Discourse on Autonomy and Statehood', *Transactions of the Institute of British Geographers*, 22 (1997), pp. 111–29.

40 For a comparative analysis of the diverse proposals for territorial separation between Israelis and Palestinians, see: D. Newman, 'Creating the Fences of Separation: the Territorial Dialogue of Israeli-Palestinian Conflict Resolution',

Geopolitics and International Boundaries, 3, 1 (1998), pp. 251–70; G. Falah and D. Newman, 'The Spatial Manifestation of Threat: Israelis and Palestinians Seek a "Good" Boundary', *Political Geography*, 14 (1995), pp. 689–706.

41 The geopolitics of water as part of the peace process has been dealt with at length. See, for instance, S. Elmusa, 'The Israeli-Palestinian Water Dispute Can Be Resolved', *Palestine–Israel Journal*, 3 (1994), pp. 18–26; H. Shuval, 'Towards Resolving Conflicts over Water: the Case of the Mountain Aquifer', in E. Karsh (ed.), *Between War and Peace: Dilemmas of Israeli Security* (London: Frank Cass, 1996), pp. 14–56.

42 G. Goertz and P. F. Diehl, *Territorial Changes and International Conflict* (London: Routledge, 1992), argue that territorial changes with high relational importance are the most likely to involve violence as indeed is the case with respect to the West Bank ('the historic and religious heartland of the ancient Land of Israel') or Jerusalem ('the eternal capital of the Jewish people, never again to be divided'). This is consistent with the logic outlined by J. A. Vasquez, *The War Puzzle* (Cambridge: Cambridge University Press, 1993), and J. D. Fearon, 'Rationalist Explanations for War', *International Organization*, 49 (1995), pp. 379–414, that indicate that conflict is more likely when issues are less tangible or divisible, or in other words when territories are perceived as being exclusively 'belonging' to one group of people and that all others are usurpers. Contextually, Jerusalem is often perceived as constituting an 'indivisible' good (C. Albin 'Negotiating Indivisible Goods: the Case of Jerusalem', *Jerusalem Journal of International Relations*, 13 [1991], pp. 45–76). For a discussion of territorial symbolism within the context of the Israel-Palestine conflict, see D. Newman, 'Real Spaces – Symbolic Spaces: Interrelated Notions of Territory in the Arab-Israel conflict', in P. Diehl (ed.), *A Road Map to War: Territorial Dimensions of International Conflict* (Nashville: Vanderbilt University Press, 1998), pp. 124–46.

43 The notions of priority and duration as bases for territorial claims are discussed by A. Burghardt, 'The Bases of Territorial Claims', *Geographical Review*, 63 (1973), pp. 225–45, and expanded further by A. B. Murphy, 'Historical Justifications for Territorial Claims', *Annals of the Association of American Geographers*, 80 (1990), pp. 531–48.

44 Peace Index public opinion survey (August 1996).

45 JMCC public opinion survey (December 1997).

46 The wider context of the Arabs' hesitations to co-operate with the Americans on this matter since Madrid was skilfully elaborated upon by the Arab-American scholar Fouad Ajami: 'A shadow of American primacy lies on Arab lands; inescapably, onto the new reforms, onto the whole structure of contemporary international order for that matter, are projected the resentments that the intellectual class harbors towards Pax Americana ... America is simultaneously the agent of political order and social revolution ... In the intervening years, America has been the thing and its opposite: Satan and redeemer; it has nurtured Arab nationalism and sustained Israel ... a foul wind has greeted Israeli-Palestinian peace, and the Arab intellectual class has, by and large, taken a dark view of Oslo and of the wider process of normalization with Israel ... To its opponents the peace was a Pax Hebraica or a joint Israeli-American project that a feeble Arab world had been unable

to resist', F. Ajami, 'The Arab Inheritance', *Foreign Affairs*, 76, 5 (September–October 1997), pp. 133–48.

47 Ibid. Peace Survey Index, April 1997.

48 JMCC public opinion survey (May 1993).

49 JMCC public opinion survey (May 1997).

50 T. Hermann and E. Yutchman-Yaar, 'On the Road to Peace? The Dynamics and Political Implications of Israeli-Jewish Attitudes toward the Oslo Process', paper presented at the MESA annual conference, Chicago (1998).

51 M. Benvenisti, 'From Belfast to Jerusalem', *Haaretz* (7 May 1998) [Hebrew].

52 D. Kuttab (July 1998), www.amin.org/pages/dkuttab/july.htm.

4
The Basque Peace Process, Nationalism and Political Violence

Ludger Mees

Introduction: Subjects and concepts

The Basque Country risked entering the new millennium as the last European Union region which was host to a violent nationalist conflict.[1] Nor was the prospect of stopping the violence and reaching a peaceful settlement on the agenda of policy-makers. Since ETA (Euskadi 'ta Askatasuna/Basque Country and Freedom) began its violent campaign in the 1960s, fatalities – including those killed by extreme right-wing death squads – totalled nearly 900. ETA's September 1998 ceasefire, its first unilateral and indefinite truce in nearly 30 years, has the possibility to transform the political arena. For the first time since 1960, the year ETA killed its first victim, the situation looks 'ripe' for the start of a peace process and a negotiated way out of the conflict. What reasons lie behind this shift? In short, what factors kick-started the Basque peace process? The following analysis focuses on these questions.

Before embarking on this analysis, several prior observations and conceptual clarifications seem necessary. First, it should be stressed that the Basque conflict did not come about through the emergence of ETA. Describing it exclusively as a conflict between 'terrorists' and 'democrats' would reduce it to an unhistorical simplification. The history of Basque political nationalism is not the history of ETA. Despite frequent appearances in the mass media, the violent expression of radical Basque nationalism cannot even be considered as the predominant feature of more than a century of Basque nationalism. As a consequence of the profound gap between the processes of (successful) early *state-building* and (unsuccessful) *nation-building* in nineteenth-century Spain, Sabino Arana founded the first cell of the Basque Nationalist Party, the Partido Nacionalista Vasco (PNV) in 1895. The PNV – together with the Spanish socialist Partido Socialista Obrero Español (PSOE) – is the oldest active party in Spain. The rise of Basque nationalism marked the beginning of a new phase in the evolution of the clash between conflicting cultural identities in the Basque region and centre-versus-periphery power struggles.[2] Since violence 'is an action, a state or a situation always generated within a conflict and exclusively qualified by that conflict', we can assume that the violent dimension is only one of a number of, mainly peaceful, dimensions in this conflict.[3] This remained the case even though 'political violence' created an autonomous dynamic of its own during the later years of the conflict. 'Political violence' is used in a broad sense, as 'acts of disruption, destruction, injury whose purpose, choice of targets or victims, surrounding circumstances, implementation, and/or effects have political significance, that is, tend to modify the behaviour of others in a bargaining situation that has consequences for the social system'.[4] Historically, political violence has adopted different forms of expression (food riots, Luddism, land occupations, violent demonstrations, revolutions, etc.), with terrorism being one of those expressions.[5] If we understand the 'process of civilisation' as 'the systematic effort of the human being and of society to submit the resolution of any kind of conflict to accepted patterns', we could define the history of (political) violence as the 'history of its progressive diminution'.[6] Terrorism, that is, 'the systematic use of murder, injury and destruction or the threat of such acts for political ends', has proved to be a type of political violence quite resistant to the effects of the already mentioned 'process of civilisation'.[7]

This perpetuation of terrorism can be expected to create contradictions within the framework of an 'open' and democratic society. This point constitutes a central argument of this study. The growing dissociation between the violent and political dimension of the conflicts, between ETA and Basque mainstream nationalism, between nationalist militarism and society, will be highlighted as one of the key factors in shaping a new social and political context in the late 1980s. It was in this context that the possibility of a peace process emerged. Thus, the analysis will focus on the evolution of nationalism in the Spanish part of the Basque Country during the 1990s. Spatial constraints mean that the historical background of the conflict must be compressed, starting with the Spanish process of *transition* towards democracy.

Transition, democracy and the perpetuation of violence

General Franco's death in November 1975 brought immense political change to Spain.[8] According to the literature, Spain entered 'the ideal type of a negotiated transition, as well as a successful and relatively unproblematic consolidation of democracy'.[9] While this description may apply to the wider Spanish state, it does not apply to the Basque Country. The authors quoted above consider that democratic politics and institutions were not yet consolidated in Euskadi in the early 1980s.[10] The *national question* and its violent expressions help explain the gap between the experiences of the Basque Country and the rest of Spain. The hostile and indiscriminate activity of the police forces in the Basque provinces, the persistence of torture in police stations, the emergence of right-wing paramilitary groups and the increase in ETA violence, all made efforts to resolve the Basque conflict during the *transition* even more difficult than it had been before. Violence was affecting more people. ETA accompanied each of the major steps on the democratic transition with an expansion of violence. Since its first fatal attack in 1960 until 1977 ETA did not kill more than 19 people per year. In the next three years, ETA killed 247 people.[11] The figure then dropped to an average of from 30 to 40 victims per year.[12] The *transition* in the Basque Country was also hampered by the rejection of the new Constitution by all sectors of Basque nationalism. The partial devolution of self-government to the Basques, through the 1979 Basque Autonomy Statute, facilitated a *de facto* integration of moderate nationalism into the constitutional consensus. The radical nationalist left, represented by the ETA-allied coalition Herri Batasuna (HB) since 1978, was the only political force campaigning against autonomy. It argued that the Autonomy Statute was based on a constitution which had been rejected in the Basque provinces. The Autonomy Statute itself, however, was backed by a broad majority of the Basque voters in a 1979 referendum. Under the Statute, the three Basque provinces of Gipuzkoa, Alava and Bizkaia, which constituted the Autonomous Community of the Basque Country – Euskadi (BAC), were awarded remarkable levels of self-government within the Spanish state. This included Basque institutions (parliament, government, court of justice), police (Ertzantza), tax autonomy and broad powers in education, culture, media, industrial policy and justice. On the symbolic level, important goals were achieved by moderate nationalism. For example, the flag and the anthem invented by Sabino Arana, the founder of the PNV, became the official symbols of the autonomous Euskadi.[13]

For ETA and the radical nationalist left, autonomy was a poisoned apple offered by Spanish centralism to moderate Basque nationalism in order to ensure the future Spanish domination of the Basques. According to this view, autonomy also perpetuated the territorial division of

Table 4.1 Nationalist vote-sharing in the elections to the Spanish (EG) and the Basque (EA) Parliaments

	EG	*EG*	*EA*	*EG*	*EA*	*EG*	*EA*	*EG*	*EA*	*EG*	*EA*	*EG*	*EA*
Year	*77*	*79*	*80*	*82*	*84*	*86*	*86*	*89*	*90*	*93*	*94*	*96*	*98*
PNV	28.8	27.6	38.0	32.0	42.0	28.0	23.7	22.7	28.5	23.9	29.9	25.4	27.9
HB	4.3	15.0	16.5	14.8	14.6	17.8	17.5	16.8	18.3	14.5	16.3	12.5	17.9
EE	6.3	8.0	9.8	7.7	8.0	9.1	10.9	8.8	7.8				
EA							15.8	11.1	11.4	9.8	10.3	8.3	8.7
Oth.			0.9		1.0								
Total	39.4	50.6	65.2	54.5	65.6	54.9	67.9	59.4	66.0	48.2	56.5	46.2	54.5

Sources: Llera (1994: 158–9); *El Diario Vasco* (24 October 1995 and 26 October 1998).

the Basque regions and impeded Basques from exercising their right of self-determination.[14]

Thus, the implementation of the Basque Statute of Autonomy did not bridge the gap between the minority wing of nationalism and the rest of the Basque society. In fact, since the split in nationalism, initiated in the 1960s and consolidated during the *Transition*, the major co-ordinates of the Basque political system have remained largely unchanged.[15] Indeed, the Autonomy Statute strengthened *both* wings of Basque nationalism.

As Table 4.1 shows despite the establishment and the consolidation of powerful autonomous institutions, a significant minority of Basque society continued to support an openly anti-system party like HB. Various attempts by the Spanish government to establish dialogue with ETA failed. ETA-militar were unwilling to follow the example of ETA político-militar (dissolved in 1982) and lay down their arms.[16]

Right-wing violence also contributed to the conflict. From 1978 to 1991 this 'counter-violence' resulted in 90 casualties. From 1983 to 1987, Grupos Antiterroristas de Liberación (GAL) killed 25 Basques, mostly in the French-Basque territories. GAL's objective was to force the French government to adopt a tougher attitude towards ETA refugees and to co-operate more directly with the Spanish police forces.[17] In the late 1990s, Spanish judges charged the former socialist Minister of the Interior Barrionuevo (1982–8) and a number of his subordinates with organising and promoting GAL. In July 1998, former minister Barrionuevo and his State Secretary Vera were sentenced to ten years in prison for their role in GAL activities. Revelations of state terrorism, together with a series of corruption scandals linked with the socialist government, especially during the last five years of President González's long mandate (1982–96), plunged the Spanish political system into a crisis of legitimacy. This, in turn, provided ETA and radical Basque nationalism with a fresh boost.

In fact, the crisis in the Spanish political system helped slow down the process of separation between ETA and Basque society. Several factors contributed to this process. First, Spain was no longer a dictatorship. It was now a parliamentary democracy with formal channels for the expression of grievances and opposition. Second, Basque society and Basque nationalism had changed. Nationalism had achieved unprecedented levels of power. Third, ETA had failed to accommodate its strategy to the new situation. It pursued a campaign of indiscriminate violence. Conceivably, Basques and Spanish, except those linked to the Basque National Liberation Movement (BNLM) were potential

Table 4.2 Votes obtained by HB in the Basque Autonomous Community

Elections	*Votes*
European Parliament 1987	210 430
Spanish Parliament 1989	186 646
Basque Parliament 1990	186 242
Spanish Parliament 1993	174 655
Basque Parliament 1994	166 147
Spanish Parliament 1996	154 853

Sources: José Manuel Mata, *El nacionalism vasco radical: Discurso, organización y expresiones* (Bilbao: Universidad del País Vasco, 1993), p. 33; *El País* (20 July 1997)

victims.[18] The bombing of a supermarket in Barcelona in June 1987 which killed 21 people provided a bloody example of the indiscriminate nature of the violence. Fourth, the pursuit of a violent strategy, without an apparent political rationale, provoked a reaction on behalf of those for whom ETA presumed to act: the Basque people. A significant outcome was the emergence of the Basque Peace Movement in the 1980s. This increasing sensitisation of society against violence was noticeable among Basque youth, and was reflected in the ballot boxes. An analysis of HB's recent electoral performances shows that the party has steadily lost votes since the 1987 European election (see Table 4.2). These figures contrast with the upward trend in the HB vote from 1979 to 1987. If the results of Navarra are included, then HB lost about 70 000, or a quarter of its 1987 total vote, in the 1987–96 period.[19]

Yet, despite the electoral haemorrhaging and the calls of the Peace Movement, ETA and HB opted for a contrary strategy: the reaffirmation of political violence. This militarisation of radical nationalist politics played a crucial role in the origins of the Basque peace process.

The counterattack

The conservative victory in the March 1996 general election was based on a hard-line attitude towards terrorism. Contact with ETA was ruled out, with policing promoted as the most effective strategy against terrorism. Improvement in co-operation between the Spanish and French police forces increased pressure on ETA. In 1997, the police captured 88 ETA members, more than half in France. Among the latter were several leading activists of the organisation: Isuntza, Urrusolo and Nervios.[20]

Despite police successes, ETA maintained a remarkable capacity of recovery and reaction. ETA strategy became increasingly indiscriminate. This was evidenced by the selection of six low-level town councillors of the conservative government party Partido Popular (PP) as easy targets. There was a resurgence in ETA activities following the election of Aznar as conservative Prime Minister of Spain. The offensive had two aims. First, to force the Government to transfer the more than 500 ETA prisoners to prisons in the Basque Country.[21] The second aim was to push the Government to the negotiating table. In the pursuit of these aims, all means were valid. In July 1997, days after ETA released a young businessman, Cosme Delclaux, after 232 days as a hostage, the Spanish police freed a kidnapped prison worker, Ortega Lara. He had been held for 532 days in deplorable conditions. His kidnappers had decided to let him die by starvation if the Government continued to refuse to transfer prisoners. Television images of an emaciated Ortega Lara were reminiscent of the victims freed from Auschwitz and Birkenau. They produced a more profound effect against ETA, even among its followers, than years of anti-terrorism communiqués.[22]

One week later, however, ETA kidnapped a 29-year-old PP Town Councillor in the Basque town of Ermua. Miguel Angel Blanco, son of a Galician working-class family, was better known as the bass-player of a local pop group than as a politician. ETA announced Blanco would be 'executed' within 48 hours unless there was an immediate transfer of all ETA prisoners to the Basque Country. Even if willing, the Government would have found this task impossible given the time constraints. As a result, the kidnapping took on the character of a televised death penalty. Despite the mobilisation of millions of Basques and Spaniards, and pleas from international mediators, and even some HB politicians and ETA prisoners, Blanco was killed a few minutes after the expiration of the ultimatum.[23]

The subordination of political reasoning to the dynamics of military activism also affected Herri Batasuna.[24] After a long process of internal discussion and after the rejection of two alternative documents, rank-and-file members of HB endorsed the Oldartzen Report in 1996. Drafted by the coalition's collective leadership, it was to be the party's political and strategic programme. The document criticised the Spanish and French states for their pursuit of 'the disappearance' (Article 81) of the Basques as a nation, and criticised all parties, organisations and institutions which collaborated in this aim. Although the authors recognised HB's 'false dependence on the activity of ETA', no attempt was made to break this dependence or articulate a more critical attitude towards violence. On the contrary, there was no doubt about the legitimacy of the ETA violence:

> As long as the Spanish and French states, besides violating the collective rights of *Euskal Herria* and the personal rights of its inhabitants, deny the possibility of a solution of the so called 'Basque problem' by democratic means, it will be legitimate for *Euskal Herria* to defend its sovereignty using all forms of struggle: the institutional one as well as the struggle in the street and the struggle of a political character developed by ETA and IK [*Iparretarrak*: armed organisation acting in the French Basque territory], that is, the armed struggle.

Furthermore, the enormously destructive street violence committed by gangs of young radicals received acknowledgement in the Oldartzen Report, which referred to it as 'expressions of the political struggle of our people'. Far from establishing a possible link between the uncritical support of violence on the one side and the increasing loss of political representativeness in the Basque society on the other, Oldartzen pointed to the opposite conclusion: it was necessary to abandon the strategy of resistance and move to a new offensive phase, 'theorizing and practising whatever allows us to accelerate the political process right now'.[25]

If political statements were ambiguous, the statistics for street violence were not. During the 1990s, the incidence of street violence increased sharply. It can be regarded as a reaction to the loss of influence by ETA/HB, and the successful mobilisation of the Peace Movement. The street violence took the form of well organised gangs, mostly made up of teenagers, which burned and destroyed hundreds of telephone boxes, banks, public buses and trains, private cars of politicians and offices and bars of the political parties. During 1996, the material damage caused by these acts of sabotage was calculated at more than 3500 million Pesetas (US$24.31 million). This was an increase of 125 per cent over the year before. The increase was largely due to the growing trend towards arson attacks. While general street violence increased by 20.4 per cent in the 1995 to 1996 period, arson attacks increased by 60 per cent.[26] Between 1992, when this type of violence began, and 1997, more than 500 youths were arrested by the police, and 100 sent to prison.[27]

According to media reports, the street violence was orchestrated by Txelis, an imprisoned ETA leader who played a key role in the development of this strategy following the capture of the organisation's Central Committee in 1992.[28] Ever since, ETA, KAS and HB supported the street violence.[29] Yet, the political aim of the street violence, if any existed, was lost on the Basque population. A May 1997 public opinion poll found that 83 per cent of the population in the Basque Autonomous Community thought that the street violence would not help to achieve the political aims of those responsible. Only 9 per cent thought that it would. Even among HB voters, 47 per cent gave a negative answer to the question.[30] If the street violence has had any effect, it has probably been the increasing ghettoisation of the Basque National Liberation Movement and the growing identification of radical nationalism with the burning of buses, banks, cars and even town halls. This growing identification of violent nationalism with criminality generated a boomerang effect against all those calling for a dialogued solution for the conflict.

The HB leadership repeatedly demonstrated its subordination to ETA and its absolute lack of political autonomy. This made it more vulnerable to juridical action. The results came soon: in December 1997, the Supreme Court sentenced 23 members of the HB Directing Council to seven years in prison for 'collaboration with an armed gang'; and in July of the following year, *Egin*, the daily paper close to HB, its radio station and a number of HB-allied enterprises were closed down after a magistrate linked these organisations to ETA's financial network.

The imprisonment of HB's Governing Council forced the coalition to elect a new Council in February 1998 and replace its imprisoned Members of Parliament. The new directing Mahai Nazionala (National Table) seemed to be more willing to draw conclusions from the political decay of the BNLM and to recover some of the lost political space through more flexible political discourse and strategies. The new tendency was also a reaction against the emergence of the Basque peace movement which, during the 1990s, proved to have a surprising capacity for mobilisation in Basque society. The business sector, which was keen to stop the damaging effects of violence and to ensure a peace dividend, also played a role in the emergence of the peace process. The relationship between violence, the economy and peace in the Basque Country, however, is much more complex than one might expect.

Violence and the economy

Until the 1970s, the Basque provinces occupied leading positions in most Spanish socio-economic indices. Certainly this was reflected in indices on growth rates, per-capita income and earnings or rates of professional occupation. Bizkaia, Gipuzkoa and parts of Catalonia were the first territories to industrialise at the end of the nineteenth century.

The second 'industrial revolution' of the 1960s and first half of the 1970s pushed Alava and Navarra, the Basque 'later-comers', into a similar position to their neighbours on the seaside, converting the Basque region into one of the most modern and dynamic centres of the Spanish economy.

Since the 1990s, economic prospects have become more optimistic. This privileged situation has changed dramatically since the end of the 1970s. The growing liberalisation of the Spanish economy, strong international competition, the technological backwardness of Basque factories and the oil crisis pushed the Basque economy into recession. Many traditional iron, steel and shipbuilding plants were closed down or restructured. About 180 000 jobs were lost in the three provinces of the Basque Autonomous Community. Unemployment reached a peak of 23 per cent of the working population. Indicators of wealth and income in the Basque Country declined in comparison with Spain. Terrorist violence was both a by-product and an active promoter of this acute crisis.[31]

Nevertheless, it is impossible to measure precisely the impact of violence on socio-economic decline in the Basque Country. On the one hand, the kidnapping and killing of businessmen and 'revolutionary taxes' levied on employers had an obvious negative impact on the economy. On the other, these factors are relative. In recent years, violence persisted and even increased alongside a vigorous renaissance of the Basque economy. Between 1985 and 1995, per-capita income in the three provinces of Alava, Gipuzkoa and Bizkaia grew by 39 per cent, about 5 per cent above the Spanish average (see Table 4.3).[32]

Euskadi even recovered its attraction for foreign investment. During the 1990s, the Basque provinces, which – not counting Navarre – make up 1.43 per cent of total Spanish territory, increased their share of

Table 4.3 Per capita income: Basque Autonomous Community, 1955–93 (Spanish average: 100)

Year	*PCI*
1955	170.89
1985	107.54
1987	107.06
1989	107.13
1991	110.1
1993	109.09

Source: *Cambio*, 16 (27 October 1997), p. 12.

Table 4.4 Rates of unemployment in the Basque Autonomous Community (end of 1997)

Province	*Unemployment*
Alava	15.5
Gipuzkoa	17.0
Bizkaia	23.4
BAC Average	20.2

Source: *El País* (17 January 1998).

inward investment to Spain from 1.01 per cent in 1991 to 7.12 per cent in first semester of 1997. Moreover, according to Basque University research, an increasing proportion of this inward investment is in the high-tech sector.[33]

Gross Domestic Product (GDP) rates confirm the Basque economic resurgence. In 1996, Basque GDP increased by 2.0 per cent. A year later, it doubled to 3.8 per cent, against the Spanish rate of 3.3 per cent and the European average of 2.5 per cent.[34]

As in the Spanish and most other European economies, economic growth in the Basque Country only slightly reduced unemployment. This peaked in 1994 at more than 25.0 per cent of the working population. At the end of 1997, the figure was 20.2 per cent, although there were remarkable inter-provincial differences (see Table 4.4). The regional peak was 27.0 per cent in the traditional industrial areas on the left bank of the river Nervión.[35]

Youth unemployment was particularly high. According to the nationalist Eusko Langileen Alkartasuna (ELA) trade union, 43.4 per cent of the Basque working population aged less than 25 years was unemployed. The European average rate was 12.5 per cent.[36]

There is no reliable sociological data on the relationship between youth unemployment and violence, especially street violence. A cause–effect relationship is unlikely, since most of the youngsters engaged in the radical nationalist street gangs had not yet entered the labour market. Nor is there any evidence of a correlation between unemployment rates and the incidence of sabotage in the different Basque areas. Street violence reached its peak in Gipuzkoa, the most nationalist province, rather than Bizkaia which recorded the highest population and unemployment rate (see Table 4.5).[37]

An end to street violence and politically motivated violence in general is likely to produce an immediate peace dividend. Basque society has

Table 4.5 Local distribution of street violence, 1992–4 (percentages)

	Population	*1992*	*1993*	*1994*
Gipuzkoa	25.8	43	55	54
Bizkaia	44.5	36	23	27
Alava	9.9	11	8	6
Navarra	19.8	10	14	13
Total	100	100	100	100

Source: Gobierno Vasco (ed.), 'Plan de Actuación del Gobierno para el desarrollo de los valores democráticos y fomento de actitudes de solidaridad, tolerancia y responsabilidad en los adolescentes y jóvenes vascos', ms., Vitoria (1997), p. 16.

had to finance massive repair bills following gang violence as well as increased security measures. Tourism suffers from the Basque Country's violent image. In 1997 the British Foreign and Commonwealth Office advised tourists against visiting the Basque Country for security reasons. After protests by the Basque Government the advice was later withdrawn.[38] A report on foreign investment blamed terrorism as the 'principal culprit' for the reluctance of foreign businesses to invest in a region with a good infrastructure and a skilled workforce.[39]

Nevertheless, spokespersons for the Basque community, a sector most affected by violence, maintain a realistic attitude. The president and the general secretary of the Employer's Association of Gipuzkoa addressed the relationship between violence and industrial investment in the Basque Country:

> Talking about investment in the Basque Country and elsewhere in Europe – and I am thinking especially about foreign investment and in general about enterprises of a certain dimension – before deciding about the placement of their capital, they check all the conditions like infrastructure, the skilfulness of the people, the industrial culture, the market and its foreseeable perspectives of growth, public subsidies, tax system ... I don't think that a great amount of investment is being diverted only because of terrorism. What is happening is that when all the other factors are weak, logically terrorism will be more important. On the other hand, if those factors are strong and favourable, at the end investment will come despite terrorism, and there are some examples to prove that.[40]

The facts seem to corroborate this impression. Basque fiscal autonomy is influential in producing a remarkable pull-effect towards Spanish and foreign capital autonomy. This capacity of financial self-management, legitimised for historical reasons and granted by the 1978 Constitution, is an absolute exception in the Spanish fiscal system and provides the Basque administration with an important instrument for the public regulation of the regional economy. According to *El País* in September 1996, at least seven multinational companies expressed an interest in investing in the Basque Autonomous Community.[41] Lower taxes in the Basque Country and public subsidies attract capital from surrounding regions, provoking protests from neighbouring regional governments. Between July and August 1996, 23 cases of capital-transfer to one of the Basque provinces were counted.[42]

To summarise, an end to violence would bring important dividends to Basque society, especially its economy. Nevertheless, Basques have learned to live with violence and to recover little by little their traditional economic strength despite continuing violence. This seems to imply a paradoxical conclusion with regards to the peace process: the peace dividend is important, but not important enough to generate stronger pressure from the Basque business community towards policy-makers to accelerate the peace process. This passivity was criticised by the Basque peace movement Elkarri who, based on a report on 'Peace and the Economy in Northern Ireland', urged Basque businesses to take a more active part in the promotion of a dialogued solution to the Basque conflict.[43] In the preliminary stages of the Basque peace process, this active part was not played by the business community, but by the peace movement itself.

Mobilisation for peace

The growing contradiction between the consolidation of parliamentary democracy, with a remarkable level of self-government, on the one hand, and increasing political violence, on the other, provoked public protests against ETA violence in the first half of the 1980s. These protests, by Basque pacifists, were isolated and marginal. Although the new political system did not fulfil the expectations of many moderate nationalists, it did provide some instruments for the articulation of discontent and the formulation of new claims. As already indicated above, autonomy marked the watershed in the separation between radical and moderate nationalism. It crystallised the separation between those nationalists who backed violence and those who did not. An early symbol of this shift in relations was the first mass demonstration against violence organised by the PNV in 1978. About 35 000 Basques demonstrated in Bilbao for a 'Basque Country in Peace and Freedom'.

This demonstration, however, was only a first timid step. In reality, over the following years, the attitude of PNV leaders towards ETA violence was not as clear as the demonstration implied. After many years of critical solidarity, it was not easy to break totally with ETA. There were two main reasons. First, many nationalists were still convinced that ETA had the same political objectives as the PNV. Secondly, terrorism was helpful as an additional pressure in negotiations with the central government. It is unrealistic to blame the PNV for the persistence of ETA violence, but the fact remained that the political parties were either unwilling or unable to find a solution to the problem. This was the context for the genesis of the Basque peace movement during the 1980s.

The first attempt to co-ordinate the different groups and initiatives came in 1989 with the foundation of the Coordinadora Gesto por la Paz de Euskal Herria (Co-ordination for a Gesture for Peace in the Basque Country). Gesto is now one of the most dynamic and representative organisations in the peace movement. It has been very successful among Basque youth. It has 160 local groups integrated in the Coordinadora, of which 40 are linked to schools or universities.[44] The name of the group refers to its decision to hold silent protest demonstrations after every fatal act of political violence. From May 1988 to February 1998, Gesto has organised 15 760 silent protest meetings at 150 points across the Basque Country.[45] A key aim is to carry the rejection of violence from the street to every-day life. The increasing success of the popular mobilisations promoted by Gesto provoked the reaction of the Liberation Movement which, afraid of losing control of the streets, started to organise simultaneous counter-demonstrations. Tensions led to the intervention of the Basque police, which would form a *cordon sanitaire* between opposing protesters.[46]

The core of Gesto por la Paz's ideology is the total rejection of violence for political aims. It is a discourse based on ethics, in which any kind of violence is condemned. Thus, the task of Gesto is of consciousness-raising to undermine the (ethical) basis of political violence in Basque society. This does not mean that the political implications of violence are denied, but, according to one Gesto veteran, 'our task does not consist of presenting concrete political solutions to the problem'.[47] In general terms, Gesto backs dialogue with ETA, and considers some kind of secret contacts necessary before the proclamation of a ceasefire.

Gesto por la Paz draws support from voters of nearly all the Basque political parties, except HB and PP. It has suffered from splits in recent years. They include Bakea Orain (Peace Now) and Denon Artean (Among All of Us), but none has matched Gesto's capacity for mobilisation.[48]

The origins of the other mass-mobilising peace group, Elkarri (One to the Other/Mutually), can be found in the Basque National Liberation Movement. Elkarri was founded in 1992, the same year that the leadership structure of ETA was dismantled. A single-issue ecologist organisation was transformed into a peace group with the principal aim of contributing to the establishment of a new political climate favourable to a negotiated solution to the conflict. At first, the group was regarded as the result of a new strategy by ETA and HB, aimed at breaking the cohesion of the democratic parties in their attitude towards ETA. This initial scepticism was fuelled by the fact that Jonan Fernández, one of the most popular Elkarri leaders, had been a HB town councillor in Tolosa (Gipuzkoa).

In recent years, however, this image of the group has changed. First, Elkarri's criticisms of ETA violence have made it a target of severe ETA and HB disapproval. Second, the Elkarri leadership has endeavoured to make linkages with all sectors of Basque society. As a result, most political observers see Elkarri in a positive light. This capacity for bridge- building between the extremes is unusual in a highly polarised society such as the Basque Country.

In comparison to Gesto, Elkarri, with a full-time staff of 13 and about 2500 members, considers politics, not ethics, the principal arena for its activity: 'Its main purpose is to promote a process of democratic dialogue in *Euskal Herria* for the transformation of conflict through social mediation'.[49] It is impossible to separate ethics from politics in the analysis of the Basque conflict.

In recent years, Elkarri has carried out a broad range of activities, including the collection of signatures, workshops with policy-makers, publications and the creation of educational materials for schools and public demonstrations. The culmination of the group's work so far has been the peace proposal, Izan (To Be), presented in November 1997. It anticipated some of the basic ideas of President Ardanza's March 1998 peace proposal.

The openly political character of Elkarri carries a double risk. First, much of its work depends on the support of the political parties. Second, and linked to the first point, this makes the group vulnerable to criticism from those reluctant to accept the intervention of organisations without an electoral mandate.

Besides Gesto, Bakea Orain, Denon Artean and Elkarri, the spectrum of the Basque peace and human rights movement is completed by other minor groups, some of which form part of the Liberation Movement, such as Senideak (relatives of the ETA prisoners and refugees) or Gestoras Pro Amnistia (organisation demanding a total amnesty for all ETA prisoners). Elkarri promoted a round-table debate between all these groups which in the Maroño Agreement (January 1994) called to 'substitute all expressions of violence for mechanisms of dialogue as the best route to peace'.[50] Subsequent attempts to introduce a more political dimension into the agreement by discussing the roots of the conflict and possible solutions (self-determination) broke the fragile union of the peace groups.[51]

The Basque peace movement raised consciousness on issues of violence. There is a new sensitivity towards violence. The level of legitimacy for the armed struggle has decreased, even among Basques close to the Liberation Movement. According to a 1997 public opinion survey, 84.1 per cent of youth in the most nationalist Basque province, Gipuzkoa, considers itself 'opposed to the violence of armed groups'.[52] Youth, traditionally more given to radical nationalism, seems to have most attachment to the new sensibility. According to sociologist J. Elzo, 'the young people have been ETA's source of supply, in the future they are going to be the organisation's gravediggers'.[53]

This new critical sensibility concerning ETA violence has also been present in the streets. The massive demonstrations during summer 1997 in response to the kidnapping of Ortega Lara and the assassination of councillor Blanco mobilised approximately six million Basques and Spaniards. In November of that year, nearly 5 out of every 10 Basques (47 per cent) said that they had participated in one or more of the demonstrations organised to protest against ETA. The so-called 'spirit of Ermua' has been interpreted as a grass-roots call to stop violence and endorse unity against terrorism. Nevertheless, the increasing rejection of violence does not close the door on a way out of the conflict based on dialogue. The total of those backing contacts with ETA, with or without a ceasefire, numbered 65 per cent in autumn 1997 (43 per cent with a ceasefire; 22 per cent without). Only 22 per cent of the Basque population reject any contact with ETA.

The pre-ceasefire situation in the Basque Country was characterised by a new dualism of a tougher rejection of ETA and all forms of violence on one side, and an increased support for dialogue as a way out of the conflict on the other. Like all social movements, the peace movement in the Basque Country has been (and still is) both a product of this process of (ideological and mental) transformation of society, as well as an actor intervening in and promoting it. The work of Elkarri, Gesto and the other groups contributed to a new context in which, unlike a few years ago, proposals endorsing dialogues as solutions to the conflict could no longer be considered wishful thinking by pacifist Utopians. The effect of the social mobilisation for peace was not limited to the streets. It also affected the political parties.

The political parties: Old polemics, new alignments

One explanation of the continuity of ETA violence and its social support after the establishment of Basque autonomy in 1979 may be the lack of a common strategy by the democratic parties, nationalist and non-nationalist, in their opposition to ETA. The major clash was between those who emphasised the political nature of the problem and those who interpreted the conflict in exclusively terrorist and criminal terms. For parties like the leading PNV, Euskadiko Ezkerra (EE) or later EA, one of the major obstacles on the way to peace was the central government's policy of blocking the full implementation of the Statute of Gernika. This argument was converted by the statewide socialist and conservative parties into a crude, polemical attack against the nationalists, who were blamed for the persistence of terrorism. The nationalists were said to have no interest in an end to violence since there would be few political benefits for them.

It took some years for the parties to realise that the only beneficiary from party political polemics was ETA. Policy-makers became aware of the growing gap between society, which was mobilising for peace, and a political system immersed in never-ending polemics. Hence, it was society and the brutality of terrorism which pushed politicians towards an agreement. Following a particularly bloody period of ETA violence, in which 32 people were killed in two bombings in the last trimester of 1987, all of the political parties in the Basque parliament, except HB, reached an agreement. The Basque president Ardanza initiated the 'Agreement for the Pacification and Normalization of Euskadi' or 'Pact of Ajuria Enea' on the 12 January 1988.

The Agreement contained three fundamental statements. First was the common rejection of all attempts to reach political aims by violent means. Second was a reaffirmation of the nexus between the full development of autonomy and the subsequent 'progressive resolution of the conflicts of the Basque society' as a contribution to the 'reinforcement of democracy and peaceful coexistence'. Third was an offer of a solution to the conflict based on dialogue 'if the proper conditions for a negotiated solution of violence are given, consisting of a clear will to put an end to violence'.[54]

In the ten years of its existence, President Ardanza chaired 32 formal meetings of the Pact's members. The Agreement's main achievement was its contribution in strengthening anti-violence sensitivity in Basque society. It created a new cleavage separating those who backed the use of violence for political purposes from those who rejected the idea. This rift cut across the historical divide between Basque and Spanish identities. Despite the party-political polemics, there was no longer any base for criticising any of the parties of the *Ajuria Enea* block for an ambiguous attitude towards violence. This was also a consequence of the fact that, during the 1990s, all of the parties, including the nationalists, became ETA targets.

The Agreement had one major deficit: it was used as a defensive instrument in the struggle against terrorism, but it failed to facilitate advances towards peace. ETA and radical nationalism have always rejected the Agreement as a badly disguised instrument 'in the strategy against the independence movement'.[55] According to this view, instead of being a real agreement for 'the pacification and normalization' of Euskadi as the title suggests, the pact has functioned as a mere anti-terrorism pact. Yet, in contrast, ETA's increasingly indiscriminate military activity and the increasing 'militarisation' of HB's political discourse could not be interpreted as an invitation to open dialogue.

It was the recognition of this deficit that pushed President Ardanza towards a more active position in the policy of pacification. In March 1998, after both secret and public contacts with the parties represented in the Basque and Spanish parliaments, and with President Aznar's conservative central government, Ardanza's peace proposal was leaked to the press.[56] The document was significant as the first serious and concrete peace proposal presented by mainstream nationalism since the beginning of the violence in the Basque Country.

The central objective of the proposal was to ask two questions. First, what can be done to ensure that ETA stops using violence and HB starts 'integrating itself definitively into the political activity characteristic of the democratic system'? Second, how can a broader political consensus in Basque society be created? A basic premise of the proposal was a recognition that the double aim would not be possible exclusively through police action. Therefore, some kind of 'political incentive' together with a complete and unlimited ceasefire was

Table 4.6 President Ardanza's peace proposal

Conditions	– unlimited ceasefire – dialogue as consequence of the ceasefire, and not vice versa
Interlocutors	– no direct participation of ETA – ETA must delegate to HB as legitimate representative of a sector of the Basque people – rest of the Basque parties – Spanish state (via Basque parties with state-wide representation) – competent agencies of the state: disposition to accept and to implement the agreements reached by the parties
Contents	– issue: 'national question' – fixed timetable – no previous (political) conditions and limitations – after a period of testing: referendum
Procedure	– 'talks before talks' between the Basque democratic parties, central government, opposition parties in the Spanish parliament, ETA (secret contacts) and HB – information on public opinion – continuous advice concerning the possibilities of consensus embedded in the Constitution and the Statute of Autonomy

Source: 'Para un acuerdo entre los Partidos de la Mesa sobre el "final dialogado"; Documento de trabajo', ms., Vitoria-Gasteiz (17 March 1998).

necessary. Table 4.6 summarises the main features of the peace proposal.[57]

Although the Northern Ireland peace process was not referred to directly, Ardanza's 16 pages of text reflect parallels between both cases. In fact, the PNV followed the Northern Ireland peace process very closely and Ardanza admitted that he and his advisers have had contacts with practically all the important actors involved in that process.[58] He incorporated several of its core ideas into his own proposals, although they were adapted to suit the Basque case: the exclusion of a direct participation of armed groups in the negotiations; the prior establishment of a peaceful atmosphere (ceasefire) as an indispensable precondition for the participation of parties linked to armed groups; the commitment of all participants in the negotiations to abide by any agreement reached; the fixed time-frame; and the referendum. The idea of exploring the juridical possibilities of political reform granted by the Constitution itself, especially by its 'First Additional Disposition' and its recognition of the 'historic rights' of the Basque provinces, was not new either: a few months before Ardanza's proposal was published, Elkarri presented its Izan/To Be document.

Political reactions to the President's proposal were mixed. The socialists and governing conservatives rejected the proposal as a political concession to ETA terrorism. These parties received the support of 300 hard-line anti-nationalist Basque intellectuals and artists, who in February 1998 constituted the 'Forum of Ermua'. This was a pressure group, well represented in the media, and opposed to any political incentives given to a 'fascist movement ... directed by ETA, HB and other organizations from their environment'.[59] The democratic nationalists backed Ardanza's plan, however, while HB criticised its own exclusion from the drafting of the document rather than the contents. In a political climate characterised by a growing confrontation between the parties just a few months before regional elections to the Basque parliament, there was no opportunity for a real debate of this first serious peace proposal: elections are bad times for good politics.

For moderate nationalists, the rejection of Ardanza's peace proposal by the non-nationalist parties had a deeper political significance. It revealed the unwillingness of the socialists and the conservatives to explore what Ardanza called the 'second phase' of the Ajuria Enea Agreement: to examine the possibilities for a 'negotiated solution' to the conflict. In other words: for the PNV and EA, the attitude of Partido Sociaista de Euskadi (PSE) and PP had fatally injured the 'Pact of the Democrats'. The prospects of a peace process were slim without the support of the two main Spanish parties and almost half of Basque voters. For a qualitative change in the Basque conflict, a shift in the political and strategic outlook of the Liberation Movement was necessary. The idea of the 'third space' helped to bring this shift about.

Constructing the 'third space'

The contemporary history of Basque nationalism is a history of a polarisation between nationalist and non-nationalist identities. Contrary to the experience of other ethnic movements on the Spanish periphery (for example, Catalan), in the Basque Country none of the political projects created to mediate between the opposite poles (Nationalist Republicanism 1910–13; Acción Nacionalista Vasca during the Second Republic; Euskadiko Ezkerra during Post-Francoism) was successful. After the events of the summer of 1997 (the release of ETA hostage Ortega Lara; the kidnapping and killing of councillor Blanco; the massive and spontaneous anti-ETA rallies) the wall that separated both political blocks was higher than ever. The only possibility of breaking the stalemate was in making the frontier between the two blocks less insurmountable and in promoting an exchange of ideas that might contribute to the de-escalation of the conflict.

This was the basic reasoning behind the idea of the 'third space' (also called the 'third way'). Attempts to define the concept are rare. It is probably more than mere coincidence that references to the 'third way' surfaced in Basque political discussion at more or less the same time as Tony Blair, Anthony Giddens and others began their search for a way out of the crisis of international social democracy. In the Basque Country, the idea of the 'third space' was neither a product of the social democratic crisis, nor was it conceived as an instrument to bridge the gap between the nationalist and the non-nationalist communities. It was imagined as a political and social area of encounter between all those in favour of Basque self-determination by peaceful and democratic means. It was a meeting point for Basques dissatisfied with the bipolarisation of society into two blocks.

Behind these basic ideas there was no concrete and tangible programme attached to the concept of the 'third space'. It was this (calculated?) ambiguity which made it so attractive to many Basques inside or close to the Liberation Movement. A second factor increased the attraction: the promoters of the 'third space' were nearly all linked to civil society and social movements, and not to the political system. This reinforces the argument that the dynamic of the Basque peace process started from the bottom of society and later impacted on the top. The principal agencies engaged in the 'third space' project were the majority Basque, moderate nationalist and leftist trade union ELA, the HB-allied union Langile Abertzaleen Batzordeak (LAB), the Basque farmers union, Euskal Herriko Nekazarien Elkartea (EHNE), the peace movement Elkarri and a number of politicians and intellectuals, some related to the extreme leftist group Zutik which was close to the aims of the Liberation Movement, but critical of its military bias.

The origin of the 'third space' project was an *entente* between the Basque nationalist unions ELA and LAB.[60] Previously, there had been a growing disagreement between ELA and its traditional partners, the socialist Unión General de Trabajadores (UGT) and the leftist Comisiones Obreras (CCOO), due to what ELA considered an extreme subordination of these unions to the directives of their mother-organisations in Madrid. Since neither UGT nor CCOO were willing to defend what ELA-leader José Elorrieta called a 'Basque framework of industrial relations', for the moderate unionists the only way of working in favour of this aim was breaking the traditional alliance with those 'Spanish' unions and constructing a new one together with the only nationalist union remaining, even if that organisation – LAB – was a part of the Liberation Movement commanded by ETA. This process of emphasising the more political, that is nationalist, dimension of the union's discourse led in 1993 to the breaking of the ELA–UGT–CCOO alliance and ELA's *rapprochement* with LAB, which became public in the first common manifestos issued by both organisations on the 'Day of the Basque Fatherland' (Aberri Eguna, Easter Sunday) and then on 1 May 1995.

This new alliance was a risky gamble for José Elorrieta, ELA's General Secretary. For many of the union's 80 000 members the reasons for this strategic change were incomprehensible. Why should a democratic and moderate union like ELA form an alliance with a worker's organisation which had been blamed for being a strong supporter of ETA? This unrest became open rebellion when ETA started its campaign against the Ertzantza, the Basque police. This campaign caused fatalities among ELA members (Gómez Elósegui, Olaciregui, Doral, Goikoetxea, Zabalza, Agirre). Since LAB was unwilling to change its traditional non-criticism of ETA, even the killing of members of its new nationalist partner, Elorrieta was under strong internal (and external) pressure to put to end the alliance with LAB.[61] After the killing of another ELA-member, prison psychologist Gómez Elósegui, in March 1997, the General Secretary admitted that 'the relationship between ELA and LAB has been seriously affected'.[62]

The 'spirit of Ermua' and the growing popular rebellion against ETA violence froze, but didn't bury, the idea of the 'third space'. In October, the conflict between the Basque and Spanish governments on the implementation of the social part of the Statute of Autonomy, especially the transfer of the national employment agency, sparked a revival of the project. While the Basque conservatives and socialists were preparing to celebrate the eighteenth anniversary of the Statute of Autonomy, Elorrieta announced a public meeting in Gernika, the historic symbol of Basque freedom, as ELA's contribution to the festivities. In previous media statements, he declared the 'death' of the Basque Statute of Autonomy and the necessity of exploring 'a new framework of self-government'.[63]

On the 18 October, 3000 nationalists turned up at the meeting organised by ELA which was supported by LAB, the farmer's union EHNE, the social democrat nationalist party EA, the philonationalist wing of the leftist Izquierda Unida (IU) (Ekaitza), HB, and Elkarri. Several PNV leaders were also present. This meeting was the public baptism of the 'third space' and Elorrieta's speech its *Magna Carta*. It was, in the words of a leftist commentator, the 'presentation ceremony of Basque sovereignism, its first public act'.[64] The ELA leader's message was threefold. First was his already mentioned diagnosis of the death of Basque autonomy, 'killed by the centralists'. Second was a message about the means of the struggle for Basque sovereignty. Days before the Gernika meeting, ETA had killed another Basque policeman who was also a member of ELA:

> ELA is completely conscious that the way towards a new self-government won't lead us anywhere unless it is democratic; unless it is peaceful, we shall never ever get the majorities and the social support we need. In consequence, ETA has to know that there is no place for it, that we don't need it, that it is an obstacle on this way to the future. The power of our reason, the support for our project, the dreams of our people, – all these are sufficient weapons to help us win. Other weapons are not necessary, they only obstruct.

After explaining the *why* (death of autonomy) and *how* (democratic and pacific means), Elorrieta defined the *who* or the social agency of his project. It was the 'majority' of all Basque citizens 'who accept that the sovereignty, the right to decide our future as a people, concerns the Basque citizens'.[65] Elorrieta's proposal to create a new nationalist, democratic and pacifist majority in favour of Basque sovereignty had an important impact on the media and the political parties. The presence of high-ranking PNV and EA members seemed to symbolise the notion of a new political and social majority beyond the traditional lines of conflict. As a consequence, the reaction of the Basque conservatives and socialists was more directed against the democratic nationalist parties and their collaboration with HB than against Elorrieta's proposals. This was understandable for two reasons. First, despite the events of the summer and speculation on possible changes within HB and the Liberation Movement, ETA had not changed its violent strategy. Second, the political instinct of conservative and socialist leaders made them aware of the possibility of a future realignment in the Basque political system. This would be motivated by discontent within moderate nationalism over traditional policies towards terrorism, and the growing desire for peace within the Basque Country.

The 'third space' was also becoming a political idea with remarkable attraction for various important sectors of Basque society. Much of this attraction lay in the ambiguity of the idea. The 'third space' was not a political programme which aimed towards the construction of a new, alternative society. It was an idea based on a number of fundamental principles (solution of the conflict through dialogue, self-determination and no violence) with three immediate political objectives: first, the creation of 'spaces of de-escalating tension'[66] – in order to contribute to the de-escalation of violent confrontation; second, the breaking of the stalemate between the 'democrats' and the 'people of violence'; and third, the design of a hypothetical new majority for the promotion of Basque sovereignty as a realistic alternative to the armed struggle. Only a sufficiently fuzzy and ambiguous concept like the 'third space' was capable of generating this majority. It was a formula for the internal use of Basque nationalism and not Basque society. Even critical commentators recognised the potential of the idea: 'It has to be fairly admitted that Elorrieta's third space is becoming configured as the only political factor that can really move ETA'.[67]

ETA paramilitaries understood the message behind the 'third space' and its potential consequences. The answer came in December 1997, when the Spanish Supreme Court sentenced 23 members of the Directing Council of HB to seven years in prison. In response to what HB considered a 'political sentence dictated by the government and signed by the judges', the party called for a general strike on the 15 December.[68] It was foreseeable that in a political climate characterised by a growing rebellion against ETA terror a general strike could not be expected to obtain remarkable levels of solidarity outside the Liberation Movement. In the philosophy of the 'third space', the general strike was considered as a step backwards, since it would consolidate the existing frontiers. Guided by this conviction, the leaders of the two nationalist unions made an alternative call for a 'national demonstration' under the slogan *Konponbidea, demokrazia osoa* (The solution is full democracy). They invited HB to cancel the general strike and to support the initiative of the unions, *Elkarri*, EHNE and others. This call was heeded by HB. The same day, ETA shot and injured a PP councillor's bodyguard in San Sebastián. The new initiative of the 'third space', however, survived the tense situation. *Egin* called the unitary act of protest an 'historical milestone' that had become possible thanks to the 'political astuteness demonstrated by HB'.[69] The demonstration marked a major step towards receiving the same broad political and social backing obtained by ELA in Gernika, even if the PNV expressed its decision not to 'share banner and street with ... those who practise aggression, insult and imposition'.[70]

Three days before the demonstration, ETA killed another PP councillor (J. J. Caso Cortines) in Renteria. Since neither HB nor LAB was willing to criticise ETA, it was impossible for ELA to maintain the call for the unitary demonstration. The situation was even more complicated for LAB. On the one hand, its leader, Rafa Díez, was reluctant to abandon the still new idea of a 'third space' and its vital axis LAB–ELA. On the other hand, LAB was still a part of the Liberation Movement and as such was obliged to respect the Movement's inner hierarchy with ETA at its top. The confused reaction of the radical nationalists reflected the nervousness of an organisation struggling for greater autonomy from the military direction of the Liberation Movement without upsetting the 'armed vanguard'. Following the shooting of Caso, LAB, but not HB, signed a communiqué calling for the demonstration to be cancelled. It did, however, fail to directly criticise ETA. On the same day these communiqués were published, LAB issued another one backing the call of the HB leadership to maintain – even without the other organisations – the demonstration, which later was banned by the Department of the Interior of the Basque Government.[71]

ETA was alert to the almost invisible shifts within the radical nationalist universe. The paramilitaries were aware that, for the first time, ETA's function was being questioned within the Liberation Movement. An ETA communiqué one week after the killing of Caso seemed to re-affirm the organisation's self-appointed position as supreme judge in the national liberation struggle. Apart from the habitual railing against PP politicians and their 'war for the destruction of Euskal Herria as a nation', the text criticised those organisations associated with the 'third space', including LAB. LAB's decision to cancel the demonstration was blamed on a 'wrong and partial humanitarian ethic'. They were said to have committed a 'political error' which was a result of their 'lack of maturity'.[72]

This was a serious blow for LAB. ETA had never delivered such an open and direct warning to an organisation which considered itself part of the Liberation Movement. Ordinarily, this would have spelt the end of the 'third space' notion and the attempt to re-align pro-nationalist politics. But when HB finally held its demonstration the party's new spokesman, Arnaldo Otegi, declared that 'here in the Basque Country there are no third ways'. 'Here, there are only two projects: the Spanish one and that of Euskal Herria'. Joseba Permach, another new HB spokesman, was more explicit. He stated that 'there is no third way, but there is a third *space*'. But what was this 'third space' for HB and LAB? For LAB-leader Rafa Díez, it was a space of 'social, trade-unionist and cultural sectors that are betting on a Basque national project and moving away from autonomous statutism which has become an important pillar of the "shared project" defended by Mayor Oreja [the Spanish Minister of the Interior]'.[73]

Behind the etymological exercise of contrasting two ambiguous concepts lay the equally confusing reality confronting the Liberation Movement. While the idea of exploring new ways into the future had growing support, links with the past were strong enough to prevent an open challenge to ETA's leadership role. ELA commentators interpreted Caso's shooting as an attempt to 'short-circuit the increasing protagonism of the third space, because ETA does not control a socio-political movement that, in the end, ... can politically harm violence a lot more than the antiterrorist discourse of the PP does'.[74] In order to recover complete control, it was necessary to establish the antagonism of the two *ways*.

Two conclusions might be drawn out of the confusing reaction of the Liberation Movement to the 'third space' idea. First, ETA seemed to have difficulty supporting initiatives towards a Basque peace process, if pushed by organisations not under paramilitary control. Second, the contradiction between armed struggle and mass movement had become so evident that it could no longer be silenced inside the Liberation Movement. Despite the ambiguity, partial failures and scarce political dividend, the idea of the 'third space' had become a rolling stone which ETA was unable to stop before it affected the Basque National Liberation Movement.

From Gernika to Lizarra, via Stormont: the final countdown

The three place names Gernika, Lizarra and Stormont represent milestones in an almost year-long journey which led to the ETA ceasefire on 16 September 1998. The period between Elorrieta's 'third space' Gernika demonstration in October 1997 and the announcement of ETA's first indefinite and unilateral ceasefire can be considered as a preparatory phase in the Basque peace process. It was a 'talks before talks' phase, in which a number of crucial decisions was taken in order to ensure the silence of the paramilitary weapons. Gernika symbolised the increasing influence of the idea that there might be other, political and (maybe) more effective ways towards Basque self-determination than armed struggle. It also symbolised that the armed struggle had become a serious obstacle to self-determination. Lizarra represented the importance of nationalist realignment as a first step towards de-escalating tension and peace; it was the Basque version of the Hume–Adams *entente*, which kick-started the Northern Ireland peace process and led to the Stormont Agreement. In fact, Stormont became a very powerful example for Basque nationalism, especially for the Liberation Movement. It is difficult to imagine the Basque peace process without the domino effect of the Northern Irish model.[75] In an *Irish Times* interview, HB's new leader, Arnaldo Otegi, confessed that

> Ireland was a mirror for us, and so was the republican movement. Negotiation was always regarded here in the Basque Country as something suspect. But Sinn Féin [SF] and the republican movement showed us that negotiation did not have to lead to political treachery. If it could happen in Ireland, why not in the Basque Country?[76]

This Irish connection of Basque nationalism provides an example of the growing interrelationship between social movements in a globalised world.[77]

Gernika, Lizarra and Stormont shaped a new situation in the Basque Country, in which for the first time since the genesis of violent nationalism in the early 1960s there was a tangible perspective for peace. The main reason for this was a major shift in the 'contextual structure' of Basque society in the 1990s.[78] As a consequence, traditional forms of politics became increasingly questioned and a new political scenario became possible. Factors contributing to the shift included: the emergence of a mass peace movement which extended to the fringes of radical nationalism; the divergence between the growing militarisation of the Basque National Liberation Movement and the eagerness for peace in broader society; the increasing pressure by police and judges on terrorism and its political 'accomplices'; the contradiction between the military strategy and the political possibilities offered within the framework of political, cultural and economic autonomy; the negative consequences of terrorism for the regional economy; the impossibility of designing a common initiative of peace shared by all (nationalist and non-nationalist) parties of the Ajuria Enea Pact ten years after its constitution; the radical and unconditional rejection of Ardanza's peace proposal by socialists and conservatives; and finally, the tempting attraction of the 'third space' project.

ETA and the Liberation Movement were unable to protect themselves against the new contextual structure. The Ermua mobilisations of the summer of 1997 were a catalyst for a timid process of internal debate on the relationship between armed struggle and politics. Evidence of this came in the form of criticism of ETA by José Luis Alvarez Santa Cristina (better known as Txelis), the former head of the political branch of ETA and one of the principal 'inventors' of the street-guerrilla. French police captured him, with the rest of the ETA leadership, in 1992. Influenced by the Ermua mobilisations, and a growing debate on future radical nationalists strategies, in the columns of *Egin*, Txelis circulated his 'Abertzaleon estrategiaz' (About our strategy as patriots) manuscript from his French prison cell in August 1997. It was signed by two other well-known ETA prisoners (Kepa Pikabea and Roxario Pikabea). The significance of the document was owing to the formerly hard-line attitude of the author. He had been regarded as ETA's principal ideologist. His analysis was guided by a will to overcome the problems of the Basque struggle by defining new ways of achieving the Liberation Movement's aims.[79]

Txelis did not question the philosophical base of ETA's activity, defending 'the right of any people to defend itself with arms against the State that is attacking it with arms'. But his analysis of the functionality of the armed struggle concluded that within the particular context of the Basque Country, Spain and Europe at the end of the twentieth century, the armed struggle – once a valid means of defending the interests of a nation – had become an obstacle on the way towards national sovereignty. In his words, violence was producing a 'boomerang effect' for the defenders of the Basque nation. The State's ability to survive the challenge of the armed struggle, and to transform its effects into the opposite of what its promoters intended, led the imprisoned ETA-leader to call for an 'unlimited, broad and lasting moment of de-escalating tension' and for the unity of all Basque patriots.

A new ETA killing in December 1997 led to greater internal and public criticism. HB could no longer silence increasing unrest within the Liberation Movement. Pressure for a strategic reorientation had become too strong and the party was urged to respond to the cumulative effects of popular discredit, police successes and judicial vigour. The first step towards a gradual abandonment of the Oldartzen strategy and a re-evaluation of the efficacy of militarism was announced by Rufi Etxeberria, a leading member of HB's Directing Council, on the Basque public radio station Euskadi Irratia in October 1997. Etxeberria declared the 'beginning of a new phase', in which HB would push forward politics of 'national construction'. After the imprisonment of Etxeberria and the rest of the HB-leadership, a new and more heterogeneous and moderate Mahai Nazionala was elected. Arnaldo Otegi, a former ETA prisoner, and since December 1997 spokesman of the new Directing Council, became the public face of the new wind blowing through HB and the Basque National Liberation Movement.

This shift in the political wing of radical nationalism would not have been possible without the consent of the paramilitaries. Although inside information on the situation within ETA in late 1997 is scarce, there seemed to be a nervousness about increasingly successful police action against the organisation. The ETA leadership was no longer safe in France and was forced to establish a 'new centre of operations' in Belgium.[80] Changes occurred within HB and its new Directing Council after an internal electoral process in February 1998. Political observers referred to a more flexible 'political waist' in the new HB leadership. Words and deeds evidenced this 'political waist'. In public appearances, Otegi and Permach again distinguished between the political project represented by HB and ETA's armed struggle. In contradiction to the traditional concept of ETA as the vanguard of the struggle, Otegi admitted 'the majority of the Basques do not share the armed struggle of ETA'. Both Otegi and Permach stated that HB did not give 'political coverage' to the 'street struggle' of the urban guerrilla.[81]

Alongside HB's efforts to stress its autonomy from ETA's militarism, HB leaders also re-assessed their attitudes towards the other nationalist parties. Perceptions of these parties changed from lackeys of the Spanish oppressors to potential allies in a new project leading towards Basque sovereignty. The Northern Irish peace process provided radical Basque nationalism with an idea, which facilitated the start of the peace process, the idea of a pan-nationalist agreement as first step towards the achievement of a solution through dialogue to the conflict. In other words, since the beginning of 1998, HB endeavoured to create the conditions in which a Basque John Hume and Gerry Adams could emerge. If this was the case, somebody would necessarily have to play the part of a Spanish Tony Blair.

The Irish mirror has been present in the history of Basque nationalism since its very beginnings.[82] With radical Basque nationalism in crisis, mass mobilisations against ETA, police successes against the paramilitary organisation, and the alternative of the 'third space' penetrating the Liberation Movement, it was not surprising that ETA and HB looked to the Irish example. With Tony Blair's election in May 1997, the Northern Ireland peace process developed rapidly. There is no precise information about ETA–IRA or HB–SF contacts, but formal and informal meetings have taken place. Certainly, the example of a nationalist movement reaching by peaceful means aims not reached by violent struggle had an immense influence on Basque radical nationalism.

In 1997 and early 1998, however, the lack of synchronism between events in Northern Ireland and Euskadi seemed total. On 20 July, one week after PP councillor Blanco was assassinated by ETA, the IRA restored its ceasefire in response to changes brought about by the Blair administration. One week after the beginning of multi-party negotiations in Northern Ireland which included Sinn Féin (7 October 1997), ETA killed a Basque policeman in front of the new Guggenheim Museum, thus aborting the planned 'third space' demonstration. Two days after Gerry Adams's first visit to Downing Street (10 December 1997), ETA shot another PP councillor dead. As Adams was being received by the first British Prime Minister since the creation of Northern Ireland, his 23 political allies in the HB leadership had just started their seven-year sentence for collaboration with terrorism. In the three months following the Good Friday Agreement (10 April 1998), ETA killed another three people.

Even during violent periods, the message from Ireland reached the Basque Country. From late 1997, it affected general political debate as well as radical nationalism. In April 1998, parallels between the Irish and the Basque cases were again evident. Two days after the Stormont Agreement was reached, Basque nationalists of all colours celebrated their supreme national festivity, Aberri Eguna, with the Northern Ireland peace process centre stage.[83] The non-nationalist parties rejected any parallelism between the Basque and Northern Irish cases. Carlos Iturgaiz, the leader of the Basque PP, put it this way:

> The situation is not comparable. In the counties of Ulster an agreement has been produced between two communities confronted one with the other, whereas here there is a fanatic minority, ETA and HB, that tries to impose by force and coercion its authority on a democratic and peaceful majority. HB and ETA have always tried to Ulsterize the Basque Country and to show a conflict between two parts which simply does not exist here.[84]

The socialists agreed with this argument and pointed to the high level of self-government already reached by Basques in contrast with the lack of autonomy in Northern Ireland. Their reaction, however, was not as categorical as that of the conservatives. This political debate was accompanied by a debate in the media. Few opinion-makers in the Spanish and Basque daily papers could resist the temptation of discussing the hypothetical lessons from the Northern Irish case.[85]

An 'Ulsterisation' of the main conflicting discourses in the preliminary phase of the Basque peace process is identifiable. The influence, however, was not only symbolic and theoretical. It also translated into concrete political practice by those who were keen to draw conclusions from abroad: the radical nationalists of HB and ETA. Their basic instinct of political survival also played a part. The bitter experience of the winter of 1997, when the Spanish Supreme Court jailed 23 HB leaders for seven years without a major reaction from those sectors of Basque society not directly involved in the Liberation Movement, accelerated the strategic reconversion of HB from intransigent militarism to compromise-oriented policy-making. Thus, in the Basque case, the initiative on the construction of a cross-nationalist axis was not taken by moderate majority nationalism, but by the radical minority wing. The Basque SDLP, that is – *mutatis mutandis* – the governing PNV, was not able to play the initial and active part in this initiative, since the party was still the most important part of the 'Democratic Bloc' built around the Ajuria Enea Agreement that, as a consequence of the Ermua mobilisations, excluded the possibility of any common initiative with those who supported violence. Furthermore, the recrudescence of terrorism in December 1997 and early 1998, as well as the absence of visible signs of a more critical attitude by HB leaders towards ETA violence, would have been poor politics by any party willing to initiate talks with HB. It was then the Basque Sinn Féin, Herri Batasuna, which made the first step. This had two parts. In February 1998, immediately after HB's new Directing Council was elected, the party's spokesmen re-issued an idea proposed in September 1997 by the previous Mahai Nazionala which invited all political parties, labour unions and other social movements to participate in a so-called 'Ireland Forum'. The purpose was to discuss the Northern Irish peace process and its application to the Basque conflict.[86] At the same time, Otegi and the new HB leaders asked the PNV for secret political talks to identify possible points of consensus with a view to establishing a broad national agreement that might serve as a framework for a future ETA ceasefire. The PNV, mindful of changes within ETA and increasingly distant from the non-nationalist parties of the Democratic Bloc, was more positive to the idea of talks with HB than in 1997. This tendency towards new approaches was encouraged by the rejection of President Ardanza's peace proposal in March 1998. But even before this point a first secret meeting between HB and PNV had been held on 26 February.[87]

PNV and HB met 12 times in the next seven months. Both parties decided to 'armour' the talks against external, violent interference. The PNV became the target of tremendous political and media pressure when news of these talks reached the media.

In fact, for the PNV the political cost of the talks increased daily and Joseba Egibar, the party's spokesman, admitted that his defence of the talks was jeopardising his political future.[88] But the PNV persevered, especially after its negotiators learned that those supporting a ceasefire and a revaluation of politics within ETA were becoming a majority.[89] Fruit of this was a parliamentary *entente* between the PNV, HB, EA and IU which was more symbolic than practical.[90] The new *entente* with a party backing terrorism prompted the Basque socialists to quit the regional government.

While HB, PNV, EA and IU were trying to build the Basque version of the Hume–Adams axis, the Good Friday Agreement was reached in Northern Ireland. Basque nationalists drew two conclusions from an analysis of the Good Friday Agreement. First, the strategy of inter-nationalist co-operation was the correct one on the way to peace. Second, after the consolidation of the HB–PNV axis it was necessary to reach a broadening of the consensus if a Basque Stormont was to be reached. The reaction of both ETA and HB was immediate: according to the Argentine daily paper *La Nación*, representatives of ETA had met IRA leaders in Montevideo to get direct information on the Stormont Agreement.[91] The IRA emphasis on politics increased pressure on ETA, since, as the *Irish Times* put it, 'the IRA ceasefire deprived it of a sense of having brothers in arms elsewhere in Europe'.[92] At the same time, HB, after attending the Sinn Féin Conference, recovered an idea already presented months ago, announcing the constitution of the 'Ireland Forum'.[93] The first meeting of the Forum took place on 20 June, with the participation of all nationalist parties, IU, the two nationalist unions, the farmers' union, the peace movement Elkarri and a number of smaller organisations close to nationalist thinking. The idea of the 'third space' and of the 'new majority' had reappeared, pushed by the Irish example. As on previous occasions, ETA was unwilling to leave this new initiative in the hands of the political, social and cultural organisations assembled in the Forum. Only a few days after the Forum's constitution, a bomb killed a PP councillor in Renteria who, a few months earlier, had substituted for a colleague shot dead by ETA.

However, this new incident, which had generated internal protests within HB, was an accident. The internal debate of the paramilitaries was about to conclude and the decision to declare a ceasefire seemed to be immediate. This conclusion had yet to be transmitted to the commandos in the underground.[94] This process of transmission took place in July and the absence of a violent reaction to the closure of *Egin*, on the orders of the Spanish Supreme Court, indicated significant changes within ETA.

An ETA ceasefire was being operationalised and HB's more flexible approach received the backing of the paramilitaries.[95] A means had to be found through which the ceasefire could be interpreted as a fundamental contribution to a future political victory rather than a surrender. The 'Ireland Forum' performed this function. The 23 members of the Forum reached the 'Lizarra Agreement' four days before ETA's ceasefire announcement. The Forum's sole objective was to reach a consensus on a draft which reflected the previous work of the Forum. In reality, there was little chance of making major changes to the draft presented by the representatives of HB and PNV Iruin and Egibar. The reason was that ETA did not know the literal text of the draft but its general outline, on which it had agreed. Since no peace process and no resolution of the Basque conflict was supposed to work without the co-operation and consent of the paramilitaries, it seemed politically inconvenient to risk this consensus by accepting major changes to the text.[96] The final document, with a first part completely dedicated to the Northern Irish peace process, was new evidence of the deep influence of Northern Ireland on Basque, and especially nationalist, politics.[97]

The declaration based on the Irish experience picks up some of the principles of Ardanza's peace proposal, such as the definition of the conflict as a political conflict, the open and unconditional agenda of the negotiations, the consideration of the Basque people as the sovereign decision-taking subject or the demand to the implicated states to accept the outcome of the negotiation process. There were, however, three remarkable differences. The first was semantic but had an acute political meaning. For Ardanza, an ETA ceasefire prior to political dialogue was an 'absolute necessity'. In the Lizarra document, ETA was not mentioned, but it was envisaged that negotiations would be carried out in the 'permanent absence of all expressions of violence'. While this was a euphemism for an ETA ceasefire, it could also be applied to 'state [that is, police] violence'. The second difference was the explicit exclusion of negotiations with ETA in the Ardanza document, against negotiations 'without excluding any of the implicated parties', in the Lizarra Agreement. This would include ETA. The participation of the paramilitaries was, however, conditional because, according to the Lizarra document, the final word rested with the 'citizens of Euskal Herria'. Finally, the third difference lay in the Lizarra document's specification of the core issues of the future negotiation process: the 'territoriality', meaning the separation of the seven (French and Spanish) Basque territories by political and administrative borders; the recognition of the Basque people as the subject of decision-making; and, finally, the acknowledgement of the Basque people's right to 'political sovereignty'. The last was another euphemism not necessarily meaning independence, since a 'sovereign' decision could also be that of a Basque republic within an Iberian federation or even that of maintaining the current *status quo*. The differences resulted from the different objectives of the two texts. Ardanza's proposal was that of a (nationalist) president trying to establish the highest possible level of consensus among nationalists and non-nationalists. The Lizarra Agreement, on the contrary, was a document written predominantly, but not exclusively, by and for nationalists (including ETA) with the implicit aim of smoothing the way to a ceasefire. It was a political manifesto in the mould of a Basque Hume–Adams document directed towards public opinion. In reality it was addressed to the local paramilitaries. It was not an institutional declaration which had to take Basque Trimble, Paisley or their Spanish allies into account.

Political reactions to the Lizarra Declaration were predictable. On the one hand, the polarisation of Basque politics into nationalist and non-nationalist blocs was again evident. Little seemed to have changed since the debate on Ardanza's peace proposal. The Spanish government and Basque conservatives blamed the PNV, EA and IU for 'breaking the consensus of the democrats' by burying the Ajuria Enea Agreement. They also criticised the 'indulgence' of ETA and radical nationalism. The socialists, anxious about the possibility of losing their non-nationalist voters to the conservatives in the imminent regional elections, used the same arguments as the PP leaders and President Aznar. In this view, the agreement was a capitulation to ETA. One Irish commentator regarded the reactions as a consequence of the impression that in the Basque Country 'democratic nationalists are being seduced by ETA, whereas ... the SDLP won over Sinn Féin to democracy in Ireland'.[98] Of the rejectionists, only the socialists of the most nationalist Basque province, Gipuzkoa, were moderate in their criticism. They asked their Madrid-based leadership and their Basque general secretary Redondo not 'to close all the doors' to the process initiated in Lizarra.[99]

On the other hand, the signatories to Lizarra championed agreement as a first step on the way to peace. The initiative also received the official support from the Basque government, which, after the withdrawal of the socialists, only consisted of the nationalist PNV and EA. The government also issued a call to ETA to lay down its arms and take notice of what the majority of the Basque people was demanding.[100]

When Mari Carmen Garmendia, spokeswoman of the Basque government, issued this statement, she probably knew that the call to ETA was superfluous, since the paramilitaries had already made their decision. On 17 September *Euskadi Información*, successor to the closed daily paper *Egin*, and *Egunkaria*, the daily paper written exclusively in Basque, published the text of a communiqué in which ETA announced its first ever complete and indefinite ceasefire.[101] The communiqué, issued four days after the Lizarra Agreement, did not actually mention the Agreement, yet Lizarra is implicit throughout the text. The first sentence reads: 'After two long decades, now there is once again an open possibility for *Euskal Herria* to take a decisive step on the way towards independence.' ETA's answer to the new scenario was a ceasefire. The character of the truce, however, would depend on 'events and the steps'.

In Gernika, the union leader José Elorrieta spoke on the idea of the 'third space' and a 'new – peaceful – majority' backing Basque sovereignty. HB and ETA were 'ripe' to enter mainstream politics, but they wanted an 'honourable way' to do so. The PNV 'threw [them] a lifeline',[102] accepting the idea of a pan-nationalist *entente* as the instrument that would kick-start the peace process and as a first key to the resolution of the conflict. The inter-nationalist party talks, the Ireland Forum and finally the Lizarra Declaration specified the proposal of a cross-party nationalist agreement. Stormont was the proof that this strategy was possible. ETA's communiqué fitted perfectly into this inter-nationalist operation, since its message was addressed especially to the nationalist community and not, as usual on previous occasions, to the Spanish government or the 'centralist' parties. On 16 September, the Basque Humes and Adams, seizing the opportunities created by a new political and social framework in which the pressure in favour of an end of violence had become stronger than ever before, reached their first success: for the first time since the beginning of the violent ethnic conflict in the Basque Country, the conditions for a negotiated solution of the problem were present. Will Lizarra lead to a Basque Good Friday Agreement? The future will provide the answer to this question. For the moment, the Basque–Irish parallels continue: in the regional elections to the Basque Parliament on 25 October, the voters rewarded radical nationalism for its new strategic image and its contribution to the achievement of the ceasefire. Herri Batasuna, rebaptised as Euskal Herritarrok, received a substantial peace dividend with 17.94 per cent of votes. It became the third-largest party in the Basque Autonomous Community behind the PNV (27.97 per cent) and the PP (20.14 per cent), followed by the PSE–EE (17.57 per cent). The party won 57 000 new voters in comparison with the regional elections of 1994 and the total of 223 264 votes was the best result ever obtained by HB.[103]

Notes

1 A certain exception might be the case of Corsica, where, however, neither the nationalist movement nor the impact of the violent conflict have reached a similar extent to that of the Basque Country.

2 For the origins of Basque nationalism, its evolution and historical context, see: Javier Corcuera, *Orígenes, ideología y organización del nacionalismo vasco (1876–1904)* (Madrid: Siglo XXI, 1979); Ludger Mees, *Nacionalismo vasco, movimiento obrero y cuestión social* (Bilbao: Fundación Sabino Arana, 1992); Ludger Mees, *Entre nación y clase: El nacionalismo vasco y su base social en perspectiva comparada* (Bilbao: Fundación Sabino Arana, 1991); José Luis de la Granja, *Nacionalismo y II República en el País Vasco* (Madrid: Siglo XXI, 1986); Juan Linz, 'Early State-Building and Late Peripheral Nationalisms against the State: the Case of Spain', in S. N. Eisenstadt and S. Rokkan (eds), *Building States and Nations: Analysis by Region* (Beverly Hills: Sage, 1973), vol. 2, pp. 32–116; Cyrys Ernesto Zirakzadeh, *A Rebellious People: Basques, Protests and Politics* (Reno: University of Nevada Press, 1991); Daniele Conversi, *The Basques, the Catalans and Spain* (London: Hurst, 1997); Marianne Heiberg, *The Making of the Basque Nation* (Cambridge: Cambridge University Press, 1989).

3 'Y es que la violencia es una acción, o estado o situación, que se genera siempre, y se cualifica de manera exclusiva, en el seno de un conflicto.' See Julio Aróstegui, 'Violencia, sociedad y política: la definición de la violencia', *Ayer*, 13 (1994), pp. 17–55 (29).

4 H. L. Nieburg, *Political Violence: the Behavioral Process* (New York: St. Martin's Press, 1969).

5 See Charles Tilly's classic *From Mobilization to Revolution* (New York: Addison-Wesley, 1978), specially Chapter 6: 'Collective Violence', pp. 172–88.

6 Aróstegui, 'Violencia', p. 32.

7 Ekkart Zimmermann, *Political Violence, Crises, and Revolutions: Theories and Research* (Boston, MA: G. K. Hall, 1983), p. 346. A good overview on the complex theoretical debate about the concept of 'terrorism' is provided in Alex P. Schmid, *Political Terrorism: a Research Guide to Concepts, Theories, Data Bases and Literature* (Amsterdam: North Holland, 1983). See the author's complex definition of terrorism on p. 111.

8 Two months before his death, Franco persevered with the execution of five political prisoners (including two ETA activists) despite widespread international protests.

9 Richard Gunther, Hans-Jürgen Puhle and P. Nikiforos Diamandouros, 'Introduction', in, Gunther, Puhle and Diamandouros (eds), *The Politics of Democratic Consolidation: Southern Europe in Comparative Perspective* (Baltimore/ London: Johns Hopkins University Press, 1995), pp. 1–32 (4). For the Spanish *transition* see also Richard Gunther, Giacomo Sani, and Goldie Shabad, *Spain after Franco: the Making of a Competitive Party System* (Berkeley: University of California Press, 1986); Donald Share, *The Making of Spanish Democracy* (New York: Praeger, 1986).

10 'Thus, within this one region... democratic politics and institutions were not consolidated at that time' (Gunther, Puhle and Diamandouros, 'Introduction', p. 11.

11 Politically, these were crucial years: 1978: Referendum on the Constitution; 1979: Referendum on the Basque Autonomy Statute and second elections to the Spanish Parliament; and 1980: first elections to the regional Basque Parliament.

12 Statistics in Florencio Domínguez Iribarren, *ETA: Estrategia, organización y actuaciones 1978–1992* (Bilbao: Universidad del País Vasco, 1998), pp. 220–3. The first fatality among ETA victims, frequently forgotten in the figures, was a young girl injured by a bomb placed in the train station of San Sebastián in June 1960. Normally it is the *Guardia Civil* José Pardines, shot dead in 1969, who is considered the first 'official' fatality.

13 On the construction of the Basque regional autonomy, see the basic analysis of Javier Corcuera, *Política y derecho: La construcción de la autonomía vasca* (Madrid: Centro de Estudios Constitutionales, 1991).

14 The three Basque regions within the French state (Lapurdi, Behenafarroa and Xuberoa) were not linked to the Basque Autonomous Community. Navarra, the fourth Basque province within the Spanish state, has constituted its own single-province Autonomous Community. The process of separation between Navarra and the other three provinces began during the Second Republic, when a small majority of the Navarrese town councils voted against the integration into the Basque autonomy, which after a long delay was finally established in October 1936, some months after the beginning of the Spanish Civil War. The position of ETA and radical nationalism towards regional autonomy is described with empathy by Francisco Letamendia (Pseud. 'Ortzi'), *Historia del nacionalismo vasco y de ETA*, 3 vols, especially vol. 2, pp. 221–493 (*ETA en la Transición*) (San Sebastián: R & B, 1994).

15 On the history of ETA, see: Jáurgegui Gurutz, *Ideología y estrategia de ETA 1959–1968* (Madrid: Siglo XXI, 1981); José María Garmendia, *Historia de ETA* (San Sebastián: Haranburu, 5th edn, 1995) (1st edn, 1979/80); Robert B. Clark, *The Basque Insurgents: ETA 1952–80* (Madison/London: University of Wisconsin Press, 1984); John Sullivan, *ETA and Basque Nationalism: The Fight for Euskadi 1890–1986* (London: Routledge, 1988); Pedro Ibarra, *La evolución estratégica de ETA: De la guerra revolucionaria (1963) a la negociación (1987)* (San Sebastián: Kriselu, 1989); Peter Waldmann, *Militanter Nationalismus im Baskenland* (Frankfurt: Vervuert, 1990); Peter Waldmann, *Ethnischer Radidkalismus: Ursachen und Folgen gewaltsamer Minderheitenkonflikte am Beispiel des Baskenlandes, Nordirlands und Quebecs* (Opladen: West deutscher Verlag, 1989).

16 For the dissolution of ETA-p.m. see Giovanni Giacopucci, *ETA-pm: el otro camino* (Tafalla: Txalaparta, 1997), and the memoirs of one of the politicians who personally participated in the negotiations, R. Castro, *Juan Maria Bandrés: Memorias para la paz* (Majadahonda: HMR, 1998).

17 Melchor Miralles and Ricardo Arques, *Amedo: el Estado contra ETA* (Barcelona: Plaza & James, 1989); Alvaro Baeza, *GAL, crimen de Estado* (Madrid: ABL, 1996); Sagrario Morán Blanco, *ETA entre España y Francia* (Madrid: Editorial Complutense, 1997).

18 The best study of the complex network of organisations and initiatives constituting the Liberation Movement with ETA at its core is José Manuel Mata, *El nacionalism vasco radical: Discurso, organización y expresiones* (Bilbao: Universidad del País Vasco, 1993).

19 This political decay has already attracted the attention of sociologists who have tried to explain it with data proceeding from biographical case-to-case studies. See Mikel Arriaga, *Y nosotros que éramos de HB: Sociología de una heterodoxia abertzale* (San Sebastián: Haranburu, 1997).
20 *El País* (27 December 1997).
21 The prisoners had been dispersed throughout Spain – often great distances from the Basque Country.
22 Belén Delgado Soto and Antonio José Mencía Gullón, *Diario de un secuestro: Ortega Lara, 532 días en un zulo* (Madrid: Alianza, 1998).
23 María Antonia Iglesias (ed.), *Ermua, 4 días de julio: 40 voces tras la muerte de Miguel Angel Blanco* (Madrid: El País-Aguilar, 1997).
24 Kepa Aulestia, *HB: Crónica de un delirio* (Madrid: Temas de Hoy, 1998).
25 'Oldartzen. Oinarrizko Txostena. Egoeraren azterketa eta ildo politikoa', manuscript (December 1994), pp. 197, 241, 212, 287, 283.
26 *El País* (9 December 1997).
27 *Egin* (30 December 1997).
28 *El País* (13 January 1997).
29 As an example, see the communiqués of ETA and KAS in *El País* (3 April 1997). The acronym KAS stands for *Koordinadora Abertzale Sozialista* (Patriotic Socialist Coordinating Council), which is a semi-legal organization created to coordinate the strategy of the political and the armed wings of the Movement. ETA-m is a full member of KAS, a fact that provides real decision-making authority to this Council.
30 Gobierno Vasco (Presidencia, Gabinete de Prospección) (ed.), 'Actitudes hacia la violencia en el País Vasco', ms. (Mayo 1997), p. 12.
31 As a briefing update of the most important dimensions of the crisis and a source for statistical data, see the article 'A pesar de ETA', *Cambio,* 16 (27 October 1997), and the chapter 'Repercusión social y económica del terrorismo', in Domínguez Iribarren, *ETA*, pp. 261–71.
32 *Cambio*, 16 (27 October 1997), p. 12.
33 Ibid. and *El País* (28 January 1998).
34 Information facilitated by the Basque Government's Minister of Economy, Francisco Egea, based on the data available for the first semester of 1997. See *El Diario Vasco* (17 December 1997).
35 *El País* (17 January 1998). The situation in the province of Navarre with an unemployment rate of 9.72 per cent was better. See *El País* (6 January 1998).
36 *Landeia*, 59 (enero 1998), p. 22.
37 Gobierno Vasco (ed.), 'Plan de Actuación del Gobierno para el desarrollo de los valores democráticos y fomento de actitudes de solidaridad, tolerancia y responsabilidad en los adolescentes y jóvenes vascos', ms., Vitoria (1997), p. 16.
38 *El Diario Vasco* (10 April 1997).
39 *El País* (28 January 1998).
40 Interview with J. M. Korta and J. M. Ruiz Urchegui (14 November 1997), tape document.
41 *El País-Negocios* (29 September 1996).
42 *El País* (23 September 1996).
43 The presentation of the report and the press-conference in *El Diario Vasco* (13 May 1997).

44 *El País* (20 July 1997).
45 *El País* (20 January 1998).
46 During the last few years there have been registered several cases of violent aggression against supporters of Gesto.
47 Interview with Xabier Azkazibar, Bilbao (9 June 1997), tape document.
48 More information about the organisational structure and the discourse of these peace groups can be found in Benjamín Tejerina, José Manuel Fernández Sobrado and Xabier Aierdi, *Sociedad civil, protesta y movimientos sociales en el País Vasco: Los límites de la teoría de la movilización de recursos*, ed. Gobierno Vasco (Vitoria: Gobierno Vasco, 1995), especially pp. 39–44, 83–9, 131–2.
49 'The Basque Conflict', ms. (report prepared by Elkarri, 1995) p. 26.
50 'Basque Conflict', p. 26. See also Bakea Orain, *De Arantzazu a Maroño, encuentros por la paz* (San Sebastián: Tercera Prensa, 1994).
51 See the statement of Bakea Orain in *El Diario Vasco* (19 July 1997). In September, a member of the same group talked about the 'recent dissolution of the Maroño groups'. See *El País* (29 September 1997).
52 *El Diario Vasco* (10 June 1997).
53 The data and Elzo's statement in *El País* (24 November 1997).
54 The text of the Agreement is reproduced in *El País* (13 January 1998).
55 See the editorial ('Diez años') in *Egin* (11 January 1998).
56 There have been rumours that the origin of this leak was the conservative Spanish Minister of the Interior or the Secret Services interested in aborting the initiative without giving it time to mature.
57 'Para un acuerdo entre los Partidos de la Mesa sobre el "final dialogado" Documento de trabajo', ms., Vitoria-Gasteiz (17 March 1998).
58 Information given in the context of a meeting with the members of the research project 'Coming out of Violence' (12 March 1998).
59 See the 'Manifesto for the Democracy in Euskadi' issued by the 'Forum of Ermua' the day of its foundation in February 1998, *El País* (14 February 1998).
60 For the history of the nationalist labour movement in the Basque Country, see Ludger Mees, 'Social Solidarity and National Identity in the Basque Country: the Case of the Nationalist Trade Union ELA–STV', in P. Pasture and J. Verberckmoes (eds), *Working-Class Internationalism and the Appeal of National Identity* (Oxford/New York: Berg, 1998), pp. 43–81.
61 There are no official figures, but it is known and admitted by Elorrieta himself that the unrest, especially of many Basque policemen members of the union, pushed quite an important number of *ertzainak* to quit the union.
62 See *El Diario Vasco* (18 March 1997).
63 *El Diario Vasco* (2 October 1997).
64 Javier Villanueva, 'Puesta de largo del soberanismo vasco', *HIKA*, 1997ko azaroa, p. 28.
65 The text of the conference in *HIKA*, 1997ko azaroa, pp. 22–3.
66 See, for instance, the interview with Elorrieta quoted above and the public conference given by Fernández in Tolosa, *El Diario Vasco* (18 December 1997).
67 See Alberto Surio's comment ('La foto borrosa') in *El Diario Vasco* (19 October 1997).

68 See the article 'España nos ha enseñado los dientes' with information about the press conference given by the HB leaders in *Egin* (2 December 1997).
69 'Hito histórico', *Egin* (6 December 1997).
70 See the communiqué of the PNV in *Egin* (11 December 1997).
71 All these communiqués can be found in *Egin* (13 December 1997).
72 The text of the communiqué, completely written in Basque, was published by *Egin* (19 December 1997).
73 'HB y LAB salvan al "tercer espacio" de sus críticas a la "tercera vía"' (Quotation in *El Diario Vasco* [30 December 1997]).
74 This opinion is quoted in *El Diario Vasco* (13 December 1997).
75 Daniele Conversi, 'Domino Effect or International Developments? The Influences of International Events and Political Ideologies on Catalan and Basque Nationalism', *West European Politics*, 16, 3 (July 1993), pp. 245–70.
76 'Basque leader sees peace process as way forward', *Irish Times* (31 October 1998).
77 Sydney Tarrow, *Power in Movement: Social Movements, Collective Action and Politics* (Cambridge: Cambridge University Press, 1994), p. 191.
78 For the concept of the 'contextual structure of society' which is a re-elaboration and modification of the more common concept of the 'political opportunity structure', see Dieter Rucht, *Modernisierung und neue soziale Bewegungen: Deutschland, Frankreich und USA im Vergleich* (Frankfurt: Campus Verlag, 1994), pp. 303–23.
79 José Luis Alvarez Santa Cristina, Kepa Pikabea Ugalde and Roxario Pikabea Ugalde, 'Abertzaleon estrategiaz', ms., 1997ko abuztua, pp. 2, 5.
80 *El País* (2 November 1998).
81 See the interviews in *El Diario Vasco* (2 February 1998) and *El País* (9 February 1998).
82 Alexander Ugalde Zubiri, *La acción exterior del nacionalismo vasco (1890–1939): Historia, pensamiento y relaciones internacionales* (Bilbao: Universidad del País Vasco, 1996); Xosé Manoel Núñez Seixas, 'El mito del nacionalismo irlandés y su influencia en los nacionalismos gallego, vasco y catalán (1880–1936)', *Spagna Contemporanea*, 2 (1992), pp. 25–58; Xosé Manoel Núñez Seixas, 'El espejo irlandés y los reflejos ibéricos', *Cuadernos de Alzate*, 18 (1998), pp. 169–90.
83 Garaikoetxea, leader of EA, criticised the 'lack of courage' that in Euskadi was impeding the negotiation; Arzallus praised Tony Blair, contrasting his example with the Spanish politicians who defended the 'military way' as the only means of fighting against ETA; HB's new leader Arnaldo Otegi confirmed that 'Euskadi is going to live the same process as Northern Ireland does'. See *El País*, *Egin* and *El Diario Vasco* (13 April 1998).
84 This statement of Iturgaiz and those of other leaders can be found in 'Los partidos vascos discrepan sobre la aplicación en Euskadi de la vía irlandesa', *El Diario Vasco* (12 April 1998).
85 Here are only four examples from the enormous bulk of press articles dedicated to this question: Imanol Zubero, 'Irlanda y País Vasco, odiosas comparaciones', *El País* (14 April 1998); Antonio Elorza, 'De Stormont a Euskadi', *El País* (17 April 1998); Miguel Herrero de Miñón, 'Método de Stormont' *El País* (18 April 1998); Manuel Castells, 'El Estado red', *El País* (20 April 1998).

86 *El Diario Vasco* (17 February 1998).
87 This, at least, is the date published later by *El País* (2 November 1998).
88 *El País* (20 September 1998).
89 *El País* (2 November 1998). The newspaper does not specify the names of the interlocutors, nor the exact date, nor the source of the information, which later was not denied by the PNV. By the end of April, ETA issued a communiqué requesting the PNV to break with its 'Spanish' allies, announcing 'profound changes' for the future of the Basque Country.
90 IU and EA had also held a number of previous separate meetings with HB.
91 Information published by *El Diario Vasco* (27 April 1998).
92 See the comments of Paddy Woodworth in 'Basques expect a new impetus to peace process', *Irish Times* (30 October 1998).
93 'HB propone un foro para extraer consecuencias del proceso irlandés', *El Diario Vasco* (23 April 1998).
94 Information published by *El País* (20 September and 2 November 1998).
95 At the beginning of September 1998, HB decided to participate in the regional elections to the Basque Parliament to be held in October under the name of *Euskal Herritarrok* (Basques Citizens). This new denomination was registered both to prevent a possible banning of HB and to open the new electoral coalition to sectors purged in previous phases or simply discontented with the extreme military bias of the HB politics.
96 Information according to 'Egibar e Iruin lo hicieron pasar a la ratificación del resto de los firmantes con la advertencia de que era innegociable e inmodificable', *El País* (5 October 1998).
97 Text in *El País* (13 September 1998).
98 See Paddy Woodworth, 'Spanish divided on Irish model as way forward', *Irish Times* (17 September 1998).
99 See the different declarations picked up by *El País* and *El Diario Vasco* (14/15 September 1998).
100 'El Gobierno vasco avala la declaración de Lizarra y reclama a ETA que deje de matar', *El País* (16 September 1998).
101 Text in *Euskadi Información* (17 September 1998).
102 Quotations from P. Woodworth, 'Basques expect a new impetus to peace process', *Irish Times* (30 October 1998).
103 Results in *El Diario Vasco* (26 October 1998).

5
Sri Lanka – the Intractability of Ethnic Conflict

Paikiasothy Saravanamuttu

Introduction

The protracted search for effective and durable groundrules for relations between the majority Sinhala ethnic community in Sri Lanka and the principal minority ethnic community the Tamils includes 15 years (at the date of writing) of armed hostilities between the predominantly Sinhala state and the main Tamil militant group the Liberation Tigers of Tamil Eelam (LTTE) or Tigers. The conflict has spilled over to affect also the position of another minority community, the Muslims.

Over the 15 years of armed hostilities there has been a series of grave human rights violations by both sides of the ethnic divide, the resort to terrorism and attrition as well as short-lived and arguably short-sighted attempts at negotiations. The search for a durable solution has invariably focused on constitutional reform for conflict resolution and, in this respect, the search for peace constitutes the definitive phase in Sri Lanka's tortuous nation- and state-building process, fifty years after formal decolonisation and the granting of independence.

Whilst the analysis of the evolution of the conflict in the last four years can be divided into subject headings, it is important to understand at the outset that there are certain factors that are common to all these issue areas. Together they make up the overarching set of factors that have militated against conflict resolution. In effect, they are the distinguishing features of the old paradigm that is wedded to the *status quo ante bellum*. Proponents of this paradigm will insist that nothing that has transpired in the last 15 years has demonstrated a case to the contrary. Rather it has confirmed their position. Critics will argue that the persistence of open armed hostilities and ethnic conflict is testimony enough to the need for a paradigm shift and new thinking on conflict resolution.

The resilience of the old paradigm ensures that there is a lengthy time lag between developments in the conflict and developments in the efforts to resolve it. As a consequence there is always the risk that tardiness in the latter allows for the former to render any progress, albeit marginal, insufficient and insubstantial. For example, the introduction of devolution entailed in the 1987 Indo-Sri Lanka Accord, an achievement in itself, has come to be seen by both the current government and the LTTE as inadequate, as too little too late. Consequently, conflict-resolution efforts have to recommence periodically the process of advocacy for constitutional arrangements that go beyond the devolution introduced by the Accord.

The old paradigm

Perceptions of discrimination

The old paradigm is distinguished by a number of features. Foremost amongst them is the pathology of insecurity of the two sides which has been characterised as a problem between a majority with a minority complex and a minority with a majority complex. Arising from this is the lack of comprehension of the ethnic nature of the conflict, the frequent denials of ethnicity at the heart of it and the ready definition of the conflict as primarily if not exclusively one of terrorism. Accordingly, the dominant view is that there can be no accommodation with terrorists or that, at the very least, a political settlement has to be preceded by the defeat of terrorism so as to disabuse any notion that terrorism does pay.

In this connection, it must be noted that there have been two armed insurgencies against the state from within the majority community, in 1971 and the 1987–9 period. Led by the Janata Vimukthi Peramuna (JVP) or Peoples Liberation Front, in both instances the insurgency was characterised as a terrorist challenge and crushed through counter-terror operations. Particularly in 1989, this entailed widespread killing and gross human rights violations. The characterisation of the LTTE as a terrorist organisation accordingly evokes a similar response and invites comparison with the defeat of the JVP insurgencies.

The extent to which the majority community too has a perception of grievance and insecurity is attested to by the establishment of a non-governmental Sinhala Commission in 1998 to inquire into the grievances of the majority community, 50 years after independence and after 15 years of armed hostilities in the ethnic conflict. The depth of this feeling must be measured against entrenched constitutional provisions relating to the unitary state and the granting of 'foremost-place' status to Buddhism, the religion of the majority, and, until the 1987 Accord, the institution of the Sinhala language as the official language of the country. This majority-community perception, with its espousal of the trinity of the land, the race and the faith, arises from perceptions of discrimination under colonial rule and the fear of being dwarfed in a region in which there are some 60 million Tamils in the South Indian state of Tamil Nadu and more in Southeast Asia. The Tamils have other options and other places to go in this perspective, whilst the Sinhalese have only Sri Lanka. Therefore, the Tamils and other minorities must accommodate to the Sinhalese and not vice versa.

Members of the Buddhist clergy or Sangha have been amongst the most forceful proponents of this perspective. Historically they have been at the forefront of the development of the Sinhala language and culture and, in the era of mass democratisation, have been drawn into politics as a legitimising force. Whilst their influence may not be as widespread now as it has been in the past, they nevertheless do retain a powerful hold on popular opinion as figures of authority and as community leaders. The close identification of the Sangha with the majority ethnic community has militated against the Sangha acting as a powerful peace constituency and one able to provide the moral impetus for conflict resolution through negotiation. The view held by leading members of the Sangha, that the conflict is about terrorism which has to be defeated as a basic prerequisite for any attempts at a political settlement, has also constrained the conflict-resolution process.

The 'minority complex' of the majority community with its perception of Tamil links to the rest of the world, has also given rise to suspicion amongst the Sinhalese of international interest and involvement in the conflict in Sri Lanka and its resolution. This is a suspicion that is nurtured by the existence of a Tamil diaspora in the West, which in turn came into being at the outset because of the official language policy in Sri Lanka and, subsequently, the armed ethnic conflict. The perception is of a prosperous diaspora which is funding Tamil secessionism and which is disproportionately influential in lobbying Western governments on behalf of the Tamil cause. Western media, NGO and government condemnation and expressions of concern, for instance, regarding human rights violations by the armed forces and the fate of refugees as a consequence of the conflict are attributed to the Tamil diaspora's superior ability at leverage in the service of Tamil nationalism.

This sentiment was clearly expressed in the attitude towards the meeting of the NGO Forum on Sri Lanka composed of European and

Sri Lankan NGOs in November 1995. The army was poised to take the northern capital of Jaffna and concern was being expressed as to a resulting refugee problem. There was a dispute with the government as to whether the Forum had been permitted to have its meeting in Sri Lanka. Furthermore, the meeting of the Forum was disrupted and the venue had to be changed more than once. Local activists who were well-known supporters of the ruling coalition were part of the Forum. They were beaten up by persons widely believed to be supporters of the government. The argument advanced was that the Forum would lobby to halt the government offensive by drawing attention to a potential refugee crisis. And this would only benefit the LTTE.

This perception of the Tamil diaspora extends to calls for the banning of the LTTE and the invariable conclusion that Western governments' reluctance to do so stems from the lobby power of the Tamil diaspora and/or from a vested and inimical interest in the territorial integrity and sovereignty of Sri Lanka.

The unitary state

Another factor associated with the trinity of the land, the race and the faith and one which has bedevilled all attempts at a political and constitutional settlement is the almost primordial attachment to the concept of the unitary state embodying majoritarian democracy. This is deeply embedded in the political culture to the extent that, in Sri Lankan politics, 'federalism' is a 'dirty word' and subversive idea. Irrespective of nation-building and the ethnic conflict, the state-building exercise and the challenge of governance has had to cope with this dominant feature of the political culture. The constitutional evolution has been such that there has been almost an axiomatic belief in the view that power and authority has to be concentrated at the centre or else national sovereignty will be adversely affected and the virility of the state impaired. The two autochthonous constitutions of 1972 and 1978 differed from the original Soulbury Constitution promulgated at the granting of independence, in terms of the degree to which the concentration and consolidation of power at the centre was effected. In Sri Lanka, the font of all power has moved from ethnic identity and party affiliation to the office of an executive president.

The aversion to pluralism and power-sharing is widespread. It is shared by the LTTE as indeed it was by the extra-parliamentary insurgency from within the majority Sinhala community, the JVP, in their two attempts at the armed seizure of the state. The LTTE brand of ultra-nationalism is exclusivist and indeed their political project of a separate state is predicated on the axiomatic assumption that there is no alternative to majoritarianism. In this perspective, the Sri Lankan state is acting as a Sinhala state, as indeed it would. Therefore, it will discriminate against the Tamils and Tamil rights can only be secured within a separate Tamil state.

Of course, the dignifying of the political project by recourse to the basic tenets and rhetoric of nationalism serves the legitimisation function. This should not obscure the assessment of the LTTE as a totalitarian group which has sought to realise its claim to be the sole legitimate representatives of the Tamil people through terror, assassination and the sustenance of a fear psychosis. Furthermore, the LTTE's forcible eviction of the Muslim population from Jaffna and treatment of that community are clear testimony that their ideology very easily extends to ethnic cleansing.

The majority community aversion to federalism and any meaningful power-sharing is reinforced by the politics of ethnicity. There is a perception among the Sinhala community that federalism is the mechanism by which the Tamils will secede and set up a separate state. This perception has been fed by the Tamil name of the Tamil political party, the Federal Party, formed in 1951 as a breakaway from the Tamil Congress over the issue of the disenfranchisement of the Tamil population of recent Indian origin who are based in the tea plantations.

The Tamil translation of Federal Party – Illankai Tamil Arasu Kachchi – contains the word 'Arasu' which also means 'state'. Sinhala nationalists contend therefore that the English nomenclature deliberately obscures the true political project whereas the Tamil one does not. (There is no separate word for federalism in the Sinhala language either.) Federalism is therefore to be avoided at all costs because it is sought as a precursor to secession. This view is unmoved by clarifications in parliament by Tamil politicians, by countervailing evidence of an armed ethnic conflict arising from the fact that governments have been unwilling and unable to share power and not the opposite, and by the entrenched constitutional provisions regarding the religion and language of the majority community.

More recently, the antipathy to federalism has been solidified by the unwillingness of the LTTE to spell out its proposals for a political settlement in the event of the recommencement of negotiations. At various times, the LTTE and spokespersons believed to represent their views have declared the Tigers' willingness to accept a federal solution, without elaborating what they understand by this. There have been a few occasions at which this elaboration has been forthcoming and it has confirmed opinion that the LTTE understanding of federalism is essentially confederalism – a political association between two autonomous and sovereign units. This lends credence to the argument that the LTTE is determined to acquire a separate state and all other statements are merely obfuscation of this basic secessionist goal. Moreover, since the concept of federalism is bandied about by the LTTE in this respect, federalism is thereby interpreted to be a stepping stone to secession, if not virtually synonymous with it.

All attempts at the devolution of power have in fact been a consequence of the ethnic conflict and been proposed as a way by which it could be ameliorated, if not resolved. Accordingly, the advocacy of every such proposal has been in terms of the ethnic conflict and not in terms of the importance of devolution and power-sharing in furthering empowerment of the people and democratic governance. Yet at the same time, based on the political calculation that if the majority is to agree to the devolution that the minority must have then the majority must have it too, devolution is extended over the entire country. Consequently, the absence of asymmetry compounds the acceptance of devolution by the minority and gives rise to arguments about the wastage of resources that the devolution exercise entails.

An argument associated with this and used increasingly frequently since the establishment of provincial councils following the 1987 Indo-Sri Lanka Accord is that devolution is far too costly an exercise which will also breed corruption. This in large part stems from the pervasive culture of patronage politics and from the persistence of the notion that real power is exercised from and at the centre – provincial politics is merely a way station to national politics. This is certainly confirmed by the meagre powers devolved to the provinces and an overarching balance of political and administrative power weighted heavily in favour of the centre. However, the dominant factor accounting for this perception is probably patronage politics.

The provision of perquisites and vehicles to provincial legislators by their respective party hierarchies in order to secure their political allegiance feeds the cynicism of the public. And this cynicism, when coupled with the suspicion of devolution as a means to resolve the ethnic conflict, is unmoved by any arguments about the economic costs of the war.

The role of the media

Any statement of the features making up the dominant paradigm militating against conflict resolution is incomplete without an account of the role of the media – in particular, the role of media in conflict resolution. There is no escaping the conclusion that the media will reflect the orthodoxy of views in society as well as alternative streams of opinion. Sri Lanka is no exception. What is clear, however, is the extent to which the media reflects the orthodoxy to the exclusion of alternative opinion with regard to the ethnic conflict. Consequently, it is a measure of the depth of ethnic differences and animosities more than it is a measure of the available common ground for conflict resolution.

Reportage of the war in the media, irrespective of whether it is the state-owned or private media, reflects popular prejudices about terrorism and ethnic grievance as well as common ethnic stereotypes. Furthermore, coverage falls well within the confines of the prevailing orthodoxy without any attempt to go out in pursuit of stories not incorporated into official accounts. There appears to be a willingness to cover the conflict from Colombo and to accept the version of events of the conflict released by the publicity organs of the principal protagonists. Independent accounts are rare. Indeed, as a result of the availability of BBC World Service Television, Sky and CNN news, the average Sri Lankan has a better idea of what war has done to Bosnia and Rwanda than of what it has done back at home in the Jaffna peninsula. The absence of this is a key factor in bringing together a critical mass of opinion that could constitute a peace constituency.

In defence of the media, the relationship that has evolved between it and the state must be mentioned. In the 17 years of effective one-party rule (1977–94) in which human rights abuses abounded and in which the crisis of democratic governance was brought to a head, the alternative media acted as a source of criticism of the regime. As a consequence, there was harassment of media institutions, and journalists were abducted and murdered. The fear of a return to this climate of fear and repression is sometimes cited as a sobering factor inhibiting the media from violating censorship regulations governing reportage of the war, for instance, or from abjuring self-censorship in the absence of such regulations. Whilst this may hold in certain cases, the extent to which the media is a repository of public prejudice and of stereotyping as far as the ethnic conflict is concerned should not be underestimated.

The immediate context

The change of regime following the August 1994 and November 1998 parliamentary and presidential elections held out the hope that a major breakthrough in conflict resolution would be effected as well as progress towards democratic governance. After 17 years of United National Party (UNP) rule, which had seen the steady erosion of democratic rights and freedoms together with the intensification of violent ethnic conflict and an armed challenge to the establishment from within the majority community in the form of the JVP insurgency (1987–9), the Peoples Alliance (PA) coalition of nine largely centre and centre-left parties, headed by the Sri Lanka Freedom Party (SLFP), was voted into office. In the presidential elections that followed in November, the UNP candidate Mr Gamini Dissanayake was assassinated by the LTTE and the leader of the PA, Chandrika Bandaranaike Kumaratunga, received an unprecedented 62 per cent of the vote.

Ms Kumaratunga received support from all sections of the population and there was a growing expectation that the direct negotiations with the LTTE that she had initiated as Prime Minister in October of 1994 would culminate in a political settlement to the ethnic conflict. This, however, was not to be. The negotiations yielded a Cessation of Hostilities Agreement which was announced on 8 January 1995. The Agreement was to be monitored by three committees which in turn were to be headed by representatives from Canada, Norway and the Netherlands. In addition to this agreement, in the effort to demonstrate benign intent and to build confidence, the Sri Lankan government agreed to lift a substantial number of the sanctions imposed against the north-east of the country where over a period of four years the LTTE had managed to establish a quasi-state under its rule.

The Cessation of Hostilities Agreement was never really put into effect and on 19 April 1995 the LTTE unilaterally resumed hostilities which continue to the time of writing. Talks between the government and the LTTE had been stalled for some time over the issue of fishing rights, the location of the Pooneryn army camp in the north and over the free movement of armed LTTE cadre in the east.

Between April 1995 and the present, the government has launched what it calls a War for Peace against the LTTE and in the conduct of that war captured three-quarters of the Jaffna peninsula, the stronghold of the Tigers. The war continues and is now focused on government attempts to open the main supply route between Colombo and the peninsula. During this war, the government also came out with an unprecedented devolution package to resolve the conflict. The package was submitted to a Parliamentary Select Committee on Constitutional Reform with a view to it being adopted as part of a new constitution promised by the PA at the 1994 hustings. The PA also promised that the new constitution would abolish the executive presidency and restore parliamentary democracy. The new constitution has yet to be adopted. Bipartisan support has not been forthcoming for the devolution package and, accordingly, the prospects for early conflict resolution have waned.

Violence and security

Whilst at one level if the conundrum of conflict resolution in Sri Lanka can be stated as the choice between the peace that can be had with the LTTE and the peace that can be had without them, 15 years of armed hostilities indicates that it is also a war that cannot be won on the battlefield. There is no alternative to a negotiated political settlement in a situation in which neither side seems able to achieve outright military victory. However, the utility of military force for both sides and the resort to violence cannot be discounted both in terms of their respective perceptions of this utility and its realisation in practice. Of course, the utility of violence and military force for each side differs. The persistent use of violence and military force, nonetheless, suggests that neither side has come to the point at which it feels that the utility of such instruments has been exhausted.

Following the LTTE's unilateral resumption of hostilities in April 1995 and early success in inflicting damage, the government of Sri Lanka felt that it had to restore the military balance in its favour as a task of the utmost urgency and as the necessary prerequisite for the employment of other means of conflict resolution. This included the resumption of negotiations. The situation of the strength/negotiation from strength rationale came to be frequently used by the government, and the very real concern for not being duped or seen to be duped by the LTTE again conditioned its attitude towards conflict resolution.

War for peace strategy

Accordingly, the government got trapped into the logic of its chosen *modus operandi* for conflict resolution – primary reliance upon the use of military force. Even the unprecedented step of proposing a devolution package as the basis of a political settlement to the ethnic conflict and acceptance of this package by the majority community became contingent upon success on the battlefield. The LTTE was to be hammered into submission or extinction. War was a continuation of politics by other means, yet the overarching political purpose risked being obscured by the 'other means' intended to secure it.

At the outset of what has come to be called Eelam War 3 (1994–), the government had both military and political ground to cover. By unilaterally resorting to arms, the LTTE immediately gained the military upper hand. Politically too it had outwitted the government. By its insistence upon confidence-building measures, the LTTE made progress towards a political settlement contingent upon the performance of certain actions on the ground by the government. This allowed them to test the limits of the government's commitment to the negotiating process to the hilt and, by pointing to weaknesses in command, control and communication on the part of the government, build up a case against government *bona fides vis-à-vis* a negotiated settlement. They in effect set the agenda and, accordingly, resorted to arms before the key issue of a political settlement was taken up.

Their political objective was clear. President Kumaratunga had received a massive mandate as the Peace President; the LTTE aimed to demonstrate that she was no different from her predecessors and was in effect a War President or someone who had no problems in playing that role. Before she could present her proposals for a political settlement they had forced her into war, claiming that she was neither willing nor able to negotiate in good faith.

The resulting government strategy was to insist that it acknowledged the existence of an ethnic conflict for which there had to be a political settlement. Yet, the LTTE was the principal obstacle to that settlement and as a terrorist organisation had to be wiped out or transformed. The War for Peace, the name the government has given to its strategy for conflict resolution, is presented as being waged against the LTTE on behalf of all the people of Sri Lanka yearning for peace. Its success depends on the effective calibration of military means with political goals. The record of the last four years suggests that the government has fallen far short in this respect, even though it has yet to acknowledge the need for realistic strategic reassessment.

There is a problem in the prevailing government strategy with regard to the coherent identification of strategic goals and with regard to the honest appraisal of the requirements for waging war against a guerrilla force. It has never been quite clear as to whether the government believes it can and therefore seeks to wipe out the LTTE, or as to whether the government thinks it cannot and therefore seeks through the use of superior military force to transform the LTTE into a reliable partner for peace along the lines of its choosing. Adding to this confusion are frequent government statements about the fanatical commitment of the LTTE to Eelam or a separate state. Were this to be the case, there is no transforming the LTTE: it is not going to metamorphose into a player, in the mould desired and designed by the government.

This smacks of *ad hoc* policy-making, strategy built on shifting sands, which in this context is oscillating military fortunes. As a consequence of there being no firm grip on its agenda and no clear strategic perspective, the government options for conflict resolution have narrowed rather than widened in the period since April 1995. This has been the case even though the army has taken three-quarters of the northern Jaffna peninsula, the government has announced an unprecedented devolution package and the international community has positioned itself squarely behind the government in declaring the LTTE to be terrorists.

The government strategy of taking territory from the LTTE, including its northern stronghold of Jaffna, may have given it short-term politico-psychological benefits with the majority community, but this has hardened attitudes towards their acceptance of a settlement with meaningful devolution and power sharing. (The LTTE forcibly evacuated Jaffna and retreated further south and to the jungles.) Devolution is what the government insists is necessary for a settlement and what distinguishes its approach to conflict resolution from that of its predecessors and the opposition. Quite clearly, devastating military success is not going to win acceptance among the majority community for devolution or power-sharing. It is more likely in the Sri Lankan context to augment calls for a restoration of the *status quo ante bellum*. The experience of the capture of Jaffna by government forces and its impact on the government's devolution package is instructive.

The government's devolution package was first mooted in August 1995 as the focal point for public debate. In this debate, the proposals, unprecedented in themselves, were hailed by advocates of devolution as the basis for a solution and by opponents as the recipe for secession. Whilst the debate raged on, in December the army captured the premier Tamil city, the northern capital of Jaffna. The LTTE forced the population to evacuate and retreated to the jungles. The event was treated with great fanfare. The national flag which bears the Lion symbol of the majority community was hoisted in the city and the deputy minister of defence, who was credited with the victory, was promoted in military rank to general.

In January 1996, the proposals were released officially as government policy and they bore the influence of the debate that had been aroused by their initial release in August 1995. The height of the government's popularity, as a consequence of the capture of Jaffna, had nevertheless not enabled it to resist the arguments put forward by the opponents of devolution. The August 1995 proposals were refashioned in January 1996 to incorporate the views of the latter and the balance of political powers was restored firmly in favour of the centre. Clearly, military victory did not facilitate political accommodation in this instance and it is probably not going to in any other.

Alternatively, if the objective is not devastating military victory but sufficient military pressure to bring the LTTE to the negotiating table eager for a political settlement in the spirit of honourable compromise, it is pertinent to ask as to whether the War for Peace strategy will achieve this.

It is clear that, even if one hammers one's opponent to the point at which they would want to talk, as long as they realise that one cannot finish the job on the battlefield and therefore one has a vested interest in talking, the opponent also realises that they have cards to play and play with them they will to the best of their ability. The point here is that as long as the LTTE realises that the government is eager for an end to the armed conflict and requires LTTE agreement to arrive at it, the LTTE will drive a hard bargain at the negotiating table. In relative terms, the LTTE may not be in a situation of strength in this scenario; neither is it in a situation of absolute weakness. The initial challenge, however, is to marshal sufficient manpower and resources to take and hold territory as well as to go after the LTTE in the jungles, defeat them in the east and simultaneously guard against terrorist attacks in the rest of the country. The inability to do this risks a 'back to the future' scenario in which the vicious cycle of ambush, attack, atrocity and attrition could yet again be the order of the day and rebound to the benefit of the LTTE.

Conventional military wisdom indicates a ratio of at least 10 to 1 of security forces to guerrillas. This has yet to be achieved in the Sri Lankan context. Furthermore, there have been desertions from the army and some eight amnesties over the last two years alone, which have only been partially successful. And evidence of disappearances and other human rights violations in the territory under army control have been recorded. There have also been battles in which the army has registered large losses – over a thousand were killed in a LTTE attack on Mullaittivu in 1996 and a similar figure has been recorded for the LTTE attack on Kilinochchi in 1998. Whilst the government has yet to deem that its War for Peace has trapped it into a 'hurting stalemate' which emphasises the imperative of resuming negotiations, the available evidence at present is of a hurtful stalemate in the vital process of conflict resolution.

In May 1997, the government launched Operation Jayasikurui (Certain Victory) to open the main supply route to the northern peninsula. The reasoning was that once this route was opened troops could be supplied with ease and greater regularity and the relief and rehabilitation of the north essential to winning the hearts and minds of the civilians there could be commenced in earnest. Seventeen months and many premature deadlines later, the army has been valiantly attempting to gain control of the remaining third of the 70-mile stretch of road. At the end of September 1998, the operation was relaunched and days before this the Tigers attacked another position, overrunning an army camp and killing over a thousand troops as mentioned above.

Whilst the government has been claiming impending victory ever since the offensive was launched in May 1997, it has had to impose censorship on the reporting of the war (June 1998) and an all-island emergency (August 1998) under which it postponed provincial council elections scheduled for 28 August. The argument provided was that elections would require the redeployment of security forces and this in turn would benefit the LTTE. In addition to the lack of progress, the chosen strategy for conflict resolution is affecting the government's ability to perform a basic duty in a functioning democracy – that of holding elections.

The government had hoped that by the beginning of 1998 the supply route would have been opened. This, coupled with local government elections in the Jaffna peninsula to signal the commencement of democratisation and the return to normality, was projected as a winning combination of events to prepare the country for a referendum on devolution in early April of 1998, just before the local New Year. The *pièce de résistance*, as it were, was to be the jubilee anniversary celebration of independence. It was to take place at the Dalada Maligawa or Temple of the Tooth in Kandy on 4 February, with Prince Charles in attendance as the chief guest.

On 25 January, the LTTE exploded a bomb at the entrance to the Maligawa and, by this single egregious act of terror, demonstrated its ability to set the agenda of politics and conflict resolution and scupper any movement to a solution that seeks either to exclude or to marginalise them. Since this bomb, the focus of Sri Lankan politics has been on elections as the means by which the political deadlock on devolution could be broken. Elections, both parliamentary and presidential, were not due until 1999 at the earliest and the LTTE has effectively placed the non-violent conflict resolution process on hold, whilst intensifying violence. The UNP opposition, sensing the political vulnerability of the government resulting from its inability to protect the most important symbol of both religious and temporal power in the land, has abandoned any pretence of achieving a bipartisan consensus on devolution. It is fully committed to partisan politics in preparation for elections.

Terrorism and the human rights situation

Two immediate consequences of the War for Peace strategy were that the incidence of terrorism by the LTTE has increased and the human rights situation in the country has been adversely affected. Whilst the government concentrated its military efforts on smashing the quasi-state the LTTE had built up in the northern peninsula since 1990 and on capturing territory which the LTTE claims to be that of Eelam or the separate Tamil state, the LTTE retaliated with increased terrorism in the rest of the country and in the capital Colombo, in particular. In effect, they were demonstrating that they did not have to play by the rules set by the government and, through their refusal to do so, set the agenda of the conflict. Their objective was to increase the costs of waging war against them and to harden attitudes against a settlement on the grounds that there could be no agreements with terrorists.

The LTTE's intensification of terrorism – the worst incident in terms of the costs to life and property was the 31 January 1996 bombing of the Central Bank – resulted in heightened security and surveillance in the city of Colombo which has a large Tamil population. In these circumstances, Tamils in Colombo and those coming to the capital bore the weight of the heightened surveillance efforts of the police and security forces – constant questioning at military checkpoints that dot the city, and interrogation and detention at night and in the early hours of the morning. A number of the arrests and detentions were not carried out according to the procedures laid down by the government and, in a number of cases, Tamil citizens were illegally detained. On the ground, petty corruption and ignorance of the law reinforced Tamil perceptions of insecurity and discrimination.

The government eventually moved to rectify the situation. It recognised that its attempts to win the hearts and minds of the Tamil people were being undermined daily by the deteriorating security situation. An Anti-Harassment Committee comprised of cabinet ministers, officials and security personnel was established with a 24-hour phone and fax line for receiving complaints. This has ameliorated the problem somewhat.

The situation in the north-east, in areas under army control, is also a cause for concern. The human rights record of the security forces in the mid-1990s is widely believed to be a vast improvement on their record in the early years of the armed conflict. Since the army took Jaffna, there have been reports of successful hearts and minds operations and of a growing sense of security on the part of the civilians with regard to the presence of the armed forces. It is also felt that the attitude of the commanding officer is a crucial factor in ensuring this. An improvement in the situation notwithstanding, there are also allegations of a mass grave, disappearances and of murder. International bodies such as Amnesty International and the UN Special Rapporteur on Enforced and Involuntary Disappearances, in addition to Tamil political parties and human rights activists, allege that from 600 to 700 persons have disappeared and have not been accounted for, since the army took possession of Jaffna in December 1995.

One such case became an international *cause célèbre*. It is an important and instructive case for a number of reasons. Krishanthi Kumaraswamy, an 18-year-old Tamil school girl in Jaffna, was abducted, raped and murdered by security personnel on her way home after sitting an exam. The same fate befell her mother who went in search of her, and a neighbour who accompanied the mother was also murdered. After much lobbying by human rights organisations, a trial-at-bar was initiated. Nine security personnel were indicted and convicted. During the case, one of the accused walked from the courthouse and he has yet to be re-arrested. The first accused in the case, Somaratne Rajapakse, on being convicted announced that he knew of a mass grave in Chenmanni, Jaffna, containing some 400 bodies.

This allegation is now being investigated. Rajapakse has been beaten in detention. According to Amnesty he was also threatened whilst in the hospital he was moved to, as a result of injuries sustained whilst in prison. The site of the alleged mass grave is being guarded by the armed forces and this has been a cause of some concern. International forensic expertise is being sought in the excavation of the site and human rights groups have also expressed concern that internationally accepted guidelines and procedures for excavation of such sites be followed. The Human Rights Commission established by the government in 1996 is involved in the case, and has opened an office in Jaffna.

The Kumaraswamy case is important for a number of reasons, the most notable being that it is the first time that security personnel have been indicted and convicted of a human rights violation in the context of the ethnic conflict. Before this, the criticism had been that the security forces operated with impunity and that government accusations of Tiger atrocities were thereby blunted. The government has understandably cited the convictions in this case as evidence of its *bona fides vis-à-vis* the human rights of the Tamil people. What transpires with regard to the allegation of mass graves will no doubt be viewed as a test of the extent of the government's commitment in this regard.

Progress towards constitutional agreements and political factors (1995–8)

As outlined above, the government has proposed an unprecedented devolution package embodying its commitment to a peaceful political settlement through constitutional reform. The devolution package forms part of a proposed new constitution, the other principal feature of which is the abolition of the executive presidency and a return to a parliamentary system of government. In this respect, the government is projecting constitutional reform as a key instrument of conflict resolution with regard to the nation- and state-building crisis in Sri Lanka.

The government's devolution package

The government is proposing that Article 2 of the existing constitution, declaring Sri Lanka to be a unitary state, be jettisoned and Sri Lanka be termed a Union of Regions. Unlike the system of provincial councils, under the new constitution there will be a clearer demarcation of powers and spheres of competence. There will be no Concurrent List of subjects over which both the Regions and the Centre will exercise jurisdiction and power will be devolved to all regions equally. The concept of asymmetrical devolution has not been taken on board.

Subjects such as defence and overall control over the economy will fall within the Centre's jurisdiction and the advocacy of secession will be prohibited. Regional Councils are to be allowed regional police forces. The Centre is empowered to take action in a region if it believes that there is a threat to the unity of the country located within that region. This action extends to the dismissal of the elected Regional Council. Whilst land is to be vested with the Regional Councils, Regional Councils are required to give up land to the Centre for use in a subject area under the jurisdiction of the Centre. Land is to be alienated by the Regional Council, in the first instance with due regard to ethnic composition in the district.

The government has also proposed a series of referenda to resolve the territorial issue pertaining to the northern and eastern provinces. These two provinces are claimed by Tamil political representation to be the 'traditional homelands' of the Tamils. In recognition of this, they were merged under the terms of the 1987 Indo-Sri Lanka Accord, pending a referendum on the issue in the eastern province. This was to be held a year later at the discretion of the President of Sri Lanka. A decade later, no referendum has been held and the two provinces remain officially, though not permanently, merged. The merger of these two provinces constitutes the territorial issue of the conflict. The northern province is predominantly Tamil with a small Sinhala population. The significant minority presence here is that of the Muslim community, which the LTTE in its version of ethnic cleansing has expelled. The eastern province is ethnically mixed. The Tamils constitute the single largest community but do not have an overall majority. The Sinhalese and Muslims together outnumber them.

Ethnic politics has affected the Muslim community as well. In the eastern province, this has given rise to the Sri Lanka Muslim Congress (SLMC), a constituent member of the ruling PA coalition, to safeguard the interests of the eastern province Muslims. The SLMC argues that accommodation between the Sinhalese and Tamils in the east should not be at the expense of the Muslims. Since 1987, the Muslims have been caught up in a Tamil-dominated, merged north-eastern province. A perpetuation of this under a LTTE provincial government is not a prospect they relish and the SLMC has held out for either a separate Muslim south-eastern region or, at the least, autonomy arrangements for the Muslims within a merged province. The latter poses practical difficulties since all Muslim villages are not territorially contiguous.

The government has tried to accommodate the SLMC, even at the risk of being accused of carving out territory to ensure SLMC membership of the ruling coalition. The devolution proposals envisage a series of referenda in which the majority Tamil administrative districts of the eastern province will be allowed to decide on their merger with the north. Depending on the result of these referenda, the same is to apply to the majority Sinhala and Muslim districts, with the latter being given the option of constituting a separate Southeastern Region. All Tamil parties oppose this, arguing that the merger of the north and east is a *sine qua non* of Tamil aspirations for autonomy. The homeland concept underpinning the merger is incorporated into the declaration of principles on self-determination issued by all Tamil parties in talks with the Sri Lankan government in the Bhutanese capital Thimpu in

1985. Only the Tamil United Liberation Front (TULF), the oldest Tamil political party represented in Parliament and the only one not to have taken up arms against the Sri Lankan state, supports the idea of a Southeast Region on pragmatic grounds. The principal opposition party, the UNP, is opposed to the merger and to any radical territorial re-demarcation of the eastern province.

The issue of territory is a highly charged one. Opponents of the government's package contend that the re-demarcation of territory on ethnic grounds is a highly dangerous precedent that will lead to similar demands in other areas and to the eventual break up of Sri Lanka. They are also incensed by the vesting of land with the Regional Councils, erroneously claiming that this would violate the right of every Sri Lankan to live anywhere in the island and also claiming that even the central government will be deprived of land for use in the interest of all communities. Maps used by opponents of the government's package illustrate the charge that it would result in the Tamil dominated Northeast Council controlling some five-sixths of the coastline and the vast majority of the available land.

A variety of factors that make up the political culture in Sri Lanka and which have stymied efforts at resolving the ethnic conflict have been noted at the outset. A further elaboration of this is necessary to understand the difficulties in completing the process of constitutional reform.

The politics of constitutional reform

Constitutional reform is beset by problems of substance and, as a consequence, problems of process as well. Moreover, it has to be carried out in a political context in which partisan allegiance is upheld above national interest and the competition between the two main parties is great.

The existing constitution was promulgated in 1978 by the UNP regime. It brought in a system of proportional representation and sets out a procedure for amendment which first requires a two-thirds majority of parliament and then approval by the people with a simple majority at an island-wide referendum. Under this system, it is quite clear that a bipartisan consensus between the two main parties is crucial to the passage of a new constitution. The UNP opposition has been unwilling to provide the necessary support and the government has on numerous occasions threatened to effect a 'constitutional revolution' to promulgate a new constitution. There is a provision in the 1978 constitution which permits the president to go to the people in a non-binding, consultative referendum on an issue of national importance. The president is prohibited from exercising this option on a constitutional question. However, there is a school of thought which believes that this option could be exercised legitimately.

In all probability, the Supreme Court will have to decide on the constitutionality of this method, were it to be attempted. Critics also point out that this procedure would allow for a new constitution of the country, which amongst other features contained entrenched guarantees to the minorities, to be promulgated by a simple majority. This could in turn be abolished at the next election by recourse to the same procedure, if the opposition so desired and was elected to government.

The damaging tradition of constitution-making in Sri Lanka, with every government on being elected to office promulgating a new constitution to suit its needs, as happened in 1972 and 1978, would be thereby perpetuated. Critics also aver that the experience of elections held under the government does not inspire confidence. The result could be 'manufactured', the opposition would cry foul and the whole process robbed of any democratic legitimacy. In this respect, the government is in a bind and unable to deliver on election promises to change the structure of the state and to bring peace. It does not have the requisite votes in the legislature to pass the new constitution and it is highly unlikely that, with a system of proportional representation in operation, it will obtain the majority in the legislature in the future.

In the politics of constitution-making, the government has not moved to strengthen its hand as it should. Arguably, it has made a weak position even weaker by its inability and/or unwillingness to forge the necessary bipartisan consensus. The government has a single-seat majority in parliament and has relied for the most part on the minority parties to support its legislative programme. Despite establishing a Parliamentary Select Committee on Constitutional Reform to produce a new constitution by consensus, the government and the president in particular have frequently engaged in partisan invective against the UNP record in government and, at times, attacked the Leader of the Opposition, personally.

The UNP opposition has repeatedly pointed to the shortcomings of the government in forging a bipartisan consensus as a key reason for the failure of consensus to materialise. They argue, that unlike in the past or indeed the PA in opposition responding to the system of provincial councils, the UNP has not whipped up public feeling against the government's devolution package or engaged in a mass campaign of extra-parliamentary agitation against it. As testimony to its good faith, the UNP also points to the agreement signed between its leader and the president. This was brokered by Dr Liam Fox, Under-Secretary of State in the last Conservative government in Britain. According to this agreement, the two party leaders agreed to abide by any agreements to resolve the ethnic conflict entered into by the other, as long as each side was kept abreast of the other's initiatives and 'concurred' with them.

Whilst the UNP argument is not without some foundation, it nevertheless is open to the charge of disingenuousness. Like the PA, it has not seen fit to transcend partisan politics and treat conflict resolution as paramount and in the national interest. The political calculation underpinning the UNP stand seems to have been made in purely partisan terms – the PA would reap all the benefits from a political solution to the conflict and consolidate its hold on power for decades. Likewise, the PA argument appears to be that there is no advantage to be gained from sharing the responsibility and reward for a political settlement to the conflict, with the UNP.

There are other reasons as well for the UNP stand. The party is not a homogeneous unit, and after 17 years in government has to adjust to drastically changed political circumstances. Moreover, it has to cleanse itself of the image of a corrupt and authoritarian organisation which it earned during those 17 years. There is also a difference of opinion within the party on devolution. At various times its stand has been that the Provincial Council system it introduced in the wake of the 1987 Accord set the limits of devolution in Sri Lanka. The government's package goes far beyond it. It is quasi-federal at least, a departure from the unitary state, and therefore should be opposed.

Currently, the UNP argues that there should be unconditional talks with the LTTE. Critics contend that this is ample proof of the UNP's bad faith. Since they do not support the government package which the LTTE rejects as inadequate, what will they talk to the LTTE about? The strategy of the UNP has been to point to the package as a dangerous irrelevance which the government will foist upon the country by foul, rather than fair, means. In order to mask divisions within its ranks over devolution, the UNP has focused on process rather than substance – on the legality of a consultative referendum as the means by which the government will introduce the new constitution, rather than on the substantive provisions of a new constitution incorporating the terms of a political settlement to the ethnic conflict.

When the government in October 1997 released its official draft of the devolution package as coming out of deliberations in the Select

Committee, the UNP disclaimed it as a consensus document and asked for a further 6 months in which to present its own proposals. The Select Committee had already been in existence for 18 months and it seemed as if the UNP was intent on derailing the whole process by talking devolution to death. The UNP proposals emerged in three instalments in 1998, each one being conditioned by unfolding political developments. According to the party, they were being presented as constructive contributions to the sustenance of necessary debate on devolution. The UNP proposals concentrated as much on other aspects of governance and, as far as the ethnic conflict was concerned, concentrated on a form of power-sharing at the centre with the unitary state intact.

With the Maligawa bomb at the end of the January 1998, the UNP sensed that the government was damaged politically, the prospects of a consultative referendum had receded and that the election season had been advanced. Opposition to devolution, however, would not play well with the minorities. The current position of unconditional talks with the LTTE lends itself to the interpretation that it is calculated to win back minority support by heightening the irrelevance of the government's devolution package, at the same time as appearing highly conciliatory to minority aspirations and the imperative of conflict resolution.

There are divisions too within the SLFP, the principal party of the ruling nine-member People's Alliance coalition over devolution. The SLFP has traditionally been the party of Sinhala nationalism. Ms Kumaratunga's father's government made Sinhala the official language in 1956 and her mother's governments of 1960–4 and 1970–7 implemented the policy aggressively to the detriment of ethnic harmony. Ms Kumaratunga has, in this respect, inherited a party in which the dominant view on the ethnic conflict was at variance with her more liberal perspective. She has catapulted to its leadership and that of the country in a short space of time – Chief Minister of the Western Province in May 1993, then Prime Minister in August 1994 and President in November of that year. The challenge continues to be to her ability to galvanise important sections of opinion in support of her devolution proposals and their implementation.

Intra- and inter-party divisions compounding the failure to arrive at a bipartisan consensus aside, there are other factors militating against acceptance of the devolution proposals. The impact of military factors has also been discussed. There are also other groups that have emerged who are opposed to devolution and committed to a military solution to the scourge of terrorism. They are made up of members of the Sangha and professionals, whose antipathy towards government is augmented by the government's failure to deliver and its shortcomings on other fronts. Indeed, one of the problems associated with the consultative referendum is that it will be seen not so much as a gauge of opinion on the devolution proposals, but on the overall record of the government so far. In both cases, the verdict may not be anywhere near so fulsome and positive as the government may wish.

The government has not delivered on a series of manifesto promises, allegations of corruption have lost it the moral high ground it occupied in 1994 and revelations of mismanagement have given rise to questions about its commitment to and capacity for governance. Therefore, the attempt to go to the people over the head of an obstructionist parliament determined to frustrate their will, as reflected in the government's agenda for reform, may not guarantee the success required or in the measure needed in terms of credibility and legitimacy. And any attempt to 'manufacture' a result nearer to the heart's desire will undermine the whole process of constitutional reform for conflict resolution and be politically self-defeating.

The politics of the North

The fate of the devolution proposals at a consultative referendum notwithstanding, the question of whether they can be implemented in the north-east – the area for which they are primarily intended – remains. It echoes the conundrum of conflict resolution in Sri Lanka, about the kind of peace that can be had with the LTTE and the kind of peace that could be had without them.

The LTTE led by Vellupillai Prabhakaran claim to be the 'sole legitimate representatives of the Tamil people'. They have in their drive for hegemony over the Tamils in the north-east of the island systematically slaughtered their opponents who also espoused the Tamil nationalist project, practised ethnic cleansing against other communities in the north-east, glorified a martial past and nurtured a cult of nationalism and loyalty to nation and leader alike, so strong that suicide bombings have been elevated to the status of the ultimate sacrifice for the liberation of the nation.

The LTTE has been able to project itself in this guise largely because of the inability and unwillingness of successive Sri Lankan governments to address genuine Tamil grievances in the fields of education and employment, in particular, and, because of the government's reliance upon military force with its attendant evils of civilian suffering and atrocity, to combat Tamil nationalism. As the Sri Lankan state has used force against what it has defined as a terrorist problem and failed to share power, the LTTE has been able to gain credibility amongst the Tamils as a defence against the government's use of force and as a catalyst for forcing devolution and power-sharing onto the agenda as a *sine qua non* of a solution.

The ability of the Tamil militants and the LTTE to sustain their nationalist project is in the ultimate analysis underpinned by the pervasive sense of discrimination felt by the Tamil population upon which ideas of nation, homeland and separatism have been grafted. Whilst the ideas of nation and traditional homeland are now articles of faith among the majority of Tamils, their total support for secession is a matter of considerable dispute, notwithstanding the LTTE assertions to the contrary.

Whilst statutory discrimination has been largely removed through the various attempts at conflict resolution – after the Indo-Sri Lanka Accord of 1987 – Tamil was also made an official language – the perception of discrimination remains strong and is the primary reason militating against a restoration of the political and constitutional *status quo* in Sri Lanka. Whether it be provincial autonomy, federalism or a separate state, the conflict has reached the point at which the unitary state in the classic sense is untenable and the Tamil minority will have to be given as much control as possible over their own affairs. This is the only assurance they would accept as the safeguard against discrimination in the future.

Whether the LTTE will scale down its avowedly secessionist goal and accept a federal solution is by no means clear. Many argue that given its ruthless single-mindedness of purpose, the horrendous sacrifices it has wrought from the people for its secessionist goal and its apparatus of political repression, there is too much at stake for it to accept anything short of a separate state. Without one, its credibility would be shattered; it would be politically suicidal for it to settle for less. A dissenting argument is one that points to the almost deliberate imprecision at times in the LTTE's definition of Tamil Eelam and the various occasions on which they have come out in favour of federalism as a solution. From what can be gleaned, the nomenclature is not so important as the constitutional status dignifying total political control. The LTTE understanding of federalism is really confederalism – an association between two sovereign entities in specific areas.

It is against this backdrop that the persistence of the LTTE as protagonist in the conflict must be measured. Despite the reversals in military and political fortunes over the last four years, resulting from the government's determination to take territory from their control and to beat them into compliance or into extinction, an end to the conflict is bound up with the future of the LTTE. And in the absence of a political settlement, regardless of the electoral arithmetic, the logic of the conflict is that the only source of leverage the Tamils have on the Sri Lankan government to effect a change in the constitutional *status quo* is the LTTE's armed resistance.

As the experience of the government's devolution package has shown, even if a government was willing, the question arises over as to whether it is able to forge the island-wide consensus required to realise constitutional reform to settle the conflict. The logic of the War for Peace strategy is to use military might against the LTTE and, accordingly, reduce antipathy towards the devolution package. It is this synthesis that the government hoped to have achieved by the first four months of 1998 and which proved elusive. Holding local elections in the Jaffna peninsula was integral to this strategy and illustrates the central conundrum referred to above. Elections held out the possibility of anti-LTTE forces emerging to provide political representation for the Tamils and thereby making devolution to the north-east more palatable to the Sinhalese.

The local government elections in the Jaffna peninsula were the first to be held there for 15 years. They were looked upon as a rare opportunity to gauge public opinion on the peninsula and, symbolically, as the first steps in the return to normality and democratic politics. There were, nevertheless, a number of factors present, indicating that the elections would not lead to the latter and in any event, apart from allowing the government a propaganda and public relations coup both locally and internationally, that much else would be accomplished.

Organised opinion in the peninsula and non-LTTE Tamil political representation lobbied against holding elections on security grounds and argued that the exercise was fraught with difficulties from the outset, especially relating to the availability of accurate voter lists. Public opinion was critical of the holding of elections. People were of the view that elections were not a priority; adequate power, water and medical supplies were and, if the government considered the needs of the people as paramount, these issues should be addressed first. Nevertheless, people voiced their determination to register their faith in the democratic process by voting. They also voiced their desire for an end to conflict and of being told how to live their lives by people carrying guns.

The non-Tiger Tamil parties echoed these concerns, as well as that of the danger of being forced into lending credibility to a propaganda exercise by the government under the guise of restoring democracy. However, mirroring this danger was also the knowledge that they had to demonstrate the political support on the ground they claimed as their *raison d'être*, or else risk being played out of the game of Tamil political representation. Neither the people in the peninsula nor the government and the people in the rest of the country would see them as serious political players if they were to opt out of the opportunity to prove their political support. Therefore, in the face of government determination to go ahead regardless of difficulties, non-LTTE Tamil parties felt they had no option but to contest.

Foremost amongst the groups that contested the local elections was the Tamil United Liberation Front (TULF). The TULF is the oldest Tamil political party with representation in Parliament and the only party not to have taken up arms against the Sri Lankan state. Moreover, as it opposed the Thirteenth Amendment to the constitution that followed the 1987 Accord as inadequate, and boycotted the provincial council elections this facilitated, the local government elections marked the TULF's return to electoral politics in Jaffna. The TULF has been supportive of the government's package from the outset and of negotiations with the LTTE as well. The chauvinist press contends that the package bears the TULF stamp. The TULF has consistently advocated a federal solution.

At one level, therefore, TULF participation in the elections was necessary to invest the contest with a legitimacy that none of the other parties could bestow. At another, TULF participation could be viewed as the desperate act of a party which finally concluded that in order to stay politically alive it had to be politically active in those areas it claims as its constituency.

The other Tamil political parties that contested the elections were all ex-militants who entered the political mainstream in 1987 as a consequence of the Indo-Sri Lanka Accord and the introduction of provincial councils. The leader of one of these parties, Mr Douglas Devananda, has referred to them, and his own party as well, as 'half-democrats'. His party is the Eelam People's Democratic Party (EPDP). It has the largest Tamil representation in the current parliament. Some of the seats accredited to the EPDP were secured at the 1994 election with a handful of votes and the EPDP was eager to dispel the notion that it had no popular base. The EPDP has aligned itself very closely with successive Sri Lankan governments and engages in military action against the LTTE. It controls a string of islands off the Jaffna peninsula.

The elections invariably provided an insight into the availability of credible Tamil political representation that could be engaged as reliable partners in a settlement. The devolution package apart, and this too is debatable, there has been no clearly identifiable political gain the ex-militants can point to that validates their jettisoning of armed militancy and thereby undercuts the LTTE politically. They have also had to cope with the government's apparent reservations about their popular appeal and guaranteed good behaviour. Therefore, in the local elections they had to demonstrate their credentials to both the government and to the people. To the former constituency they had to prove popular support and aptitude for democratic politics. And in doing so they had to present themselves to the latter constituency as something more than mere extensions of the government. They had to define themselves as credible and independent, if they were to show that they were popular. In effect, they had to define themselves and their relationship *vis-à-vis* the LTTE – either as a bulwark against them or as a bridge to them entering the mainstream and agreeing to a settlement.

In the campaign, the ex-militants were keen to project themselves as not so much opposed to the LTTE as dissatisfied with the devolution package and the delay in its passage and implementation. None of them or the TULF has presented themselves openly and officially as alternatives to the Tigers at the negotiating table. They all maintain that the LTTE must be brought into the mainstream of politics in order to arrive at a settlement. In the election campaign, their reluctance either to oppose or to criticise openly the LTTE may well have been in the nature of an insurance policy against assassination and to ensure that people actually came out and voted for them, rather than stayed away for fear of LTTE retribution.

It was widely believed that the LTTE would disrupt the elections. On two occasions they launched armed attacks. The first was on an EPDP camp in the islands in which nine persons including an EPDP candidate were killed and the second was on the day of elections, delaying polling. Some 106 000 people in the peninsula voted and the very act of holding elections itself was hailed as victory for democracy and for the government in its campaign against the LTTE. The TULF, after legal proceedings regarding the eligibility of some of its candidates, emerged the victor in the two local bodies it contested, including the municipality of Jaffna. The EPDP emerged as the overall victor.

What has happened since the election has validated the warnings of critics and sceptics alike. It would seem that the holding of elections was a self-contained exercise in itself designed to provide short-term political benefit for the government outside the Jaffna peninsula, and not as the commencement of the return to normality and the restoration of democracy on it. The vast majority of the elected councillors has not taken their oath of office and, as a consequence, the local bodies are not functioning. Those that attempted to have been effectively shut down.

There are a number of reasons for this. In the first instance, the majority of candidates put forward by the ex-militants were armed cadre. Once the elections were over, the argument was advanced that the ex-militant political parties wanted these elected candidates to resign in order that more suitable individuals could be nominated to positions in local government. Another argument advanced was that the flow of funds from the central government was puny. MPs in the national legislature from the north-east were being told to disburse funds to the local councils from moneys allocated to them for constituency work. This has never been suggested for the rest of the country. Furthermore, the LTTE, through political assassination and the sustenance of a fear psychosis, and the government, in its unwillingness to provide support for democratisation and normality, have together obliterated any promise held out by the elections in January 1998.

The TULF, having entered the fray late, was keen to commence working in Jaffna. However, the TULF mayor of Jaffna, Ms Sarojini Yogeswaran, too, expressed her disappointment with the government's demonstrable commitment towards local government in Jaffna. On a number of occasions she complained in the media about inadequate financial resources and delays in disbursement. Determined nonetheless to do whatever she could, she sacrificed her life. On 18 May she fell victim to an LTTE assassination squad. Her husband, a TULF MP, had also been assassinated by the LTTE. The TULF nominated a successor to Ms Yogeswaran, Mr Sivapalan, who encountered the same fate, along with the superintendent of police in Jaffna and a brigadier. There have been other assassinations too of army officers and local party officials, as well as internecine fighting between factions of the ex-militant political parties. The courts have also declared that they will not operate and one local body, Valikammam North, has declared that it will not function until peace is achieved.

The experience of these elections and their aftermath indicate that though the LTTE is not in control of the peninsula it still retains a hold on it through fear and terror, if nothing else. Any attempts to operate a system of civilian administration in the peninsula, as part of a broader strategy of marginalising them, is bound therefore to fail, especially if it is not backed up in word and deed by a cogent commitment on the part of the government.

In this respect, the government's strategy for conflict resolution at the moment is stuck, militarily and politically. Showing no evidence of being appreciably chastened or chastised by the War for Peace, the LTTE is still very much a force to be reckoned with on the ground. From the perspective of the guerrilla, not losing is sufficient, whereas for the government a stalemate can be fatally damaging and especially for one which has banked on its credentials for conflict resolution to consolidate its hold on power.

External factors

Indian policy

Apart from the interest of India in the Sri Lankan conflict arising from geopolitical reasons and domestic security concerns, the conflict has not attracted international involvement for its resolution. This probably stems from the dominant strategic perspectives that inform the prevailing global power structure and its determination of a relatively low strategic significance for Sri Lanka. The irony, nevertheless, is that the most successful attempt at conflict resolution came about because of decisive external intervention.

The 1987 Indo-Sri Lanka Accord which led to the Thirteenth Amendment to the Sri Lankan constitution and paved the way for the establishment of a system of provincial councils and the merger of the north and east also led to the introduction of an Indian Peacekeeping Force (IPKF) into the merged province. Within two months of its induction and till it left the island in 1991, the IPKF was engaged in hostilities with the LTTE. In the fighting, the IPKF incurred some 1100 fatalities.

Whilst India's strategic and geopolitical concerns with respect to the conflict in Sri Lanka remain unchanged, the prospects of a further Indian intervention along the lines of 1987 are remote. New Delhi's attitude is now largely one of 'once bitten twice shy' – the LTTE aside, Indian intervention aroused the JVP insurgency in the south and led to Sri Lankan President Premadasa demanding the immediate removal of the IPKF in 1990. Non-Congress governments in Delhi, too, have been keen to be less assertive in the prosecution of Indian interests in the region. However, New Delhi's interest in the Sri Lankan conflict should not be underestimated. Any attempts at resolving the conflict through external assistance and facilitation must take this into account and India kept abreast of developments.

The Indian attitude to the conflict can be broadly divided into the period before the Accord and the period after, in which the IPKF was withdrawn and the Tigers assassinated Rajiv Gandhi. At the outset of armed ethnic conflict, India was concerned to ensure that there would be no military solution which would have adverse repercussions on the politics of the state of Tamil Nadu. For similar reasons, as well as because of the host of other centrifugal pressures in India, New Delhi also wanted to ensure that there would be no successful secession by the Tamils in the north-east of Sri Lanka. India hoped, therefore, to contain militant Tamil aspirations within the framework of a united Sri Lanka. The extent of the constitutional settlement envisaged approximated to the quasi-federal arrangements operating in India, and New Delhi went to the extent of providing sanctuary, arms and training camps for Tamil militants in order to ensure that there would be no military solution and no Eelam.

There was another dimension to this Indian policy of limited support for Tamil militancy. The Sri Lankan government in the 1980s was pro-Western and had embarked on a policy of economic liberalisation at home. It hoped to secure Western support against terrorism to counter Indian support for the militants.

This invariably aroused Indian paranoia about extra-regional involvement in subcontinental security matters and, by obscuring the real congruence of strategic perspective between New Delhi and Colombo on secession, delayed fruitful co-operation between them in the 1980s on an issue of fundamental and common interest. It was only once relations with the West improved under the premiership of Rajiv Gandhi and the economic argument against the conflict was cogently articulated to the Sri Lankan government by members of the cabinet and international donors that the configuration of circumstances emerged for the Accord. And in the Accord, in the letters exchanged between the heads of government, India's strategic concerns were reflected in the inclusion of a veritable veto over the direction of Sri Lankan foreign policy.

With the assassination of Rajiv Gandhi and, more recently, the establishment of a PA government in Colombo, relations between the two neighbours have improved vastly and are at their best, for the last decade and a half. New Delhi has co-operated with the government in

Colombo on patrolling the waters between India and Sri Lanka against Tiger infiltration and has been highly supportive of the devolution package and the War for Peace.

The indictments of the LTTE leader Vellupillai Prabhakaran in the Rajiv Gandhi murder case and the revelations of the Jain Commission further hardened Delhi's attitude towards the LTTE. As always, a variable in all of this was the relations between the central government in Delhi and the state government in Chennai, Tamil Nadu. Tamil political parties at the state level have used the Sri Lankan Tamil question in their political rivalries and in their relations with the central government. With the growing strength of regional parties and their increased leverage in the formation and survival of coalition governments at the centre, there has been concern evinced in Sri Lanka that the government in Delhi could be pressurised into softening its antipathy towards the LTTE as a result.

There was concern that this would apply to the current Bharatiya Janata Party (BJP) government and that the Tigers had made overtures to the BJP. This was heightened by the Hindu fundamentalist dimension to the BJP and the danger that the Tigers could make out or manufacture a religious factor to the conflict in Sri Lanka, in order to secure BJP support. There is no evidence that the LTTE has done this. The LTTE is a secular organisation and draws support from Christian Tamils as well.

The BJP in its manifesto stated that it would support Tamil aspirations for self-determination. It did not say that it would support secession. The BJP government has relied on Tamil party support in the Lok Sabha for its survival. Since its formation it has had to contend with threats of that support being withdrawn, from the leader of the Anna Dravida Munetra Kazam (AIDMK) led by the former Chief Minister of Tamil Nadu, Jayalalitha Jeyaram.

Jayalalitha is determined to have the government of Karunanidhi, her arch-rival in Tamil Nadu politics, dismissed by the centre. The BJP has so far resisted. It is not that Jayalalitha is enamoured of the LTTE and will use her leverage to effect a substantial shift in Indian policy away from hard, strategic realities. Rather, it is a question of how far she would go in the pursuit of power in Tamil Nadu and, indeed, how much political clout she will continue to be the beneficiary of, given the vicissitudes of current Indian politics. The latter factor suggests that the foreign policy establishment in Delhi will retain control over geopolitical and regional policy and that continuity in overall strategic perspective will be upheld.

The Indian Defence Minister at the time of writing, George Fernandes, has also been viewed by certain sections of opinion in Colombo as being pro-LTTE. This stems from him associating himself with a pro-LTTE conference in Delhi whilst in Opposition, to the extent of holding it at his residence when the government of India banned the meeting. Fernandes, though, is a maverick politician and his personal views on the Sri Lankan conflict are not underpinned by domestic political considerations.

Other actors

International opinion has swung behind the government and against the LTTE. This is attributable to the promise projected by the PA for democratic governance and its unprecedented devolution proposals. In contrast, the LTTE unilaterally broke off negotiations in April 1995, has not disavowed secession, has rejected the devolution package and continued with terrorism. This has lent credence to the government argument that the War for Peace was foisted upon it and that the War for Peace is not against the Tamil people but the terrorist LTTE, who glory in being the impediments to a settlement.

The government contends that the LTTE is well organised internationally and, through consent or coercion, freely raises funds abroad for armed resistance. It has lobbied hard to get the LTTE banned as a terrorist organisation – an action it only took itself after the Maligawa bomb in January 1998. So far, this campaign has succeeded in the US. The LTTE is contesting this action in court. It is not clear as to whether the US ban is having a fatal impact on LTTE fund-raising or as to whether it has any effect outside US domestic jurisdiction. The US also provides training to the Sri Lankan armed forces. The Sri Lankan government has also focused international attention on the LTTE's regular use of children as combatants.

Apart from India, the large and influential Tamil diaspora is located in Britain and Canada and to a lesser extent in Europe. The government hopes that the anti-terrorist legislation in Britain will also serve as a deterrent to Tiger fund-raising. The perception of an influential international Tamil lobby on behalf of the Tigers has also coloured the government's attitude towards offers to facilitate negotiations from Norway and Canada. The military and political situation has not been deemed propitious for this and the Tigers have shown no disposition towards accepting the conditions laid down by the government for the resumption of talks. The LTTE has nevertheless maintained that facilitation is necessary and the government has also moved to a position in which it agrees to this, though the preconditions remain.

Whilst offers to facilitate the resumption of negotiations remain, it is often reiterated that no state would want to actively embark on playing such a role, until it was convinced that the parties to the conflict were ready for negotiations and that there was a reasonable chance of success for facilitation. The recantation of impractical conditions by both sides – renunciation of secession and violence on the one hand and the withdrawal of the army from territory captured since 1995 on the other – are more than political rhetoric. This reflects the perception on both sides that they can and must effect a change in the balance of forces on the ground, before they can move towards negotiation.

Another element to be considered is the facilitation of a bipartisan consensus on conflict resolution. There is a recognition that, without it, the conflict resolution process cannot be moved forward and the initiative by Dr Liam Fox, the former British Under-Secretary of State at the Foreign and Commonwealth Office, was an acknowledgement of this. The Fox agreement has yet to be utilised in the service of conflict resolution. Nevertheless, it has not been officially revoked either. It can be resurrected when circumstances improve in favour of negotiations.

Economic factors

The costs of the war have been steadily increasing and with it the costs of living. Defence spending currently accounts for nearly 13.26 per cent of the estimated budgetary expenditure for 1999. Of an estimated Rs47.3 billion (US$723 million approximately) for defence, Rs39 billion is allocated for recurrent expenditure and Rs8.3 billion for capital expenditure. Total government expenditure for 1999 is estimated to be Rs339.2 billion (US$5.18 billion) at the current exchange rate.

In 1983, defence expenditure was Rs1.2 billion, in 1987 Rs6.8 billion, in 1994 Rs21.4 billion and for 1996 Rs31.7 billion. On 23 September 1998, the cabinet approved an additional Rs12.2 billion for defence, increasing the total figure to Rs57.2 billion or US$874 million approximately for 1998.

A number of studies on the real economic costs of the war have been undertaken. There are variations in the methodology used. Nevertheless, the verdict is clear. Peace may not be a panacea that will usher in prosperity, but an end to war is a necessary condition of economic development. There are other factors to be taken into account – at present a widespread complaint is the impact of a General Sales Tax on the cost of living. There is also the argument that peace dividends turn out to be quite elusive and that in any event, war, in terms of soldiers' salaries and pensions, has transformed the rural economy into a remittance economy.

The opportunity costs of war, consequently, provide a more accurate reflection of the economic costs of war. A study by Dr Saman Kelegama of the Institute for Policy Studies, an economic think-tank, tabulates the costs of war with respect to primary costs (investment and production opportunities foregone), secondary costs (damage to physical and social infrastructure as well as losses to the tourist industry) and tertiary costs (affecting the population directly, including rehabilitation of displaced persons and the loss of skilled manpower due to emigration).

Kelegama estimates that the opportunity costs of war in terms of lost output during Eelam War 1 (1983–7) would have amounted to US$1.2 billion which was 20 per cent of 1988 GDP. In the period 1990–4, otherwise known as Eelam War 2, the figure would be US$12.0 billion. He estimates the secondary costs of war for the period 1983–94 at US$3.6 billion and the quantifiable tertiary costs at US$315 million. Kelegama concludes that the overall approximate costs of Eelam Wars 1 and 2 is close to US$16 billion, that is the equivalent of 131 per cent of 1995 GDP. A study by the National Peace Council (NPC) concluded that the continuing annual cost of the war in 1996 was approximately Rs165 billion or about 21.3 per cent of GDP in that year.

As mentioned above, in the only instance where an attempt at conflict resolution was taken to conclusion, the economic argument was used in support of a settlement by influential sectors both at home and abroad. This has yet to materialise in full measure.

Although Sri Lanka has not realised its full potential and achieved the goal of becoming a Newly Industrialised Country (NIC) as promised, it is also argued that, despite the war, the island has not done as badly as some projections feared. This has been attributed to the price of tea, the remittances from migrant workers in West Asia and from garment exports. There is a fear that the full effects of the late 1990s Asian economic crisis will have a severe impact on Sri Lanka, in the aftermath of which the economic argument with regard to the cost of war will be re-canvassed to a more receptive audience.

Conclusion: The Management of Peace

John Darby and Roger Mac Ginty

The terrain of peace

A peace process is often compared to climbing a mountain, but a mountain range is a better metaphor, and the first peak is usually the ending of violence. All previous expeditions have failed. There are no obvious tracks to the top, nor any maps to provide guidance. The climbers, previously preoccupied with the arts of war, are unaccustomed to compromise and must pick up the skills as they go along. They must rely on each other's co-operation for survival. To make matters worse, the mountaineering team is composed of people who have previously been at each others' throats, often literally, and who must now overcome their suspicions and fears to accomplish a common task for the first time. For many, the ending of violence is more than enough.

If they succeed a ceasefire may follow. At last the travellers are able to peer over the summit. But they will not see a tranquil panorama of gentle hills. Instead, the view reveals new mountains, some apparently more formidable than the one just climbed. It becomes evident that the successful conquest of each new peak requires different skills and different guides. Those who negotiated a ceasefire are not necessarily the appropriate people to negotiate political agreement or to achieve economic regeneration and redistribution.

It would be easier if the mountains to be tackled were ranged in obvious sequence. Peace processes are often regarded as following three phases: first, the ending of violence; then, negotiations leading to a political/constitutional agreement; and, finally, what is often referred to as post-settlement peace building. The reality is less ordered. Unexpected peaks emerge through the mists and demand the immediate attention of the climbers. Each peace process has its own distinctive terrain and its own priorities. The decommissioning of weapons became one of the most formidable obstacles in Northern Ireland, yet it was bypassed at a brisk trot in South Africa. In the Basque Country significant reforms in policing and administrative devolution were achieved before inclusive negotiation was possible. Many of Northern Ireland's fair employment grievances had been improved long before the 1998 Agreement was reached.

The five studies

This book attempts to identify some direction posts along this difficult terrain. While it is the outcome of a co-ordinated research project, it sought to find an approach which allowed each contributor to tell the story in the most appropriate way. The aim was to try to understand why some peace processes have been less successful than others, what obstacles emerged and how they were or were not overcome.

Each of the five conflict settings has a different history, demographic structure and socio-economic profile. All may have embarked on a journey towards peace, but their progress along it was far from uniform. Each was at a different stage of the conflict resolution cycle, and had its own experience of conflict management. They also shared common features: they were all essentially internal conflicts; all have been subject to serious violence; and, most relevant, all had embarked on at least one attempt to reach peace within the last decade and had encountered similar obstacles to achieving it.

This last chapter draws on the five individual studies. It will attempt to discover what it is possible to say about peace processes in general. This will be approached along two analytical paths.

The primary analysis will be based on the six themes identified in the original research design. The importance during the process of these six factors – violence, external influences, economic factors, popular responses, symbolic factors and progress towards political settlement – will be considered in turn, and then in relation to each other. The last of them, progress towards political settlement, focuses on the central task of any peace process, and will be singled out for special attention as the sixth theme, forming a bridge between the primary and secondary analyses.

The secondary analysis will focus on the dynamics of negotiations. It will chart them through the process of getting into talks, during the negotiations themselves and into post-settlement peace building.

The role of violence

Bertie Ahern, the Irish Taoiseach (Prime Minister), suggested in 1998 that 'it is an observable phenomenon in Northern Ireland, and elsewhere, that tension and violence tend to rise when compromise is in the air'. The greatest political violence in South Africa occurred during the transition to agreement between 1990 and 1994, when almost three times as many people were killed as in the previous four years. The use of terror also rose dramatically during the Middle East peace process, and more than two-thirds of victims were killed during the Rabin–Peres era; indeed Hermann and Newman claim that 'attacks carried out from the 1990s onwards were seen by Israelis as different to those of the 1960s, 1970s and 1980s, because they occurred against the background of the peace dialogue, rather than in the context of armed conflict'. Apparently the only indisputable prediction about the likely direction of a peace process is that violence will continue after the declaration of a ceasefire.

The issues in dispute and the forms of violence, however, both change. New substantive issues emerge, most of them security related – notably early prisoner releases, decommissioning of illegal weapons and policing. The South African peace process actually began with the release of prisoners, when Nelson Mandela and other ANC leaders were set free in February 1990. The rate of prisoner releases has been a constant source of bitter dispute in Israel/Palestine, but was implemented relatively smoothly in Northern Ireland. Decommissioning of weapons is a more complicated matter. The 1991 South African National Peace Accord did not ask the ANC to disband paramilitary units nor hand over their arms caches; it required only that firearms should not be displayed at public meetings. The stubbornness of Ulster Unionists in demanding decommissioning and of Sinn Féin in rejecting it in Northern Ireland, however irritating, arose from the need of each side to keep its primary constituency on board, and on the symbolic association between decommissioning and surrender. Police reform is an equally emotional issue in negotiations. It is axiomatic that divided societies require a police force which reflects the divisions. Section 195 of the 1996 South African constitution, for example, insisted that the police and defence forces 'be broadly representative of the South African people' and by 1996 16000 former guerrillas had been absorbed into the army. There are plenty of other examples of former combatants entering the security forces, although not all attempts at integration succeeded.

The forms of violence also take on new guises as peace processes evolve. The security apparatus established during the period of violence – heavy recruitment of military, police and prison personnel, emergency legislation and procedures, information gathering, sometimes abuses of power including direct involvement in acts of terror – often become ingrained into the system. When negotiations start the security system faces the dismantling of norms developed and unchallenged for years. Militants are released instead of imprisoned. The security forces augmented during the violence are abruptly reduced in number, endangering their jobs and personal security. Demands are made to reform the police force which regarded itself as the bastion against terrorism. Unless handled carefully, disaffection within the security forces has the potential to undermine the peace process itself.

Disaffection within paramilitary organisations is a more obvious threat to progress. These are rarely the monoliths presented by their opponents. They are complex organisms performing different functions and providing umbrellas for different interests. The diversity allows paramilitary leaders to assume the high moral ground by emphasising their political and civil roles, while turning a blind eye to punishment beatings and murders. It also helps to explain strategic shifts between war and negotiation, as different elements within the organisations win temporary dominance.

During ceasefire periods the varied interests diffuse and fragment. At least four pose separate threats to peace processes:

Political violence

Ceasefires are never unanimous, so the most obvious threat is that they will break down and political violence will return. The more disaffected members of the militants may desert to splinter groups or perform individual acts of violence. The less affected may go along with the majority view, but their agreement is conditional. Their continuing allegiance depends on measurable rewards from negotiation, including prisoner releases and the dismantling of the security apparatus. These rewards are rarely immediate. Consequently the pendulum may swing back towards the militants. The talks broke down in both Northern Ireland and South Africa, leading to periods of renewed violence in 1996 and 1992 respectively, before the peace process resumed.

'Strategic' violence

The exploitation of background violence is a common feature during peace negotiations. When the Irish parliamentary leader Charles Stuart

Parnell was jailed during the Home Rule campaign in the 1880s he forecast correctly that 'Captain Moonlight will take my place', thus positioning himself as the only alternative to revolutionary violence.[1] A common fear among constitutional parties is that the pace of negotiation will be determined by the gunmen outside the negotiating rooms, and that their political surrogates may use the threat of violence to get their way; to paraphrase Clausewitz, that paramilitary negotiators were approaching politics as the continuation of war by other means.

Acts of violence during the process are taken as confirmation of this fear. The early stages of the Oslo process were hampered by Israeli suspicion of the PLO's motives, and later the government regarded Hamas's atrocities as evidence that Arafat either was unable to control his own people or was colluding with it for strategic advantage. During the early stages of the Northern Ireland peace process, Unionists constantly warned that Sinn Féin would use IRA violence to remind other negotiators of their power. Even acts of violence claimed by groups other than those participating in negotiations were cited as evidence of conspiracy. Nevertheless, as the negotiations progressed it became increasingly clear that violence threatened Sinn Féin's interests as much as those of the Unionists. The complaints diminished, as had happened in South Africa.

Family feuding: Internal paramilitary violence

The determination of paramilitaries to exercise control over their own communities does not diminish when they enter a negotiation process. They are unlikely to hand over this key negotiating card, even at the risk of destabilising the peace process itself. The expulsion of one of the former ETA leaders, Txelis, who had advocated a ceasefire from prison just a few days before the ceasefire was actually declared, was an attempt to make clear that only ETA leadership could make authoritative statements. Violence between factions within the Palestinian community continued after the first transfer of land to Palestinian control in 1995. Punishment beatings persisted in Northern Ireland after the Good Friday Agreement as both Loyalists and Republicans exercised what they regarded as their policing role.

The violence resulting from paramilitary in-fighting is often exceptionally vicious and always difficult to police. It erodes respect for law and order and retards the transition to normality. The integration of ex-militants into the security system can be a two-edged sword. It eased the transition in South Africa but the PLO, when it assumed responsibility for policing the Palestinian territories, found itself in direct confrontation with Hamas and other Palestinian militants. If paramilitaries are not integrated into the security forces, the struggle may degenerate into warfare between well-armed rivals, and the police force is often powerless to control them.

Spoilers: Zealots versus Dealers

In essence spoiler violence[2] is carried out by those who remain outside the negotiations from choice. Their aim is not to influence the content of a peace agreement. It is to ensure that agreement is not reached or, if reached, is derailed. Consequently peace processes are very vulnerable to spoilers, especially in their early stages.

The very involvement of paramilitary interests in negotiations implies that the purity of their cause has been compromised. It imposes strains on organisations which are essentially military, and it is difficult to find any instances when such a move was not accompanied by a split between two main groups – the Zealots and the Dealers. The Zealots often comprise radical groups, like the 'Real' IRA and the Continuity IRA in Northern Ireland, who picked up the torch (sometimes literally) they believed had been surrendered by the Dealers. In Sri Lanka the result was a succession of assassinations of Tamil rivals by the Tamil Tigers, who in 1998 murdered the Tamil mayor of Jaffna, having previously killed her husband, and then her successor as mayor. All major attempts to start negotiations in Israel/Palestine were accompanied by Palestinian attempts to bomb them away, but the killing of 28 Muslims by the Israeli settler Baruch Goldstein in 1994 and the assassination of the Israeli Prime Minister Rabin in 1995 showed that Zealots from both communities were eager to capsize the process. Both white and black dissidents threatened the South African process, although spoiler violence by blacks was relatively well controlled during the period of negotiation, perhaps a reflection of the dominance of Nelson Mandela and the ANC. The picture is often complicated by maverick militants who carry out unauthorised crimes for personal gain or from habit, especially in the period immediately following the declaration of a ceasefire.

A major step in removing the threat of spoiler violence is when negotiators representing militants feel strong enough to condemn their violence. The gradual swing away from Herri Batasuna since the late 1980s encouraged Basque leaders who had previously supported ETA to advocate negotiations with the government, and to pressurise ETA towards a ceasefire in 1998. Nelson Mandela calmed his furious supporters after the murder of the ANC leader Chris Hani in April 1993 by pointing out on television that an Afrikaner woman had provided the information necessary for the arrest of his assassins.[3] The universal fury at the Omagh bomb in August 1998, and the marginalisation of the bombers, allowed Sinn Féin to condemn a Republican bomb for the first time. The strength of Hamas as an alternative to the PLO in Israel/Palestine prevented Arafat from such an unqualified condemnation. Strong leadership is necessary, but is more easily supplied when the peace process has become entrenched.

The fragmentation of paramilitary organisations is not the only violent accompaniment to peace processes. Two other forms of violence may also seriously undermine them – the revival of direct confrontations between ethnic rivals and a rise in the conventional crime rate.

Return to the streets

In deeply divided communities the ending of political violence by ceasefire often raises the level of face-to-face street violence. During the early months of negotiation in South Africa sectional violence was partly orchestrated between the ANC and the IFP, but spilled over into tit-for-tat killings and more general violence. The emergence of what Mees described as the 'street guerrilla', mostly teenagers, in the Basque Country arose partly from ETA's weakening authority, but was also partly a reaction to the popularity of the peace movement. In Northern Ireland the declaration of the ceasefires, and the ending of direct violence between organised paramilitaries and the security forces, was marked by a return to more direct violence between Catholics and Protestants, especially during the marching seasons from 1996 to 1998.

The change is not surprising. During the period of organised violence, paramilitaries must be dominant and disciplined to be effective. For the Tamil Tigers in Sri Lanka, ETA in the Basque Country and the Provisional IRA in Northern Ireland, the initial targets for elimination were rival groups from their own community. During the later years of struggle, control of their own territory continued as an absolute necessity for paramilitary groups. When a ceasefire is declared the discipline of the military campaign diminishes, but the underlying sectarian hatred remains, taking the form of riots and undisciplined confrontations with ethnic rivals or the police. They can become a serious threat to a peace process. The paramilitary representatives who enter negotiations are not divorced from the instincts and antagonisms of their communities, and may feel the need to support them. The danger is that confrontational violence may swing the balance from negotiation back towards a military campaign.

'Ordinary decent crime'

A rise in conventional crime may appear to present a less obvious danger. The discipline imposed by paramilitary organisations during their freedom struggle is often imposed with a level of severity which could teach Mayor Giuliani of New York some lessons about zero tolerance. Years of violence leaves a vast stockpile of arms – in 1996 there was at least one firearm in 20 per cent of South African households and in Uganda an AK-47 could be bought for the price of a chicken.[4] The security services have become more geared to political than to regular crime. The criminal aspects of paramilitary campaigns often transmute into organised crime. Underlying all of this, people have become accustomed to violence as a routine social phenomenon. Expectations of immediate economic and other improvements are often raised during the period of negotiations, and often disappointed after the accord is reached.

The crime rate has risen to such a degree in South Africa as seriously to undermine post-settlement peacebuilding. It is a threat to inward investment, tourism and general confidence. By the mid-1990s the high level of conventional crime had far outpaced political violence as a destabilising factor. By 1998 the daily homicide rate was 52, and still rising. More ominously, the barrier between ordinary crime and South Africa's underlying racial tensions, never sharp, became increasingly blurred. Fifteen hundred white farmers were attacked between 1994 and 1998, resulting in more than 200 murders, and threatening to create a loop back from post-settlement civil violence to the racial violence familiar from the earlier struggle.

All of the forms of violence detailed above are separate threads in a single weave. The pattern that unites them is the central role of violence both before and after the declaration of a ceasefire. Paramilitaries and the state security system may use violence to gain advantage in negotiations. Ceasefires may collapse from the actions of spoilers or from opinion shifts within paramilitary structures. If they continue, political violence may be transformed into factional turf wars, sectarian confrontations or normal crime. A range of contentious issues under negotiation – the very inclusion of terrorists in the negotiations, early releases of prisoners, decommissioning of weapons, policing – have the potential to undermine the process.

External influences

In August 1993, four Israelis, four Palestinians and four Norwegians initialled a Declaration of Principles, which were formally signed one month later on the White House lawn. The Oslo Accords were launched. The process had started in 1992 when the PLO, seeking external facilitation, approached a group of Norwegians. At that time it was illegal for Israelis and Palestinians to meet in Israel. The resulting negotiations evolved their own ground rules: a cover project was invented as camouflage; both sides agreed not to dwell on history; to ensure secrecy they met in private homes rather than hotels, and the media were not informed; the teams were kept small, and the pressure maintained; negotiations even continued during mealtimes.[5]

The Oslo process, initially involving academics and NGOs and later politicians, was unique, but the exercise of external influence to facilitate or to apply pressure for a settlement is not. In South Africa the effect of UN sanctions in ending apartheid is disputed. Zartman marks it as the 'turning point' which started the search for alternatives.[6] The balance of evidence leans towards du Toit's view that the ending of the Cold War enabled the United States effectively to present an ultimatum to De Klerk: negotiate or face the consequences.

No ethnic conflict is exclusively internal. All operate within a regional or international context, and are influenced by it. Similarly, all peace processes may be generally influenced by external factors. The white South African fear of communism, if exaggerated, was genuine and the ending of the Cold War eased the initiation of the peace process there. The strategic and electoral importance of the Middle East for the United States ensured that both the conflict there, and attempts to resolve it, attracted general attention. Hermann and Newman argue that both depended more on external than domestic initiatives, and point out that 'all Israeli–Arab wars were brought to an end by external mediation'.

The 'armed struggles' in Sri Lanka and Northern Ireland depended heavily on financial support from diaspora populations. In Sri Lanka the proximity of massive Tamil populations in India helped to precipitate the Indian military intervention in 1987, with unfortunate consequences for both countries. Even today, although both the Sri Lankan government and the LTTE claim to believe that external mediation is necessary to start a peace process, they both impose mutually unacceptable preconditions, and the government has rejected offers of facilitation from Canada and Norway because of the perceived influence of

Tamil diaspora in both countries. These fears may be displaced. Irish-Americans played an important role in persuading the IRA to call a ceasefire and in bringing Sinn Féin into negotiations. Both Israeli-Americans and Irish-American communities swung around to become more enthusiastic advocates of the peace processes than the people actually living in the Middle East and Northern Ireland.

Neither the United Nations nor any major regional organisation has had direct involvement in any of the five Coming out of Violence cases, but the United States has become involved in the peace processes in South Africa, Israel–Palestine and Northern Ireland. This intervention was particularly helpful in the infant stages or to massage particular sticking points, as when the United States helped to bring the Inkatha Freedom Party into the South African process in 1992 and Clinton's two morale-raising visits to Northern Ireland. His flight into the newly built Gaza airport in December 1998 came at a point when the Wye River Accord, signed just a month earlier, needed a jump-start. The visit had no material content – no treaty was signed, no economic rewards offered. The significance was entirely symbolic. Clinton's statement – 'I am profoundly honoured to be the first American president to address the Palestinian people in a city governed by Palestinians' – was a carefully gauged warning to the Netanyahu government that the United States was not exclusively bound to Israel, and a counter to Palestinian charges of bias.

Internal disputes are often a proxy for larger disputes, or at least a historical echo of them – between the Irish and the British, Israel and the Arab countries, Sri Lanka and India. Consequently neighbouring countries often have a vested interest in encouraging or resolving conflicts. The roles of neighbouring Arab states in Israel (with quite different influences coming from Syria, Lebanon, Jordan and Egypt) were at times critical. Northern Ireland and Sri Lanka stand at the ends of the spectrum of external influence. All the interested external powers – the United States and the European Union, even the United Kingdom and the Irish Republic if they can be regarded as external to the province – gave unanimous support for a negotiated settlement in Northern Ireland. Contrast this with Sri Lanka, where the Indian intervention altered the problem without improving it, and no other neighbouring state has exercised a comparable influence for peace. Of the five areas studied, external influence was greatest in Israel/Palestine and Northern Ireland, and least in the Basque Country and Sri Lanka. The best explanation is located in the United States foreign policy and electoral politics.

Economic factors

One of the arguments most often used to encourage the ending of violence is that peace will lead to new jobs, more tourism and greater investment. It has been estimated that the cost of the war in Sri Lanka will reach $723 000 000 in 1999, 13.26 per cent of the state's budget, an intolerable burden for a Third World country; it is hard to disagree with Saravanamuttu's view that 'an end of war is a necessary condition of economic development'. The promise of a peace dividend was consciously used during the years of violence in all five areas to stimulate a peace process. The business community in Northern Ireland, predominantly Unionist, was at the fore in urging an agreement. In South Africa, the first approaches to the ANC came from the white business community.

Delivery is another matter, and the 'peace dividends' which were expected to follow the ending of violence in the Palestinian Authority and in South Africa were disappointing.[7] The heavy dependence of Palestinians on Israel, including the frequent barriers to their travelling to work, demonstrates the asymmetrical nature of many peace processes and the difficulty of improving structural inequalities. Indeed, the economic expectations which are routinely raised to encourage progress during a peace process are often frustrated after it has been agreed. Initial hopes of greater prosperity in Israel were raised by a growth of international investment after the Oslo Accords, but were dashed by a severe downturn from 1996 as the process stalled; Gross National Product in the Palestinian Autonomy Areas in particular fell dramatically. The inability of the South African administrations to implement speedy economic improvements, and therefore to secure more equitable distribution in housing, employment and general prosperity, led to increased levels of social and political unrest. The crime rate soared and has become a major post-settlement problem. This crime was often directed against those who continued to control the economy, the whites, and the racial dimension threatens a return towards pre-settlement tensions.

By way of contrast, Northern Ireland benefited initially from substantial European Union grants to buttress the negotiations from 1994, and from increased external investments: tourist revenue rose by 30 per cent in the year following the 1994 ceasefires. Still, it is hard to find evidence that peace dividends move the process forward significantly. It might be speculated that the significant reduction in economic differentials between Catholics and Protestants in Northern

Ireland before the 1998 Agreement removed a potential stimulus for Catholic disaffection after it. Certainly the Catholic community was much more enthusiastic about the Agreement than the Protestant. The evidence across the five areas suggests that a background of economic depression is a serious obstacle to peace processes. It is more difficult to prove that economic stimuli are a significant encouragement to them.

Popular responses

'Mobilising for conflict is much easier than mobilising for peace, notwithstanding the initiators of the mobilisation efforts'. This observation by Hermann and Newman lies close to the heart of one of the most contested current questions about peace processes. Are they essentially bottom-up or top-down exercises? Is it possible to stimulate a peace initiative by groundswell pressure, and does a strong civil and democratic infrastructure help to sustain it? Or is peace managed by leadership from the political elites, as appears to have happened in all five cases studied? Of course this is a false dichotomy. Lasting peace depends on both leadership and popular support.

The desire for peace expressed by the Sri Lankan government and the Tamil Tigers was undermined by their different interpretations of what constituted peace. There and in Northern Ireland opinion polls have consistently indicated a popular desire for peace, suggesting that ethnic politics encourages leaders to take up more intransigent positions. The Troubles in Northern Ireland were accompanied by the creation of many peace organisations, most notably the Peace People formed in August 1976, but it would be difficult to argue that any of them seriously diverted the direction of events. In Israel, Hermann and Newman claim that 'when the formal negotiations did not progress smoothly or reached a dead end, no significant pressures from below were exerted on the decision makers to make greater concessions in order to push the process forwards'. The decision in South Africa to enter negotiations with the ANC arose from an altered view by National Party leaders rather than their followers.

The ineffectual demonstrations of the early peace movements in the Basque Country had become more organised and effective by the 1990s. The level of activity alone marked out the Basque Country from the other areas. Between 1995 and 1998 the co-ordinating peace body Gesto had held more than 15 000 silent protest meetings. Around six million people protested against the murder of the local councillor Miguel Angel Blanco in 1997, provoking counter-protests supporting

ETA. As Mees points out, decline in support for ETA provided the opportunity for the peace movements to mobilise public protest and ultimately to influence political initiatives.

Public opinion is an amorphous concept. The generality of a population may flounder ineffectually in the face of political violence, but elements within it sometimes find it possible to make more strategic interventions. The strong civil society in Northern Ireland allowed reforms in the fair allocation of housing, employment and education to be implemented during the years of violence, prevented a bad situation from becoming worse, and reduced the roster of problems to be tackled during the peace process. South Africa's business community made the first informal approaches to the ANC in the 1980s. Other mediators – church leaders, academics and trade unionists – helped to establish the first informal meetings between political opponents in all five countries, and at least allowed them to pursue 'what-if' scenarios within relatively risk-free settings. It is also difficult to assess the influence of community relations policies and approaches, notably in Northern Ireland, in creating an appropriate atmosphere for negotiations.

The Basque experience aside, there is little evidence that a groundswell desire for peace has pressurised leaders towards the necessary compromises. One important qualification is necessary. The effectiveness of popular opinion is enhanced after an agreement has been reached, or even when a peace process is in the air. In such circumstances it is worth paying attention to those catalytic events when an atrocity not only provokes universal condemnation but also galvanises popular reaction against the perpetrators. After decades of kidnappings and murders, it took the kidnapping of Basques by ETA and Blanco's murder in 1997 to bring hundreds of thousands of Basque protesters onto the streets in opposition to ETA's violence. After almost thirty years of violence in Northern Ireland, the public reactions against the murder of three children in Ballymoney and a bomb in Omagh in 1998 had a major influence in undercutting opposition to the Good Friday Agreement. The murder of 28 ANC supporters in Bisho in 1992 was not followed by the same violent protests after the massacre of 48 people at Boipatong three months earlier. Instead it became a stimulus for the negotiations rather than a cause for withdrawal.

What is the nature of these atrocities, which converts them into catalysts for peace? To some degree it is war-weariness, but this condition can continue for years without stimulating compromise. The reason why certain violent events, at certain times, become catalysts for peace lies not in the nature or severity of the violence – there had often been worse atrocities in the past – but in its timing. The public demand for a renewal of negotiations after Bisho arose directly from the reminder of the alternative presented by the Boipatong massacre and from fear that the process might collapse. The Omagh bomb closely followed two referenda and an election massively supporting negotiations. The point is this; courage in condemning atrocities is not enough. What converts outrage to action is condemnation within the context, or at least realistic hope, that agreement is possible, and that further violence could threaten it. It is also clear that such moments are transitory. The often-mentioned 'window of opportunity' is barely ajar and soon slams shut.

Symbols and rituals

In May 1994, just as Nelson Mandela was sworn in as president of South Africa, part of the ceremony was a ritual flyover by the South African air force. Their exhausts released the red, green and black of the new South African flag. For some ANC supporters the planes had previously been associated with bombing their bases in the border states. 'It was the moment when I felt South African', said one of them.[8]

Why has South Africa been so skilled at identifying the appropriate gesture to cut across sectarian and racial barriers? A great part of the credit belongs to Mandela, who clearly manipulated symbols to encourage reconciliation. He had an unerring eye for the uniting gesture which would heal the wounds of conflict. His attendance at the Rugby World Cup final, the sport of white South Africa, and donning a Springbok shirt, showed a generosity of spirit that set an example in the uneasy new state.

It is not easy to find the telling gesture which unites antagonists and signifies a flood change. Indeed rituals and symbols more often obstruct than assist reconciliation. Ritual has demonstrated its potential to disrupt the peace process in Northern Ireland. Orange processions metamorphosed into a focus for Protestant opposition to the peace process. The change was a response to the empowerment of the Catholic minority and its new determination to prohibit parades. Protestant confidence had been eroded by what they saw as concessions to their opponents; they felt an increased need to demonstrate their heritage and unity. The differences became communal rather than political, and the highly ritualistic and predictable nature of parades resulted in a serious threat to community harmony.

One of the most difficult tasks in any peace process is how to confront the sins of the past without compromising the need for reconciliation. 'I have one great fear in my heart', said the black priest in Alan Paton's *Cry the Beloved Country*, 'that one day when they are turned to loving, they will find we are turned to hating'.[9] In the early Oslo negotiations the negotiators agreed not to dwell on past grievances. Other negotiations have built into the timetable what might be described as venting time, to allow the inevitable bitterness to be expressed and then, hopefully, set aside. The South African Truth and Reconciliation Commission was established in 1995 and did not shrink from identifying atrocities from all sides, and the Northern Ireland Victims' Commissioner made a number of recommendations to identify and support victims of the Troubles. Both arose from the same root – the need to acknowledge feelings of hurt and loss and the importance of grieving – and both attempted to find ways of dissociating these feelings from guilt and acrimony, not an easy task. Their experience supports Hermann and Newman's view that 'a much longer time scale is required for the general public to join the peace process bandwagon, endorsing the course of reconciliation with the former enemy'.

What is the nature of the successful symbolic gesture? It must appear to transcend or cut across tribalism – to reach across to the other side in a way which runs counter to cultural expectations. It is the imaginative and magnanimous gesture which touches the opposite communities and erodes its suspicions. It only works if there is no suggestion of triumphalism or condescension, and if there is no obvious – or at least apparent – short-term political advantage. Only time can answer the more nagging question – do such gestures have a permanent or passing effect on stalled peace processes?

Progress towards political settlement

If pluralist societies were charted on a graph, according to how effectively they function, the pattern might be presented as an ascending line. At the bottom of the line are peacefully regulated multi-cultural societies currently experiencing little or no violence, such as Switzerland, Canada and Australia; all of these have experienced ethnic tensions, and sometimes violence, in the past and may experience it again in the future, because permanent stability is unattainable. Moving along the ascending line, a large number of communities suffer relatively low levels of ethnic violence, including in the present or recent past the Basque Country and Northern Ireland. In these places violence has been conducted by paramilitary organisations against the state or ethnic rivals, but has been controlled by the presence of an army or by indigenous social and economic mechanisms. At the top of the graph are societies in which the violence has spiralled out of control, such as recently experienced in Bosnia, Rwanda and Burundi. These are often characterised by open warfare by organised armies.

Individual societies may move along the line of the graph in either direction. Some have completed the full course more than once, while others oscillate around one point over prolonged periods. Low-violence ethnic conflicts can be smothered temporarily, but may rekindle in the future. It is sometimes possible, especially during the earlier phases of ethnic violence, to address grievances by the introduction of appropriate reforms. But if ethnic grievances are not addressed rapidly they tend to accelerate along the line of grievance and to become increasingly violent. When this happens, it becomes difficult to return to the fundamental causes of conflict, and the priority may shift to reducing the casualties and planning for post-war negotiations.

This section will discuss the process of negotiations in three stages: pre-negotiation; the negotiations themselves; and post-settlement peacebuilding. Each stage brings its own problems and requires different approaches. Pre-negotiation, for example, often includes 'Track-two' approaches (non-governmental contact by such mediators as the business community, academics or churches), external pressure and secret talks, as well as the declaration of ceasefires. The negotiations themselves may have to tackle disputes about inclusion, violence and techniques for moving the process forward. Peace accords are not only concerned with the clauses in the agreement; equally important are their validation through elections or referenda and the schedule to deal with the remaining problems. Post-settlement arrangements often include issues such as reform of policing and the administration of justice, arms decommissioning and economic reconstruction, all of which carry different weights in different contexts.

But peace processes are not strictly linear, and different societies sometimes tackle problems outside the normal sequence. If every peace process had to wait for a complete ending to violence, none of the five would have started. The individual histories peculiar to each country account for the distinctive sequencing of each process – why the policing and administrative autonomy were tackled in the Basque Country before peace negotiations started; why minority grievances on housing, employment and educational reforms were carried out in Northern Ireland during the years of violence. Indeed, not only is it possible to tackle traditional 'post-settlement' tasks early in the process, but the momentum created by this may assist the move towards negotiations.

It is the deviations from the normal model which sometimes provide the most instructive insights into the business of making peace.

Pre-negotiation: Getting into talks

The process of moving out of violence presupposes a new readiness of combatants to accord some form of recognition and legitimacy to their opponents. After that, the process can start at any of a number of alternative points. Imagine the set of factors required to end ethnic violence – a ceasefire, agreement to negotiate, mediation, demilitarisation, decommissioning – as a circle of dominoes standing like the stones at Stonehenge. The ending of violent conflict requires all the dominoes to topple. The process can be triggered by moving any one of the dominoes forward, creating a momentum which collapses its neighbour, and so on to the next one, and the next. The dominoes are more numerous, and more entrenched, in some conflicts than in others.

Zartman has argued convincingly that a 'most striking characteristic of internal conflicts its asymmetry: one party (government) is strong and the other (insurgents) is weak'.[10] Peace processes most often occur when both these circumstances have changed, when both government and paramilitaries recognise the others' ability to frustrate their success. This has been described as a 'mutually hurting stalemate', where 'both sides perceived themselves to be in a stalemate that was painful to each of them and they saw a better alternative through negotiation'.[11] This may be allied to the concept of the 'ripe moment', that brief moment when the playing field is acceptably level for both sides and talks become possible.[12] This point was reached in South Africa in 1989 when, du Toit argues, both sides recognised that the cost of continuing stalemate was greater than any unlikely military gain, and De Klerk became leader of the National Party. Sri Lanka's experience supports this argument from the opposite perspective, in that both protagonists still appear to believe that their objectives are most likely to be achieved through war. However, ripe moments and hurting stalemates are more easily identified in retrospect than in advance. It is possible to argue that, in any conflict, a number of ripe moments come and go, and hurting stalemates demonstrably continue for years – in Northern Ireland for at least fifteen years before the 1994 ceasefires. The danger is that the argument is too passive and may discourage initiatives during periods of violence – reforms in the allocation of resources, informal attempts at mediation or mediation, Track Two approaches – which may help to prepare the ground for later negotiations. Why bother if the meal must wait for the fruit to ripen?

The peace processes in South Africa, Northern Ireland and Israel/ Palestine began with secret talks. These have certain advantages over traditional diplomacy as a preliminary to substantive talks: the formal barriers imposed by protocol are dropped; the temperature of the water and the temper of one's opponents may be tested with limited risk; 'what-if' scenarios can be floated without commitment; secret talks can be a useful transition process for those who rose to leadership as security or insurgent leaders, and who often have little or no experience of the art of compromise; working relationships are allowed to evolve between antagonists. The exclusion of the media helped to keep the talks in Oslo and Northern Ireland secret. Secret talks are attractive because, in du Toit's words, they 'held low exit costs'.

There are alternative approaches, of course, which may run in parallel to secret talks. Intermediaries such as the business community, the churches and academics were active in mediating in South Africa and Northern Ireland. Peace movements and civil society were less influential in both places. Despite 75 meetings between Democratic Alternative for South Africa (IDASA) and the ANC, du Toit's conclusion that 'they in fact did little to move the primary protagonists to the negotiating table' applies with equal strength to similar initiatives in Northern Ireland and Israel, and even more strongly in Sri Lanka.

Under what circumstances can external or internal mediation help to massage a movement towards negotiations? The involvement of Norwegian academics was critical in starting the Oslo talks in 1993. Northern Ireland benefited from both internal mediation – the two clergymen who helped to broker the deal which brought Republican and Loyalist paramilitaries into the process – and external mediation, initially by Irish-Americans and later by the notable part played by George Mitchell during negotiations. The first white approaches to the ANC came from the South African business community. Nothing of this significance can be identified in the Basque Country or Sri Lanka. Basque nationalists favour external mediation more than the Spanish government – not an unusual circumstance; and while both parties in Sri Lanka declare the need for mediation, they impose mutually exclusive conditions. One general point emerges from the comparison: mediators are more necessary, and more effective, during the preliminaries of a peace process than later, although the Northern Ireland process profited from George Mitchell's role as chairman during the negotiations themselves, and the International Committee on Arms Decommissioning performed a role which would have been impossible for a local body.

It is not uncommon for the constitutional and paramilitary opponents of the existing government to form a temporary alliance in advance of negotiation. In Northern Ireland a 'pan-nationalist front' operated between the SDLP, Sinn Féin and the Irish Government following the Hume–Adams talks. Even the TULF in Sri Lanka insisted that talks could not be confined to constitutional parties but must include the Tamil Tigers. The dominance of the ANC in South Africa, with the important exception of the Inkatha Freedom Party, made alliances unnecessary as Mandela spoke for most black South Africans. These alliances help to compensate for the asymmetrical nature of negotiations, where the initial advantage leans towards the government side. They apply pressure to force a reluctant government into talks, but carry a price. The long-term cost may be increased bitterness between ethnic protagonists during negotiations and in post-settlement peace building.

The preliminaries to peace processes are not subject to standard formulae. Chance can play a critical role. Most of the ingredients for negotiations were already in place under the Conservative administration of John Major, but it began only after a Labour government was elected with a commanding majority in 1997. A strong argument could be made that De Klerk's election as President in 1989 started the peace process in South Africa, and that the Israeli process started with the election of Rabin in 1992 and stalled after Netanyahu's election four years later. The point is that these changes of government were not exclusively related to peace, although they profoundly affected the peace process. They were chance developments.

These changes in government did not in themselves lead to negotiations. If the ground had not been prepared in advance a breakthrough was unlikely to happen. It is the combination of preparing for and seizing on the moment of opportunity that makes a peace process.

Negotiating the settlement

Spoiler violence often reaches its climax during the first weeks of actual negotiation, when the peace process is at its most vulnerable. During the years of violence which precede talks, cross-ethnic contacts diminish and hostile stereotypes are entrenched; these include the belief that one's opponents are united, cohesive, devious and successful, while one's own side is divided and frustrated. Saravanamuttu points to the 'pathology of insecurity of the two sides which has been characterised as a problem between a majority with a minority complex and a minority with a majority complex', almost identical language to that used by Jackson in 1971 to describe the Northern Ireland problem.[13] The overriding view on both sides is that their opposing aspirations are mutually exclusive and that compromise means giving in to extremists on both sides. These are not ideal conditions for negotiations. Indeed one measure of successful progress is the extent to which the antagonists move away from cohort behaviour – voting along sectarian lines on every issue regardless of its sectarian content – towards cross-cutting allegiances when, although they continue to contest the fundamental differences, they allow agreement on neutral non-controversial subjects.

The initial need at this stage is to build confidence in the fledgling process, and to establish rules and procedures to move it forward. Israel's recognition of the PLO as legitimate representatives of the Palestinian people in Oslo A, coupled with acceptance of the Palestinian right to self-determination, had immense symbolic significance. There and elsewhere the fact that negotiations are taking place at all presumes an acceptance, often implicit rather than acknowledged, that paramilitary representatives have been admitted to negotiations in return for giving up violence. The imposition of a 'good behaviour' test before full admission acknowledges the point, but is resented by the militants; they prefer to argue that their inclusion is justified by their popular support rather than because they have the power to frustrate any agreement made in their absence by the use of violence. In practice it is often motivated by both considerations. Either way, the inclusion of the militants in talks, whatever pressures it imposes on the process, admits them to the common enterprise and applies a moral pressure on them to preserve the process in the face of violence from dissidents or spoiler groups.

The inclusion of militants does not presume that the mechanics of their admission had been determined, and they are often required to surmount a tortuous series of tests and symbolic encounters. Peace processes are littered with 'historic' handshakes – Sadat–Begin, Rabin–Arafat, Adams–Mayhew, Netanyahu–Arafat – taken as sanctifying a break with the past. Probation periods were set before Sinn Féin was admitted to talks, and the Spanish President authorised talks with ETA six weeks after its ceasefire in 1998. It is necessary to agree to rules which regulate the resumption of violence. The South African process, while not requiring arms decommissioning, insisted that arms should be banned from public meetings. In Northern Ireland the Mitchell Principles were devised, and imposed, as conditions for entry to talks and for punishing breaches by paramilitaries associated with negotiating parties.

The issue of transparency is especially critical. Hermann and Newman point out that 'the messages which constitute part of the negotiation process with the other side of the conflict are not, and cannot be, the same as those used as a means of gaining the support of the domestic audience'. So how can a compromise be struck between the need for secrecy before agreement is reached and the obligation of public accountability? As a general rule, secrecy diminishes in importance as negotiations proceed, and the need to involve the community in the forthcoming compromises increases. An excess of publicity entrenches party differences before an agreement is reached. An excess of secrecy not only encourages conspiracy interpretations but may encourage hard-line mobilisation within each negotiating community. It also fails to prepare public opinion for compromise or to mobilise the public in favour of a peace process. Saravanamuttu has pointed out the difficulties created in 1994 by the variance between the Sri Lankan Freedom Party and the more liberal perspective of its leader Ms Kumarutunga. More progress may be achieved by hard-line than by moderate leaders, because concessions by the former are more convincing to their community. F. W. De Klerk, Nelson Mandela, Gerry Adams and David Trimble, all had previous associations with intransigent positions but were able to lead their respective followers into peace agreements.

Although the issues to be negotiated reflect the distinctiveness of each conflict, some themes are constant. The early release of prisoners is almost always a *sine qua non* for paramilitaries engaged in talks; it is also a highly emotive reminder to victims of violence that their sensibilities have been pushed into the background in the interests of securing peace. Reforms in policing, security and the administration of justice are also constant features if an accord is agreed. No clear pattern is discernible on decommissioning; it emerged as a major threat to the process in Northern Ireland, but hardly rated as a problem in South Africa.

The prime responsibility for preparing discussion papers on procedures for negotiation usually falls on government, especially if the talks involve a number of competing parties. This may require distance brokerage, often in two phases. Shuttle diplomacy may be needed to establish the preconditions and ground rules for participants. If these can be agreed, proximity talks are often necessary before the participants are willing to meet in plenary sessions, although *ad hoc* meetings on specific aspects of the negotiation process provided a useful middle way in Northern Ireland. Proximity talks were unnecessary in South Africa, but it took three years to complete what du Toit describes as 'talks about substantive talks' – the conditions, ground rules and rules of engagement. Substantive negotiations actually started in 1991 before the preliminaries had been completed.

Pierre du Toit identifies a number of innovative negotiation devices developed to cope when the South African process stalled, among them: the 'bush summits' designed to smooth out bilateral disagreements; the 'channel', a subcommittee of three which met daily to maintain momentum; and the creation of new institutions such as the Transitional Executive Council and the Independent Electoral Commission to counter the asymmetrical nature of power structures in South Africa. Some of these were consciously imitated in other places. The concept of 'sufficient consensus', for example, designed to keep dissenters in the process if they were outvoted on a specific issue, was effectively applied in Northern Ireland. Northern Ireland itself developed distinctive procedures, notably the use of George Mitchell as an external chairman for the talks, and the development of the Mitchell Principles as a procedure to enable parties previously associated with violence to enter talks under specific conditions; it also created new institutions such as the Parades Commission and the International Decommissioning Body to tackle issues which had not been resolved in the Accord.

Thereafter timetables and deadlines are essential to maintain momentum. In their absence the 1994 ceasefires in Northern Ireland were followed by a fatal lack of urgency which eventually led to the ending of the IRA ceasefire. Contrast that with the precise deadlines established during the resumed negotiations in 1998. In Israel/Palestine the 1993 Oslo A Accord set a specific date (May 1999), five years from the start of its implementation, for the transfer of authority and land. The deadlines were not always met, but they imposed an obligation on parties which carried substantial weight in all three cases. The Wye River Accord modified the original commitment by imposing a five-stage time frame linking Israeli withdrawals to specific security pledges from the Palestinians, a reflection of altered political demands.

One by-product of establishing deadlines is that negotiations sometimes advance in surges rather than by gradual increments. This encourages the emergence of a brinkmanship style of negotiation, conspicuous in Northern Ireland, when all-night sittings became *de rigueur* for signpost agreements along the path to settlement; sometimes the deadlines were missed by a few days. This approach carries obvious risks, as when the parties failed to meet the April 1999 date for transferring powers, but has some incidental benefits. It demonstrates how a deadline focuses attention. In addition, brinkmanship confirms to a divided community that their leaders are fighting a tough fight, thus helping to prepare them for the compromises to come.

Freidman remarked in reference to the South African process that 'however bitter conflict became, however unbridgeable the divide between negotiating parties seemed to be, somehow the abyss always seemed to hold less appeal than the option of shifting ground'.[14] A similar development was evident in Northern Ireland and, less consistently, in the Middle East. At an advanced stage of the peace process, it may be more difficult for the negotiators to leave the process than to stay in it; by the more optimistic reading, the engagement of the negotiators in a common enterprise creates a common bonding; more cynically, the failure of the peace process and a return to war places those who initiated the strategy in personal danger from militants within their own community.

Post-settlement peace-building – cementing the peace

Peace negotiations are about substantive disagreements as well as about process. The root problem in many negotiations is that the aggrieved party wants independence, which governments are usually reluctant to concede. The apparent compromise of federalism may not be acceptable to either party. As negotiations proceed, it is tempting to defer this and other sensitive issues to post-settlement negotiation. During the Oslo negotiations, for example, five critical issues, including Jerusalem, settlements and refugee return, were 'blackboxed' to enable the two sides to move forward on other less inflexible issues. In Northern Ireland the deferred issues included some very divisive matters – cross-border structures with the Irish Republic, reforms in policing and the administration of justice, arms decommissioning and the sharing of executive power. Deadlines were set for most of these – two years in the case of decommissioning – but this runs the risk of timetabling a series of post-settlement crises in the interests of short-term gain. The South African agreement transferred potentially deadlock issues, including affirmative action and the integration of the armed forces, to the agenda of the first elected government – described by du Toit as 'deliberate ambiguity'. By 1996 it might be claimed that the two-phase process set up in 1993 had been completed, but even there the controversy surrounding the Truth and Reconciliation Commission demonstrates the time bombs which are secreted in even the most carefully crafted peace accord.

The South African experience illustrates that the settlement can be seriously threatened by developments which were both unanticipated and unrelated to the conflict. The inability to deliver either economic regeneration or greater social equality led to a growing sense of disillusion with peace itself. The parallel rise in conventional crime was even more destabilising, and not unrelated to economic grievances. The transfer of ex-paramilitary activists into the police and security forces in the Palestinian Territories and South Africa was a tangible acceptance of past abuses and an effective way to convert a potentially destabilising armed threat into support for the new structures. It is also a tangible demonstration of fair employment practices by the new administrations.

Apart from having to confront these continuing disputes, post-settlement administrations are also confronted by the problems left by years of violence and confrontation. The Truth and Reconciliation Commission in South Africa and the Victims Commission in Northern Ireland were attempts to deal with victims and the injuries of the past. The controversy surrounding both bodies demonstrates the cliché that it may take as long to repair community dysfunction as it took to create it, and that means decades rather than years. In 1998, five years after the famous handshake between Rabin and Arafat, 42 per cent of Israelis still saw Arafat as a terrorist against 26 per cent who saw him as a statesman.

Relative importance of the factors

Coming Out of Violence monitored six features of five peace processes – violence, progress towards a political settlement, the economy, external actors, public opinion and symbols. The list is not exhaustive; disputes about territory, for example, are central to the conflicts in Israel/Palestine and Sri Lanka, and have less influence in Ireland, South Africa and the Basque Country. Nor do the factors carry equal weight. The balance varies within each setting and depending on the stage through which it is progressing. Nevertheless some general observations and some tentative suggestions may be made:

- Of the six variables, economic factors appear to have the lowest influence on the success or failure of a peace process. The correlation between background economic conditions and political progress is weak, although economic grievances can fuel opposition to compromise, as it did in Israel/Palestine. The promise of economic regeneration after an accord is often disappointed; even in

Northern Ireland, where there was a significant peace dividend, its beneficial effect on the process was marginal.

- The influence of external powers is often inconsistent. Diaspora support for ethnic intransigence, notably in Sri Lanka, Israel and Northern Ireland, can be swung round to support peace initiatives, as in the last two cases. The beneficial mediation of external powers was also a strong factor in both places, especially in the early stages, and its absence in Sri Lanka is a barrier to progress.
- The importance of symbols and rituals, for good or bad, is often underrated. The key positive variable is the ability of a post-settlement regime to create unifying symbols, as South Africa has done with its flag and anthem and through sport. The alternative is that rituals will become the property of one or other faction, as happened when marches and other rituals undermined the negotiations in Northern Ireland.
- The most disputed factor is the influence of developments on the ground in initiating and advancing peace processes. All five cases in the Coming Out of Violence study resulted from elite accommodations between political leaders rather than from popular pressure, although the Basque peace movements were an important influence in mobilising public opinion there.
- Violence and progression towards a political settlement are the main determinants of success or failure, and they are inextricably linked. Violence was usually the lever which moved governments to talks. It is more easily turned on than switched off. The demand from one side that violence should end, and from the other that prisoners should be released and security policies changed, dominated the early stages of negotiations and frustrated progress in Sri Lanka, Israel/Palestine and Northern Ireland. It is impossible to separate the negotiations strand from the violence strand.

Conclusions

This book had specific objectives. The five studies which form its basis shared a number of common characteristics. They were all experiencing peace processes. All of these were taking place within a relatively narrow time frame. The studies were evolutionary rather than retrospective. They were essentially attempts to resolve internal ethnic disputes, although external actors played critical roles in some of them.

UN-brokered settlements were excluded because they were, we believe, significantly different in their dynamics and outcomes and because they were already adequately covered in the research literature. Our aim was to supplement that literature by highlighting characteristics of an approach to peace processes which, we argued in Chapter 1, emerged during the 1990s and was likely to become even more common in the future.

The conclusions are presented as a series of propositions chosen to illuminate these processes.

Proposition 1: Most ceasefires collapse in the first few months. The survivors are likely to deliver some level of success.

A successful peace process is organic and cumulative. The public euphoria following the ending of violence contrasts with the mutual suspicion of the early negotiations. Constitutional politicians are forced to negotiate with people they regard as criminals. They may overlook the high risks which also confront the militants who have entered negotiations, and whose position is severely diminished if the talks collapse. Tests were imposed in Israel, in Northern Ireland and in the Basque Country before militants were admitted into talks. These delays may be understandable but can be dangerous, as the breakdown of the first IRA ceasefire demonstrated.

If the process survives the first nervous contacts, it tends to strengthen. Sometimes it is reinforced by internal pressure from public opinion, as happened in South Africa when the process faltered in 1992, and sometimes by external support, an essential element in Northern Ireland. This dynamic does not mean that the negotiators have become friends; for the entire duration of negotiations Unionists refused even to speak directly to Sinn Féin representatives. It is enough that they can define a common problem and agree to negotiate an accommodation. The dynamic of achieving this position locks those involved in negotiation in an uncomfortable embrace. The participants become more attracted to the positive rewards of a historic breakthrough. It becomes increasingly difficult for any of them to contemplate a return to the earlier violence. Failure to make progress would rule out another initiative for the foreseeable future. It would also probably mean the end of their political careers and, sometimes, threaten their lives. In addition, working relationships develop between the negotiators as they concentrate on the practical minutiae of negotiations and become better acquainted with the boundaries within which their opponents operate. These benefits depend on maintaining momentum and forward tempo. Opportunities are infrequent, and short, as shown in South Africa and Northern Ireland. Their experiences underline the importance of preparation, and moving speedily when opportunities arrive. The risk of making mistakes on the details is a necessary one.

The further the process develops the stronger its shock-absorbent facility and the more capable its ability to withstand the inevitable atrocities designed to undermine it. This resilience in turn weakens the spoilers. Political fatalities in South Africa more than doubled during the peace negotiations, but diminished even more rapidly after the 1994 elections. The policy implication is to focus economic and political support on the initial stages of the process.

Proposition 2: A lasting agreement is impossible unless it actively involves those with the power to bring it down by violence. As it is never possible to include all those who threaten the process, a principle of 'sufficient inclusion' is necessary.

Is it possible to make a settlement without including parties associated with political violence? Most recent peace processes have included those who were in a position to prevent a settlement – the veto holders. Almost invariably the vehicle for their involvement is secret negotiations through mediators or with political parties representing the gunmen. The absence of a political front for the Kosovo paramilitaries in early 1998 was a serious obstacle to initiating peace talks with the Serbians.

The settlement in South Africa started with the release of Nelson Mandela and the ANC prisoners from 1990. In Northern Ireland there were seven unsuccessful attempts to reach agreement through negotiation between constitutional politicians, until the inclusion of Sinn Féin and the Loyalist parties led to the Good Friday Agreement. The unwillingness of the Spanish government to treat directly with Basque separatists was a serious obstacle to negotiations during most of the 1990s.

In all these areas the criteria were broadened to include political representatives of militants. The question then arises about how to respond when more extreme groups – Hamas in Israel/Palestine, the Real and Continuity IRA and the Loyalist Volunteer Force in Northern Ireland – continue or resume campaigns of violence. The relationship between governments and militants presents an uncomfortable moral ambiguity. Having accepted the principle of amnesties for earlier terrorists in order to attract them into negotiation, the negotiators then assume a stern approach to the use of terror in the future. At the same time they must also keep the door open to the inclusion of late converts. At this point the creation of a mechanism is necessary to regulate the process – who should be allowed to enter talks, the conditions for expulsion and the future inclusion of spoilers. The Mitchell Principles provide a useful model for future peace processes.

The reality is that total inclusion is never possible. There are always Zealots who cannot compromise. So the demand for inclusive talks is always a qualified one. In practice the term should be modified to 'sufficient inclusion'. This does not mean the inclusion of all parties using or threatening to use violence. The principle of 'sufficient inclusion' is that a peace process includes both all actors who represent a significant proportion of the community, and all actors who have the ability to destroy an agreement.

Proposition 3: Spoiler groups can only be neutralised with the active involvement of ex-militants.

Agreement by violent groups to negotiate is never unanimous. It often leads to the formation of splinter groups determined to continue the armed struggle. If they in turn enter the process, further breakaway spoilers emerge. The actions of spoilers move increasingly towards the margins during and after the process of peace negotiations. This traffic raises the question of how spoiler violence will be tackled by a coalition government which includes ex-militants.

At some point during the process, when all the splinter groups likely to join the process have done so, two rumps may remain – militants who are engaged in crime for personal advantage and ideological spoilers. They pose different problems. It is relatively straightforward to criminalise the former and to confront them through a police force and justice system acceptable across the community. It is much more difficult for ex-militants to turn against groups who share their general orientation but have refused to buy the peace process. It would not be easy for Sinn Féin, for example, to support strong military or policing measures against other Republican organisations, even those which had been their rivals. The idea of participating in an 'anti-terrorist' government would sail uncomfortably close to old revolutionary taboos.

One key aspect is the size of the spoiler group and the seriousness of its threat to the peace process. If the spoilers carry significant popular support, as Hamas does, the authority of negotiators such as the PLO is seriously circumscribed. The ANC's dominance of political protest in South Africa, in constrast, made condemnation a lot easier. If the spoiler groups have lost popular support, ex-militants may be emboldened to condemn them, as Sinn Féin condemned the Omagh bombers. Their acquiescence with security action against spoilers may be the ultimate test of a peace process.

Proposition 4: During peace negotiations the primary function of leaders is to deliver their own people. Assisting their opponents in the process is secondary.

In any internal peace process there are power holders and power seekers. Power holders represent those – usually but not always the state – who have traditionally controlled the reins of government. The power seekers want to alter the prevailing political, economic, legal and cultural arrangements, usually by force.

Power seekers who abandon violence and enter talks are always vulnerable to accusations of betrayal. In the emotional atmosphere it is a powerful challenge to their leaders. As Berkowitz observed, 'political leaders cannot lead where their followers are unwilling to go'.[15] The work needed to prepare their followers for the shift usually starts many years before it becomes public. It might be argued that peace in Sri Lanka, the Basque Country and Israel/Palestine will have to wait for the emergence of leaders willing to move their followers away from violent protest, as militant leaders have done in South Africa and Northern Ireland. It is equally true that the delivery of power holders needs leaders with hard-line credentials.

The transitional problems facing both power holders and power brokers are superficially similar. In both cases extremists rather than moderates' leaders are more likely to deliver suspicious followers. Reluctant converts, like Buthelezi and Viljoen in South Africa, are more convincing, and more trusted by the extremes. At that point the similarity ends. The power holders – usually the state – enter negotiation because they recognise the inevitability of change before their followers do; their main difficulty is to convince their supporters that the resulting changes are minimal. The power seekers – usually paramilitary leaders – get into negotiation because they recognise the advantages of negotiation before their followers do; their main difficulty is to convince their supporters that the negotiations are achieving major concessions. If the process moves too slowly, it hurts the power seekers. If it moves too speedily, it hurts the power holders.

In navigating this complex journey the primary function of leaders is to deliver their own followers. It is true that both sets of leaders are more likely to recognise the difficulties of their opponents as negotiations evolve. They also come to realise that a peace process cannot be completed unless their opponents also have enough to satisfy their followers. This mutual dependency is in tension with the risk that assisting their opponents may alienate their own supporters. The reality is that the loss of their followers is a greater threat to party leaders than the collapse of the process. As in the story of the scorpion and the frog, it is in the nature of political leadership.[16]

Proposition 5: Members of the security forces and paramilitary groups must be integrated into normal society if a peace agreement is to stick.

The problem of re-integrating militants into society is sharpened by their ability to threaten the peace process. In Gaza and Jericho, and in South Africa, the problem was partially addressed by transferring ex-guerrillas into the regular army and police force. The transfers were relatively smooth because there was substantial support for local policing. The sectarian divide in Northern Ireland, and the continuing reminders of the brutality of 'policing' by paramilitaries, may rule it out as an acceptable option there.

There are other options. Prudence demands that those who were engaged in the war must be provided with jobs and training. The ending of violence leaves an inheritance of high risk. The shrinkage of the security industry – army, police, prison officers and private security guards – brings onto the unemployment register people skilled in the use of arms. Similarly redundant are the paramilitaries whose lives have been devoted to armed resistance. Their speedy return to civil society is essential, less because they deserve compensation than because they have the means to destabilise the peace process.

Proposition 6: Peace accords need to address the needs of victims of violence.

Historically two distinct approaches have been applied to the victims of violence – what John Groom has called the Nuremberg Tribunal way and the South African way.[17] The punishment of war crimes continues today through the United Nation's international tribunal in the former Yugoslavia. In South Africa, as in Chile after Pinochet's fall, a new model was created in a Truth and Reconciliation Commission. Northern Ireland's Victims' Commission approached the problem from a rather different angle. All these approaches focused on individual victims, but violence also leaves a collective heritage. The creation of war memorials needs to be treated with particular care in divided societies, or they may become shrines to division rather than to common suffering.

If there is a need to re-integrate ex-militants and members of the security forces into society, there is also a need to anticipate society's response to this process. The early releases of prisoners in Northern Ireland, for example, provoked a strong sympathy for the victims of their crimes. In the interests of equity, but also in order to manage the peace process successfully, any moves to reintegrate militants into society must be balanced by recognition of the needs of their victims. The Truth and Reconciliation Commission was appropriate to the needs of South Africa, but each society must find a form appropriate to its traditions and circumstances.

Proposition 7: The search for comparative models is likely to be an increasingly important feature of internal peace processes.

There has been a high level of 'borrowing' from one peace process to another. The negotiators in Northern Ireland looked for guidance to South Africa, the founding father of modern peace processes, and successfully adopted 'sufficient consensus' as a device for advancing the process. Sometimes approaches developed in an area still experiencing violence, such as the Basque policing reforms, have influenced approaches in another. In the main, however, borrowings operated as a cascade effect from the earliest to the later negotiations.

The Basques adoption of Northern Ireland as the model for their emerging process demonstrates the phenomenon. The 'Third Space' was established to welcome into negotiations all who favoured Basque self-determination by peaceful means, a process not dissimilar to the 'pan-nationalist' front in Northern Ireland. Herri Batasuna's leader Arnaldo Otegi confessed that 'Ireland was a mirror for us, and so was the Republican movement', and Mees argues that the Basque peace process is almost unimaginable 'without the domino effect of the Northern Irish model'. In 1998 when Herri Batasuna invited all political parties and other movements to participate in an 'Ireland Forum', explicitly to explore the relevance of the Northern Ireland process to the Basque Country, the Lizarra Agreement which followed borrowed heavily from the Irish example. Four days later ETA declared a ceasefire.

The search for comparative models has become a boom industry in recent years for countries entering peace processes. It carries a risk that relatively successful processes will be perceived as a template for their own endeavours, and applied with insufficient attention to different settings.

Proposition 8: A peace process does not end with a peace accord.

When the 1994 elections were held in South Africa, the preceding negotiations had resulted in a remarkably broad range of agreements – political, administrative, security and cultural – although the issues of truth and reconciliation lingered well into the post-Accord years. The agreements in Northern Ireland and Israel, in contrast, were only made possible by postponing some contentious issues for later resolution. Some of these, including North–South relations and internal governmental structures, were resolved in Northern Ireland during the year following the Good Friday Agreement, but the issues of decommissioning and policing reform turned out to be delayed time bombs during the post-Accord negotiations. The situation was similar in Israel where, despite the transfer of policing powers and some land to the Palestinian Authority, the peace process became soured by acriminonious disputes over settlements and security during Netanyahu's administration.

There are no rules about the best time to reach formal agreement during a peace process. If the negotiators wait until all major issues have been agreed, the process may collapse from mutual distrust or violence before it reaches a conclusion. If they defer complex and divisive issues for later resolution, they know that it will be more difficult to contain negotiations and that the debate will transfer from the negotiating chamber into the public arena; there, extreme elements can exploit the mutual fears and suspicions which are endemic during peace processes. In either case post-settlement euphoria may be followed by post-agreement tristesse and the all-important momentum lost.

To make sure that agreements are fully implemented sustained post-agreement political activity is required. The danger is that parties may wish to disregard or re-negotiate some provisions in an agreement which they find unpalatable. Some peace accords attempt to anticipate such problems by building safeguards or penalties for non-compliance into the agreement. The bottom line, however, is a strong political will to implement an agreement.

The custom of violence

> Blood and destruction will be so in use
> and dreadful objects so familiar
> that mothers shall but smile when they behold

their infants quartered with the hands of war,
all pity choked with custom of fell deed.

(William Shakespeare, *Julius Caesar*, III. 1)

Protracted periods of violence are not limited to the perpetrators and their victims. They create circumstances where 'custom of fell deeds' alters fundamentally the entire society's norms of acceptable behaviour.

The custom of violence is further entrenched when it passes on to second and third generations. A young man's decision to enter the war is no longer the life-change decision taken by his father. It becomes more natural than exceptional. In some districts of Gaza and Belfast the social deviants were those who did not become involved in violent protest.

Many people in such wars do not live in the war zone, but all are also affected by the custom of violence. This does not mean that large numbers of people become engaged in violent actions. It does not even mean that they acquiesce in those actions. It means that violence and its effects have worked their way into the very fabric of society and become part of normal life so that they become accustomed to the routine use of violence to determine political and social outcomes.

Consider peace processes – all peace processes – within this framework. They may best be understood as the state of tension between the custom of violence and the resolution of differences through negotiation. The relative strength of each – in South Africa, the Middle East, Northern Ireland – determines the pace of a peace process and ultimately its success or failure. Its central task is to alter human behaviour from a helpless acceptance of fell deeds to the civilised conduct of human relationships.

Notes

1 Parnell's imprisonment in Kilmainham jail in 1881 was accompanied by increasing agrarian and political violence. He was released the following year after the 'Kilmainham Treaty' was agreed with the British Prime Minister Gladstone.

2 For a fuller discussion of the role of spoiler violence, see S. J. Stedman, 'Spoiler Problems in Peace Processes', *International Security*, 22, 2 (Fall 1997), pp. 5–53.

3 The authors are grateful to Brandon Hamber for drawing our attention to this reference in B. Frost, *Struggling to Forgive: Nelson Mandela and South Africa's Search for Reconciliation* (London: HarperCollins, 1998), p. 7.

4 Naylor, R. T., 'The Rise of the Modern Arms Black Market and the Fall of Supply-Side Control', in V. Gamba (ed.), *Society under Siege: Crime, Violence*

and Illegal Weapons (Johannesburg: Halfway House, Institute for Security Studies, 1997), pp. 43–72 (61).

5 This process was described by Dr Jan Egelund, former Deputy Foreign Minister of Norway, at a presentation in the Institute of Irish Studies, Belfast, on 19 November 1997.

6 I. William Zartman, 'Dynamics and Constraints', in I. William Zartman (ed.), *Elusive Peace Negotiating and End to Civil Wars* (Washington, DC: Brookings Institution, 1995), pp. 3–29 (18).

7 The issue is discussed in the proceedings of *Coming out of Violence: Peace Dividends* (Northern Ireland: INCORE, 1995).

8 Story related to the author by Deon Seals, ANC activist and South African diplomat.

9 A. Paton, *Cry the Beloved Country* (London: Penguin, 1958), p. 116.

10 I. William Zartman, 'Conclusions: the Last Mile', in Zartman, *Elusive Peace Negotiating and End to Civil Wars*, pp. 332–46 (333).

11 Zartman, 'Conclusions', p. 334.

12 For a useful discussion of 'ripe moments', see H. Miall, O. Ramsbotham and T. Woodhouse, *Contemporary Conflict Resolution* (Cambridge: Polity Press, 1999), pp. 162–3.

13 H. Jackson, *The Two Irelands* (London, Minority Rights Group, 1972). This important pamphlet has been periodically updated by the MRG, most recently with A. McHardy in 1995.

14 S. Friedman, 'Afterword: the Brief Miracle', in S. Friedman and D. Atkinson (eds), *South Africa Review, 7* (Johannesburg: Ravan Press, 1994), pp. 331–7, 333.

15 L. Berkowitz, *Aggression: a Social Psychological Analysis* (New York: McGraw Hill, 1962), p. 183.

16 A Scorpion asked a frog to carry him over a river on his back. 'How can I be sure that you will not sting me?' the frog asked with appropriate scepticism. 'Think about it', replied the scorpion. 'What would be the advantage to me? If I stung you, we would both drown.' In the face of such logic the frog agreed to provide the lift, but half way over the river the scorpion stung him. 'Why?' cried the frog. 'Now we will both die.' 'Couldn't help it', said the scorpion as they both went down for the third time. 'It's in my nature.'

17 J. Groom, 'Coming out of Violence: Ten Troubling Questions', Proceedings of the International Peace Studies Symposium, *Coming out of War and Ethnic Violence* (Okinawa: Okinawa International University, 1996).

Bibliography

African National Congress, *ANC Statement to the Truth and Reconciliation Commission* (August 1996).

African National Congress, 'Commission on Armed Struggle, Discussion Document DI/II(a)', Kabwe papers (South Africa: University of Western Cape, Mayibuye Centre, 1985).

ANC, 'The Place of Armed Struggle, Discussion Document DI/I', Kabwe Papers (South Africa: University of the Western Cape, Mayibuye Centre, 1985).

Ajami, F., 'The Arab Inheritance', *Foreign Affairs*, 76, 5 (September–October 1997), pp. 133–48.

Albin, C., 'Negotiating Indivisible Goods: the Case of Jerusalem', *Jerusalem Journal of International Relations*, 13 (1991), pp. 45–76.

Aróstegui, Julio, 'Violencia, sociedad y política: la definición de la violencia', *Ayer*, 13 (1994), pp. 17–55.

Arriaga, Mikel, *Y nosotros que éramos de HB: Sociología de una heterodoxia abertzale* (San Sebastián: Haranburu, 1997).

Atkinson, D., 'Brokering a Miracle? The Multiparty Negotiating Forum', in Friedman and Atkinson, *South African Review*, 7, pp. 13–43.

Aulestia, Kepa, *HB: Crónica de un delirio* (Madrid: Temas de Hoy, 1998).

Alvaro, Baeza, *GAL, crimen de Estado* (Madrid: ABL, 1996).

Barber, J., and J. Barratt, *South Africa's Foreign Policy – the Search for Status and Security 1945–1988* (Bergvlei: Southern, 1990).

Bar-Siman-Tov, Y., *Peace Policy as Domestic and as Foreign Policy: the Israeli Case, Davis Occasional Papers*, 58 (Jerusalem: The Leonard Davis Institute, 1998).

Bell, T., 'The Impact of Sanctions on South Africa', *Journal of Contemporary African Studies*, 12, 1 (1993), pp. 1–28.

Benvenisti, M., 'From Belfast to Jerusalem', *Haaretz* (7 May 1998) [Hebrew].

Ben-Eliezer, U., *The Making of Israeli Militarism* (Bloomington: Indiana University Press: 1998).

Ben Tzur, E., The Road to Peace Goes through Madrid (Tel Aviv: Yediot Aharonot, 1998) [Hebrew].

Berkowitz, L., *Aggression: a Social Psychological Analysis* (New York: McGraw Hill, 1962).

Burghardt, A., 'The Bases of Territorial Claims', *Geographical Review*, 63 (1973), pp. 225–45.

Castro, R., *Juan Maria Bandrés: Memories para la paz* (Majadahonda: HMR, 1998).

Clark, Robert B., *The Basque Insurgents: ETA 1952–80* (Madison/London: University of Wisconsin Press, 1984).

Collier, D., and J. Mahoney, 'Insights and Pitfalls: Selection Bias in Qualitative Research', *World Politics*, 49, 1 (October 1996), pp. 56–74.

Coming out of Violence: Peace Dividends (Northern Ireland: INCORE, 1995).

Conversi, Daniele, *The Basques, the Catalans and Spain* (London: Hurst, 1997).

Conversi, Daniele, 'Domino Effect or International Developments? The Influences of International Events and Political Ideologies on Catalan and Basque Nationalism', *West European Politics*, 16, 3 (July 1993), pp. 245–70.

Corcuera, Javier, *Orígenes, ideología y organización del nacionalismo vasco (1876–1904)* (Madrid: Siglo XXI, 1979).

Corcuera, Javier, *Política y derecho: La construcción de la autonomía vasca* (Madrid: Centro de Estudios Constitutionales, 1991).

Cormack, R. J., and R. D. Osborne, 'The Evolution of the Catholic Middle Class', in A. Guelke (ed.), *New Perspectives on the Northern Ireland Conflict* (Aldershot: Avebury, 1994).

de la Granja, J. L., *Nacionalismo y II República en el País Vasco* (Madrid: Siglo XXI, 1986).

Delgado Soto, B., and A. J. Mencía Gullón, *Diario de un secuestro: Ortega Lara, 532 días en un zulo* (Madrid: Alianza, 1998).

De Tocqueville, Alexis, *Democracy in America* (Hertfordshire, UK: Wordsworth Editions Limited, 1998).

Domínguez Iribarren, F., *ETA: Estrategia, organización y actuaciones 1978–1992* (Bilbao: Universidad del País Vasco, 1998).

Doyle, M. W., I. Johnstone and R. C. Orr (eds), *Keeping the Peace: Multidimensional UN Operations in Cambodia and El Salvador* (Cambridge: Cambridge University Press, 1997).

Du Toit, P., 'Feeling Safe', *Leadership South Africa*, 9, 6 (1990), pp. 74–8.

Du Toit, P., *State Building and Democracy in Southern Africa – Botswana, Zimbabwe and South Africa* (Washington DC: United States Institute of Peace Press, 1995).

Elmusa, S., 'The Israeli-Palestinian Water Dispute Can Be Resolved', *Palestine–Israel Journal*, 3 (1994), pp. 18–26.

Falah, G., and D. Newman, 'The Spatial Manifestation of Threat: Israelis and Palestinians Seek a "Good" Boundary', *Political Geography*, 14 (1995), pp. 689–706.

Fearon, J. D., 'Rationalist Explanations for War', *International Organization*, 49 (1995), pp. 379–414.

Feldman, S., 'Israel's Changing Environment: Implications for Arms Control', in S. Feldman (ed.), *Confidence Building and Verification: Prospects in the Middle East* (Boulder, CO: Westview Press, 1994), pp. 195–206.

Finlay, F., *Snakes and Ladders* (Dublin: New Island Books, 1998).

Firth, R., *Symbols Public and Private* (London: Allen & Unwin, 1973).

Frameworks for the Future (Belfast: HMSO, 1995).

Friedman, S., 'Afterword: the brief miracle?', in Friedman and Atkinson, *South African Review, 7*, pp. 331–7.

Friedman, S. (ed.), *The Long Journey – South Africa's Quest for a Negotiated Settlement* (Johannesburg: Ravan Press, 1993).

Friedman, S., and D. Atkinson (eds), *South African Review, 7: The Small Miracle, South Africa's Negotiated Settlement* (Johannesburg: Ravan Press, 1994).

Frost, B., *Struggling to Forgive: Nelson Mandela and South Africa's Search for Reconciliation* (London: Harper Collins, 1998).

Galbraith, J. K., *The Affluent Society* (London: Hamish Hamilton, 1958).

Gamba, V. (ed.), *Society under Siege: Crime, Violence and Illegal Weapons* (Johannesburg: Halfway House, Institute for Security Studies, 1997).

Garmendia, José María, *Historia de ETA* (San Sebastián: Haranburu, 5th edn, 1995) (1st edn, 1979/80).

Geddes, B., 'How the Cases You Choose Affect the Answers You Get', in J. Stimson (ed.), *Political Analysis* (Ann Arbor: University of Michigan Press, 1990), pp. 131–50.

Geldenhuys, D., and H. Kotzé, 'Aspects of Decision-making in South Africa', *Politikon*, 10, 1 (June 1983), pp. 33–45.

Geller, D. S., and J. D. Singer, *Nations at War: a Scientific Study of International Conflict* (New York: Cambridge University Press, 1998).

George, A., 'Domestic Constraints on Regime Change in US Foreign Policy: the Need for Political Legitimacy', in O. Holsti, R. Siverson and A. George (eds), *Change in the International System* (Boulder, CO: Westview Press, 1980), pp. 233–62.

Giacopucci, Giovanni, *ETA-pm: el otro camino* (Tafalla: Txalaparta, 1997).

Glazer, N., and D. Moynihan (eds), *Ethnicity* (Cambridge: Cambridge University Press, 1976).

Goertz, G., and P. F. Diehl, *Territorial Changes and International Conflict* (London: Routledge, 1992).

Goodenough, C., 'Mystery That Surrounds the Armed Robberies', *KwaZulu-Natal Briefing*, 10 (February 1998), pp. 2–6.

Guelke, A., 'The United States, Irish Americans and the Northern Ireland Peace Process', *International Affairs*, 72, 3 (July 1996), pp. 521–36.

Gunther, Richard, Hans-Jürgen Puhle and P. Nikiforos Diamandouros, 'Introduction', in R. Gunther, H.-J. Puhle and P. Nikiforos Diamandouros (eds), *The Politics of Democratic Consolidation: Southern Europe in Comparative Perspective* (Baltimore/London: Johns Hopkins University Press, 1995), pp. 1–32.

Gunther, Richard, Sani Giocomo and Goldie Shabad, *Spain after Franco: the Making of a Competitive Party System* (Berkeley: University of California Press, 1986).

Gurr, T. R., *Minorities at Risk* (Washington DC: United States Institute of Peace, 1993).

Gurutz, Jáurgegui, *Ideología y estrategia de ETA 1959–1968* (Madrid: Siglo XXI, 1981).

Hadden, T., and K. Boyle, *The Anglo-Irish Agreement: Commentary, Text and Official Review* (London: Sweet & Maxwell, 1989).

Hampson, F. O., *Nurturing Peace: Why Peace Settlements Succeed or Fail* (Washington DC: United States Institute of Peace, 1996).

Hansson, D., and D. van Zyl Smit (eds), *Towards Justice? Crime and State Control in South Africa* (Cape Town: Oxford University Press, 1990).

Harrison, S., 'Four Types of Symbolic Conflict', *Journal of the Royal Anthropological Institution*, 1, 2 (1995), pp. 255–72.

Heiberg, Marianne, *The Making of the Basque Nation* (Cambridge: Cambridge University Press, 1989).

Hermann, T., and E. Yuchtman-Yaar, 'Do They Lend It Their Consent? Israeli Public Opinion and the Political Process', in D. Caspi (ed.), *Communication and Democracy in Israel* (Jerusalem: Hakibbutz Hameuhad, 1997), pp. 191–222.

Hermann, T., and E. Yuchtman-Yaar, 'On the Road to Peace? The Dynamics and Political Implications of Israeli-Jewish Attitudes toward the Oslo Process', paper presented at MESA annual conference, Chicago (1998).

Hermann, T., and E. Yuchtman-Yaar, 'Two People Apart: Israeli Jews' and Arabs' Attitudes towards the Peace Process', in Peleg, *Middle East Process*, pp. 61–86.

Holsti, K. J., *Peace and War: Armed Conflicts and International Order, 1648–1989* (Cambridge: Cambridge University Press, 1991).

Horowitz, D. L., *The Deadly Ethnic Riot* (California: University of California Press, forthcoming).

Horowitz, D. L., *Ethnic Groups in Conflict* (Berkeley: University of California Press, 1985).

Horowitz, D. L., *Israel's Concept of Defensible Borders*, Jerusalem Papers on Peace Problems, no. 16 (Jerusalem: Hebrew University of Jerusalem, Leonard David Institute for International Relations, 1975).

Huntington, S. P., 'One Soul at a Time: Political Science and Political Reform', *American Political Science Review*, 82 (1988), pp. 3–10.

Ibarra, Pedro, *La evolución estratégica de ETA: De la guerra revolucionaria (1963) a la negociación (1987)* (San Sebastián: Kriselu, 1989).

Iglesias, María Antonia (ed.), *Ermua, 4 días de julio: 40 voces tras la muerte de Miguel Angel Blanco* (Madrid: El País-Aguilar, 1997).

Jackson, H., *The Two Irelands* (London: Minority Rights Group, 1972).

Jeffrey, A. J., *Spotlight on Disinformation about Violence in South Africa* (Johannesburg: South African Institute of Race Relations, 1992).

Kane-Berman, J., *Political Violence in South Africa* (Johannesburg: South African Institute of Race Relations, 1993).

Karsh, E. (ed.), *Between War and Peace: Dilemmas of Israeli Security* (London: Frank Cass, 1996).

Kopytoff, I., 'The Cultural Biography of Things: Commoditization in Process', in A. Appadurai (ed.), *The Social Life of Things: Commodities in Cultural Perspective* (Cambridge: Cambridge University Press, 1986).

Kotzé, H., 'Culture, Ethnicity and Religion: South African Perceptions of Social Identity', *Occasional Papers* (Johannesburg: Konrad Adenauer Stiftung, 1997).

Kotzé, H., and P. du Toit, 'Public Opinion on Security and Democracy in South Africa after Transition: the 1995/96 World Values Survey', *Strategic Review for Southern Africa*, 19, 2 (November 1997), pp. 52–75.

Kotzé, H., and A. Greyling, *Political Organizations in South Africa, A–Z*, 2nd edn (Cape Town: Tafelberg, 1994).

Kotzé, H., and L. Hill, 'Emergent Migration Policy in a Democratic South Africa', *International Migration*, 35, 1 (1997), pp. 5–36.

Kruger, B. W., 'Prenegotiation in South Africa (1985–1993): a Phaseological Analysis of the Transitional Negotiations', unpublished MA thesis (University of Stellenbosch, 1998).

Letamendia, Francisco (Ortzi), *Historia del nacionalismo vasco y de ETA*, 3 vols (San Sebastián: 1994).

Linz, Juan, 'Early State-Building and Late Peripheral Nationalisms against the State: the Case of Spain', in S. N. Eisenstadt and S. Rokkan (eds), *Building States and Nations: Analysis by Region*, vol. 2 (Beverly Hills: Sage, 1973), pp. 32–116.

Mac Ginty, R., 'American Influences on the Northern Ireland Peace Process', *Journal of Conflict Studies*, 17, 2 (Fall 1997), pp. 31–50.

Makovsky, D., *Making Peace with the PLO: the Rabin Government's Road to the Oslo Accord* (Washington, DC: Washington Institute for Near East Policy; Boulder, CO: Westview Press, 1996).

Malan, M., 'Die Aanslag teen Suid-Afrika', *Strategic Review for Southern Africa,* (November 1980), pp. 3–16.

Mallie, E., and D. McKittrick, *The Fight for Peace: the Secret Story behind the Irish Peace Process* (London: Heinemann, 1996).

Mata, José Manuel, *El nacionalism vasco radical: Discurso, organización y expresiones* (Bilbao: Universidad del País Vasco, 1993).

Mees, Ludger, *Entre nación y clase: El nacionalismo vasco y su base social en perspectiva comparada* (Bilbao: Fundación Sabino Arana, 1991).

Mees, Ludger, *Nacionalismo vasco, movimiento obrero y cuestión social* (Bilbao: Fundación Sabino Arana, 1992).

Mees, Ludger, 'Social Solidarity and National Identity in the Basque Country: the Case of the Nationalist Trade Union ELA–STV', in P. Pasture and J. Verberckmoes (eds.), *Working-Class Internationalism and the Appeal of National Identity* (Oxford/New York: Berg, 1998), pp. 43–81.

Miall, H., O. Ramsbotham and T. Woodhouse, *Contemporary Conflict Resolution* (Cambridge: Polity Press, 1999).

Michie, J., and M. Sheehan, 'The Political Economy of a Divided Ireland', *Cambridge Journal of Economics,* 22 (1998), pp. 243–59.

Minnaar, A., 'Violence in Tsolo and Qumbu (Transkei)(1993–1997): Lawlessness, Criminality, Economic Survival and Incipient Democracy at Work', paper presented at the Biennial Conference of the South African Political Studies Association, Mmabatho 8–10 October 1997.

Minnaar, A., 'Witchpurging in the Northern Province of South Africa: a Victim Profile and an Assessment of Initiatives to Deal with Witchcraft', paper presented at the 9th International World Symposium on Victimology, Amsterdam, The Netherlands (24–9 August 1997).

Minnaar, A., S. Pretorius and M. Wentzel, 'Violent Conflict in South Africa 1990–1995: a Vicious Circle without End?', *In Focus,* 4, 5 (March 1997), pp. 6–9.

Miralles, Melchor, and Richardo Arques, *Amedo: el Estado contra ETA* (Barcelona: Plaza & James, 1989).

Morán Blanco, Sagrario, *ETA entre España y Francia* (Madrid: Editorial Complutense, 1997).

Morison J., and S. Livingstone, *Reshaping Public Power: Northern Ireland and the British Constitutional Crisis* (London: Sweet & Maxwell, 1995).

Murphy, A. B., 'Historical Justifications for Territorial Claims', *Annals of the Association of American Geographers,* 80 (1990), pp. 531–48.

Naylor, R. T., 'The Rise of the Modern Arms Black Market and the Fall of Supply-Side Control', in Gamba, *Society under Siege,* pp. 43–72.

Newman, D., 'Creating the Fences of Separation: the Territorial Discourse of Israeli-Palestinian Conflict Resolution', *Geopolitics and International Boundaries,* 3, 1 (1998), pp. 251–70.

Newman, D., 'The Geographical and Territorial Imprint on the Security Discourse', in D. Bartal, D. Jacobson and A. Klieman (eds), *Concerned with Security: Learning from the Experience of Israeli Society* (Connecticut: JAI Press, 1998), pp. 73–94.

Newman, D., 'Real Spaces – Symbolic Spaces: Interrelated Notions of Territory in the Arab–Israel Conflict', in P. Diehl (ed.), *A Road Map to War: Territorial*

Dimensions of International Conflict (Nashville: Vanderbilt University Press, 1998), pp. 124–46.

Newman, D., 'Shared Spaces – Separate Spaces: the Israel–Palestine Peace Process', *Geojournal*, 39 (1996), pp. 363–76.

Newman, D., and G. Falah, 'Bridging the Gap: Palestinian and Israeli Discourse on Autonomy and Statehood', *Transactions of the Institute of British Geographers*, 22 (1997), pp. 111–29.

Nieburg, H. L., *Political Violence: the Behavioral Process* (New York: St. Martin's Press, 1969).

Núñez Seixas, Xosé Manoel, 'El espejo irlandés y los reflejos ibéricos', *Cuadernos de Alzate*, 18 (1998), pp. 169–90.

Núñez Seixas, Xosé Manoel, 'El mito del nacionalismo irlandés y su influencia en los nacionalismos gallego, vasco y catalán (1880–1936)', *Spagna Contemporanea*, 2 (1992), pp. 25–58.

Orain, Bakea, *De Arantzazu a Maroño, encuentros por la paz* (San Sebastián: Tercera Prensa, 1994).

Paton, A., *Cry the Beloved Country* (London: Penguin, 1958).

Peled, Y., and G. Shafir, 'The Roots of Peacemaking: the Dynamics of Citizenship in Israel, 1948–93', *International Journal of Middle Eastern Studies*, 28, 3 (1994), pp. 391–413.

Peleg, I. (ed.), *The Middle East Peace Process: Interdisciplinary Perspectives* (Albany, NY: SUNY Press, 1997).

Peters, J., *Pathways to Peace: the Multilateral Arab-Israeli Peace Talks* (Chatham House, London: Royal Institute of International Affairs, 1996).

PIOOM (The Interdisciplinary Research Program on Causes of Human Rights Violations) (Leiden: University of Leiden, 1997).

Potgieter, J., 'The Price of War and Peace: a Critical Assessment of the Disarmament Component of United Nations Operations in Southern Africa', in Gamba, *Society under Siege*, pp. 129–68.

Pretorius, S., and A. Minnaar, 'Loaded Issues! An Analysis of the Proliferation of Weapons in South Africa: 1993–June 1995', unpublished paper, n.d.

Pundik, R., Is Oslo Alive? The Security Dimension. Is Oslo Alive? Panel Deliberations (Jerusalem: The Konrad Adenauer Foundation, the Harry S. Truman Institute and the Palestinian Consultancy Group, 1998).

Rantete, J., and H. Giliomee, 'Transition to Democracy through Transaction?: Bilateral Negotiations between the ANC and the NP in South Africa', *African Affairs*, 91, 365 (October 1992), 515–42.

Republic of South Africa, *Interpellations, Questions and Replies of the National Assembly*, Second Session, Second Parliament (Cape Town: Government Printer, 18 February 1998).

Republic of South Africa, *White Paper on Defence 1977* (Cape Town: Government Printer, 1977).

Rolston, B., 'Culture as a Battlefield: Political Identity and the State in the North of Ireland', *Race and Class*, 39, 4 (1998), pp. 23–35.

Ruane J., and K. Todd, *The Dynamics of Conflict in Northern Ireland: Power, Conflict and Emancipation* (Cambridge: Cambridge University Press, 1996).

Rucht, Dieter, *Modernisierung und neue soziale Bewegungen: Deutschland, Frankreich und USA im Vergleich* (Frankfurt: Campus Verlag, 1994).

Savir, U., *The Process* (Tel Aviv: Yediot Aharonot, 1998) [Hebrew].

Schärf, W., 'The Resurgence of Urban Street Gangs and Community Responses in Cape Town during the Late Eighties', in Hansson and van Zyl Smit, *Towards Justice?*, pp. 209–31.

Schmid, Alex P., *Political Terrorism: a Research Guide to Concepts, Theories, Data Bases and Literature* (Amsterdam: North Holland, 1983).

Shamir, J., and M. Shamir, *The Dynamics of Israeli Public Opinion on Peace and the Territories*, Research Report Series, no. 1 (Tel Aviv: The Tami Steinmetz Center for Peace Research, 1993).

Share, Donald, *The Making of Spanish Democracy* (New York: Praeger, 1986).

Shikaki, H., 'Palestinian Public Opinion, the Peace Process and Political Violence', *MERIA on-Line journal*, www.biu.ac.il/SOC/besa/meria.htm, 1998.

Shuval, H., 'Towards Resolving Conflicts over Water: the Case of the Mountain Aquifer', in Karsh, *Between War and Peace*, pp. 14–56.

Sidiropoulos, E. et al., *South Africa Survey 1996/97* (Johannesburg: South African Institute of Race Relations, 1997).

Sidiropoulos, E. et al., *South Africa Survey 1997/98* (Johannesburg: South African Institute of Race Relations, 1998).

Sisk, T. D., *Democratization in South Africa – the Elusive Social Contract* (Princeton, NJ: Princeton University Press, 1995).

Sluka, J. A., 'The Writing's on the Wall: Peace Process Images, Symbols and Murals in Northern Ireland', *Critique of Anthropology*, 16, 4 (1996), pp. 381–94.

Sollenberg, M., *States in Armed Conflict* (University of Uppsala: Department of Peace and Conflict Research, 1997).

Stedman, S. J. 'Spoiler Problems in Peace Processes', *International Security*, 22, 2 (Fall 1997), pp. 5–53.

Sullivan, John, *ETA and Basque Nationalism: the Fight for Euskadi 1890–1986* (London: Routledge, 1988).

Tambo, O. R., *Render South Africa Ungovernable*, Message of the National Executive Committee of the African National Congress on the Occasion of the 8th January, 1985, pamphlet.

Tarrow, Sydney, *Power in Movement: Social Movements, Collective Action and Politics* (Cambridge: Cambridge University Press, 1994).

Tejerina, Benjamín, José Manuel Fernández Sobrado and Xabier Aierdi, *Sociedad civil, protesta y movimientos sociales en el País Vasco: Los límites de la teoría de la movilización de recursos*, ed. Gobieno Vasco (Vitoria: Gobieno Vasco, 1995).

Tilly, C., *From Mobilization to Revolution* (New York: Addison-Wesley, 1978).

Tilly, C., 'Reflections on the History of European State-making', in C. Tilly (ed.), *The Formation of National States in Western Europe* (Princeton, NJ: Princeton University Press, 1975), pp. 3–83.

Van Creveld, M., *The Transformation of War* (New York: The Free Press, 1991).

Vasquez, J. A., *The War Puzzle* (Cambridge: Cambridge University Press, 1993).

Villanueva, Javier, 'Puesta de largo del soberanismo vasco', *HIKA*, 1997ko azaroa, p. 28.

Waldmann, Peter, *Ethnischer Radidkalismus: Ursachen und Folgen gewaltsamer Minderheitenkonflikte am Beispiel des Baskenlandes, Nordirlands und Quebecs* (Opladen: Westdeutscher Verlag, 1989).

Waldmann, Peter, *Militanter Nationalismus im Baskenland* (Frankfurt: Vervuert, 1990).

Waltz, Kenneth, *Man, the State and War* (New York: Columbia University Press, 1952).

Williams, P., 'Transnational Organised Crime and International Security: a Global Assessment', in Gamba, *Society under Siege*, pp. 11–42.

Zartman, I. William, 'Dynamics and Constraints', in I. William Zartman (ed.), *Elusive Peace Negotiating and End to Civil Wars* (Washington DC: Brooking Institution, 1995), pp. 3–29.

Zartman, I. William, and J. Lewis Rasmussen (eds), *Peacemaking in International Conflict: Methods and Techniques* (Washington DC: United States Institute of Peace, 1997).

Zimmermann, Ekkart, *Political Violence, Crises, and Revolutions: Theories and Research* (Boston, MA: G. K. Hall, 1983).

Zirakzadeh, Cyrys Ernesto, *A Rebellious People: Basques, Protests and Politics* (Reno: University of Nevada Press, 1991).

Zubiri, Alexander Ugalde, *La acción exterior del nacionalismo vasco (1890–1939): Historia, pensamiento y relaciones internacionales* (Bilbao: Universidad del País Vasco, 1996).

Index